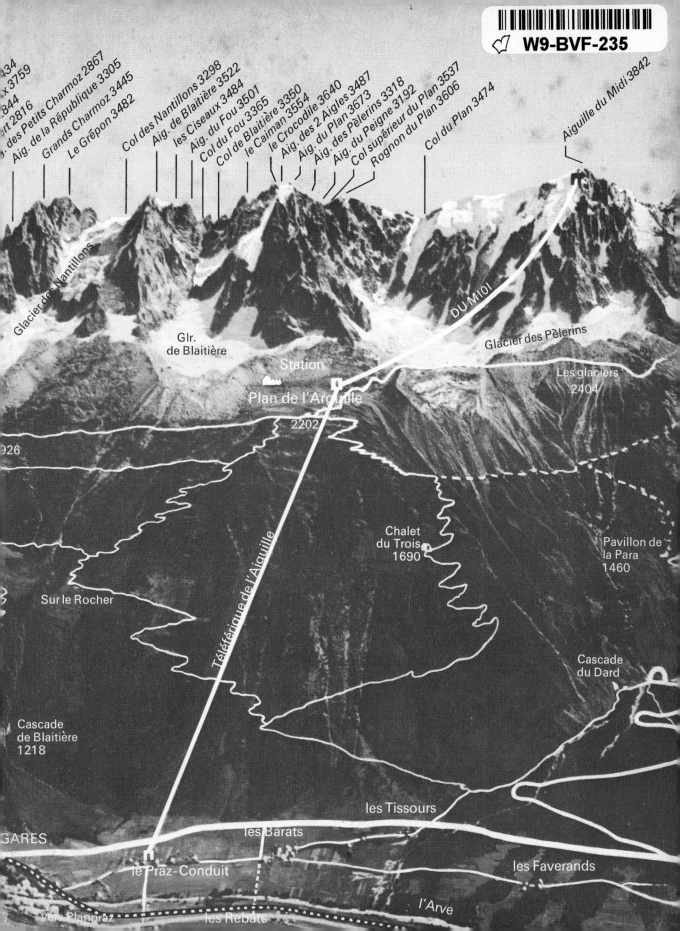

The Alps

Frontispiece The Pelvoux
(left) and the Pic Sans Nom
in the Dauphiné photo-
graphed by Vittorio Sella at
the end of the 19th century.

Jacket illustration (front):
Looking west from the
slopes above the Alpe-
d'Huez; (back): Glacier
Seracs.

THE ALPS

Ronald W. Clark

New York : Alfred A. Knopf

1973

THIS IS A BORZOI BOOK
PUBLISHED BY ALFRED A. KNOPF, INC.

Published in the United States by
Alfred A. Knopf, Inc., New York. Distributed
by Random House, Inc., New York. Published in
Great Britain by Weidenfeld and Nicolson,
London.

Library of Congress Catalog Card Number:
73-5213

ISBN 0-394-46107-X

Printed in Great Britain
First American Edition

Contents

Acknowledgements

Contemporary photographs are by the author. Historic photographs and other illustrations are from his collection of Alpine photographs, books and prints, with the exception of those acknowledged below:

The Pelvoux (frontispiece), Vittorio Sella (p. 167), Queen Margherita (p. 188), the Ecrins (p. 256) and Mont Blanc (p. 266): *Instituto di Fotografia Alpina Vittorio Sella;* Leonardo's 'Mountain Chain' (p. 29): *The Royal Collection at Windsor, reproduced by gracious permission of H. M. the Queen;* Lory prints from the Lewis Lloyd Collection (p. 54): *the Trustees of the British Museum;* Passing a Crevasse on the Glacier des Bossons (p. 60) and American party at the Grands Mulets (pp. 64–5): *the American Alpine Club;* Bisson's photographs of the Dru and the Verte (p. 84) and the Chamonix Aiguilles: *the Eastman Historical Photographic Collection;* George Leigh-Mallory (p. 115) and the Aiguille du Géant by Donkin (p. 159): *the Alpine Club;* Rescue work (p. 124), the Postal Bus at Gletsch (p. 135) and the Rigi at Sunrise (p. 202): *the Swiss National Tourist Office;* Geoffrey Winthrop Young and Joseph Knubel (p. 216): *Emile Gos;* Albert Smith (p. 275): *Gernsheim Collection.*

The author also wishes to thank Edward C. Pyatt for reading the manuscript and for making a number of useful suggestions, and the Swiss Alpine Club for permission to quote Professor Charles Baehni.

We love Nature, it is true, but put into vases, into cages, into aquaria. It goes without saying that we agree with the commission for the protection of special sites, but only when it protects vague areas; we are all members of the Society for Nature Reserves – but only on condition that the existence of these reserves inconveniences neither fishermen nor hunters, neither foresters nor walkers, neither you nor I.

Professor Charles Baehni,
Revue de la Ligue pour la Protection de la Nature,
June 1962, No.3.

The Alps from the Jura –
Hilaire Belloc's 'sight in the
sky that made me stop
breathing ...'

A Quick Look at the View

There is a slope in the Graian Alps, somewhere above the back end of the Valgrisanche, long if not particularly steep, below the permanent snowline and burrowed with holes from which the marmots whistle at each other like a ventriloquist's chorus. It goes on interminably, and you begin to doubt the wisdom of walking uphill at all. But you know you are high; with each breath you know you are higher, and it is only a minor feat of imagination to believe you are higher than anything else in Italy or Europe or even the world. Then you stop and look round. Then you look up. At least you feel you look up, which is what matters psychologically. What you gain, from an almost impossible thirty miles away, is an overwhelming impression of rock and rib, ice and arête and snowfield—the huge south face of Mont Blanc, as far away as a good man could walk in a day but hanging high in the sky like a medieval painter's dream.

The involuntary gasp of surprise is one expression of the long contemplative enjoyment of fine sights that has been part of the Alpine reward since men first began to take mountains seriously. More than four centuries ago Conrad Gesner, the Zurich natural scientist, wrote to a friend that he had decided to climb at least one mountain a year so that he could contemplate 'the great spectacles of this earthly paradise', among which he rated highly the 'steep and broken mountain tops, the unscalable precipices, the vast slopes stretching towards the sky, the dark and shady forests'. Gesner relished his views. So did his successors, the interested and interesting company of men and women who were drawn to the Alps while others still shuddered at the thought of them. Scientists like de Saussure and Agassiz came with their instruments and stayed with their passions. Ruskin caught his first sight of the Glarus Alps from above the Falls of Schaffhausen and after that was unable to escape a love-hate relationship with the 'great cathedrals of the earth, with their gates of rock, pavements of clouds, choirs of stream and stone, altars of snow, and vaults of purple traversed by the continual stars' – the Alps which either fear or other failing caused him to worship only from below.

Ruskin's successors, the mountaineers of the Golden Age, visited the Alps to exercise their physical powers of endurance and their intellectual powers of leadership. But from Wills onwards the best of them had as good an eye for a

view as the eighteenth century had for landscape layout. Frederic Harrison wrote in the early 1900s of his first sight of the Alps as 'one of the turning points in my life, the beginning of that passion which has beset me now for fifty-six years'. Mr Cook's tourists, ooh-ing and ah-ing at the Jungfrau behind its foreground of Interlaken hotels, also loved the view, if Cynara-like, in their own fashion. Today it still keeps the packaged-tour industry in fine fettle.

It is difficult to analyse the factors which transform a mountain scene, of which the Alps have hundreds of thousands, into a great view of which they have tens of thousands. Unexpectedness is one of them, as in Hilaire Belloc's revelation of the mountains from the Weissenstein, the 'sight in the sky that made me stop breathing, just as great danger at sea, or great surprise in love, or a great deliverance will make a man stop breathing'. Driving up the northern flank of the Weissenstein today, more than half a century after Belloc walked his way to Rome, you find few essentials changed. You crest the ridge and come on to one of the grandstand balconies that the Jura provides between the Col de la Faucille behind Geneva and the Wisenberg above Olten. If you are lucky you see the Alps as Belloc saw them above Switzerland's plain, 'sky beneath them and sky above them', almost sixty miles away, pin-sharp and visions from another world.

Unexpectedness makes a view stick in the memory, so that a quarter of a century later you see, clear as a picture on the study wall, the long frieze of Dauphiné summits that, approached from the north, appear one by one above the horizontal skyline dividing the Maurienne and Romanche valleys; peaks of a setpiece transformation scene rising above green waves as you breast the col. Contrariwise the expected show-sights take longer to recall; but their images harden as recollection pulls up the detail like developer working on a print. The Oberland from the Terrace at Bern; the Alps from Nyon, a horizontal display sectioned above the Lake of Geneva like a folding

Previous pages Typical Dolomite scenery.

panorama in a pre-war Baedeker, a thin slice of country going on and on as though God had forgotten to stop making mountains; the postcard Wetterhorn and Matterhorn, each standing above its respective foreground as though a celestial photographer had put them in to produce the accepted format; all are, in capitals, views worth seeing. Certainly they have become weather-worn with repetitive description, certainly they can be savoured with the expenditure of little cash and less energy; yet they have survived the sieve of many generations and they have done so because they genuinely have the splendid quality of great scenery.

But effort counts as well as accessibility, and an argument could be made for the greatest views of the Alps being those which demand at least a modicum of puff and blow. As Arnold Lunn said in *Mountains of Memory* – and not only, one feels, to start an argument: 'How frequently the reward of beauty is associated with the dignity of toil, as if nature consciously reserves her noblest effects for those who take some trouble to earn them.' Effort alone provides what Sir Claud Schuster called the 'moment of ecstasy when your head reached the level of the arête, and all the glorious spires and domes, ramparts and battlements leap into view at once. You gasp at them', he went on, 'partly from admiration and partly from lack of breath, and then let your eye look down at the mighty ice-basin below and the long cool stream of the Aletsch, the treasure-house of the frost.' A particular revelation creeps into the view which has been reached on one's own two feet – even if panting hard and praying that the top does not lie beyond that next little ridge, a whole ten paces away. This may be unfair on the fat, the elderly and the infirm but, as Bertrand Russell has pointed out, one must at some point admit that most of life is unfair. And just as there is an immutable law in physics which ordains that every action provokes its own equal reaction, so does the way in which you reach a view control the intensity and understanding and delight; easy

Part of the Dolomite panorama which awaits the motorist at the top of the road leading from Lake Misurina to the lower slopes of the Drei Zinnen.

come, less delight, a law of scenery as inescapable as the swings and round-abouts of more mundane affairs.

Yet if the greatest ecstasy is gained by the greatest effort, this is not to say that the lesser delights are not worth experiencing. The motorist driving into the view-point car park below the Rosengarten, and the crowds debouching from the train at the top of the Rigi, all content with their own form of endeavour, may not appreciate the scene with the satisfaction of the climber who in C. E. Montague's words 'hangs safe by a single hand that learnt its good grip in fifty thousand years of precarious dodging among forest boughs'. What they can do, the mob as well as the mountaineer, is appreciate a good view on its simple panoramic value.

Martin Conway, mountaineer and art critic in almost equal parts, claimed that at least on one side of a view 'there should be green and fertile land. If a lake is visible so much the better. The great ranges should not spread themselves out like a procession but should be grouped in masses.' He might have added that there should be an item whose lack so frequently confounds the mountain photographer: a decent foreground which sets off or frames or gives depth and contrast to the receding planes of peak and pasture; a foreground, moreover, which in the age of colour photography must have something more than form alone. Here, of course, the painter has an edge on tourist and photographer; conjuring up the mountain chalet and dumping it wherever he wishes, moving minor features of the foreground from east to west if they are more convenient that way, introducing at will the highlights for which the photographer waits indefinitely while his companions grow colder and more critical.

This ability to re-arrange a landscape, to select and emphasise, to transform so that one man's vision may illuminate what another may miss, can add a new element to the scene. If there is any doubt that the eye of the beholder can create something more for those who come after, it can be removed by comparing two of the most famous panoramas of the Alps. From Superga, above Turin, the eye takes in a huge spread of peaks, from Monte Viso in the south-west, along the crest of the Graians to the Gran Paradiso north-west, to the Pennines with Monte Rosa distinct and recognisable, and eastwards more Alps in ever-diminishing array until the curve of the earth puts a stop to the game. It is fine. It is very moving. But the comparable view from the rooftop of Milan Cathedral, a hundred miles to the east and roughly the same distance from the main chain, has a difference in quality that has nothing to do with the distant white fuzz on the horizon. After Tennyson had 'climb'd the roofs at break of day' and seen

> How faintly-flush'd, how phantom-fair,
> Was Monte Rosa, hanging there,
> A thousand shadowy-pencill'd valleys, and
> Snowy dells in a golden air

After that how could it ever be less than one of the great views of Europe? In much the same way the Italian plain itself, seen from the mountains, has an additional quality when one knows how Conway saw it with the painter's eye

Members of the British party who made the first ascent of the highest peak of Monte Rosa in 1855 and, shortly afterwards, the first guideless ascent of Mont Blanc. They are, left to right: Charles Ainslie; John Birkbeck; Charles Hudson; E.S. Kennedy; Stevenson; C. Smyth; F.G. Smyth; and V. Lauener.

Far left Sir Leslie Stephen.
Left Sir Martin Conway who in 1894 traversed the Alps from end to end.

from the Cottian Alps. A storm had dropped away behind and the plain emerged, 'a faint vision, through a veil of falling snow; in another moment it was a clear actuality, shining in sunlight, with its lines and dots of trees, its straight, ruled roads, its glittering rivers, encircled by far away hills and masses of cloud, domed and bright above, flat and purple-shadowed beneath'. What a lucky man was Conway, to see, to feel and to be able to record.

In the Alps it is not merely painters and writers and poets who have looked at the view for centuries and obligingly suggested what others could look for with profit. Many of the scenes themselves are not only pleasant prospects but have become, through association, part and parcel of Europe's history. Frederic Harrison's claim that 'to know, to feel, to understand the Alps is to know, to feel, to understand humanity', is no over-statement. It is impossible to look across the Chamonix Valley from the Brévent towards Mont Blanc without seeing not only a mountain face but the stage on which de Saussure's long plans for the first ascent were played out by others. Even the European Route N2, twisting up the St Gotthard, over and through a network of concrete viaducts and avalanche tunnels on its way from the northern plains to Italy, cannot remove the memory of Suvorov and his Russians, fighting down the Schöllenen Gorge in one of the most desperate battles the Alps has ever known. Monte Disgrazia is not only a fine mountain from almost any angle; its first ascent in 1862 was the subject of a historic paper, to be found on the first page of the first issue of the *Alpine Journal* whose colourful opening splendidly mirrored the times: 'as the strokes of midnight were clanging from the Campanile at Sondrio, a carriage rolled heavily into the court-yard of the Hotel della Maddalena'. Belalp, above the Rhône Valley, is not only a supreme vantage-point but the spot which the great John Tyndall made especially his own, and one where he could be seen 'holding a sort of little court in the hall before going up to his chalet for dinner'. The Meije in the Dauphiné, the last major summit of the Alps to be conquered, is not only a mountain but an object whose first ascent was an almost pathological obsession of Miss Meta Brevoort, that pioneer climber and American expatriate who could write with deep passion to her nephew of how the Meije 'must keep herself for me'. Travellers in the Alps, scientists who first climbed to measure the effect of high altitude or the creep of the glaciers and who continued to climb for the fun of the thing, leaders of armies and of tourist parties, the 'hard men' of modern mountaineering, and the painters, the writers, the potterers and the mere stand-and-starers have all added their quota to our view.

The Alpine people have added much. The best hoteliers, sniffing the morning air and watching the early mists disperse, do not regard the scene solely in terms of cash and bed-nights. For almost two centuries many great guides have shown an appreciation of mountain scenery equal to that of their employers, although most of them have revealed it by the chance phrase rather than the rounded essay. It was Luc Meynet, Edward Whymper's hunchback porter, who on reaching the Col du Lion for the first time fell on one knee 'exclaiming in ecstasy, "Oh beautiful mountains"' – an account that

The imposing finger of the Dru, with the mass of the Aiguille Verte rising to the left. On the right skyline is the Grandes Jorasses from which the Mer de Glace curves down through the centre of the picture.

does not spring entirely from Whymper's ability to make the best of a good story.

Not all guides, not even all great guides, felt the same. Melchior Anderegg, one of the heroes of the Golden Age, loved the mountains as dearly as any member of that bright company. Yet when Leslie Stephen, looking out over the rooftops of central London with his visitor, commented 'That is not so fine a view as we have seen together from the top of Mont Blanc', Anderegg's reply was: 'Ah, sir, it is far finer.'

A view is a view is a view, even though one man's relish is another man's disappointment. They come in various shapes and sizes, with regrets and ecstasies in almost equal measure; from bright daylight and the unparalleled splendour of the Viso shining above the Lombard Plain to the crepuscular Dents du Midi, standing clear to the last moment above the lake and the gathering darkness below. To each his own Alp. There are more of them than most of us realise.

The pageantry of a field of
early summer flowers in the
Vajolet valley, Dolomites.

PART ONE
From End to End

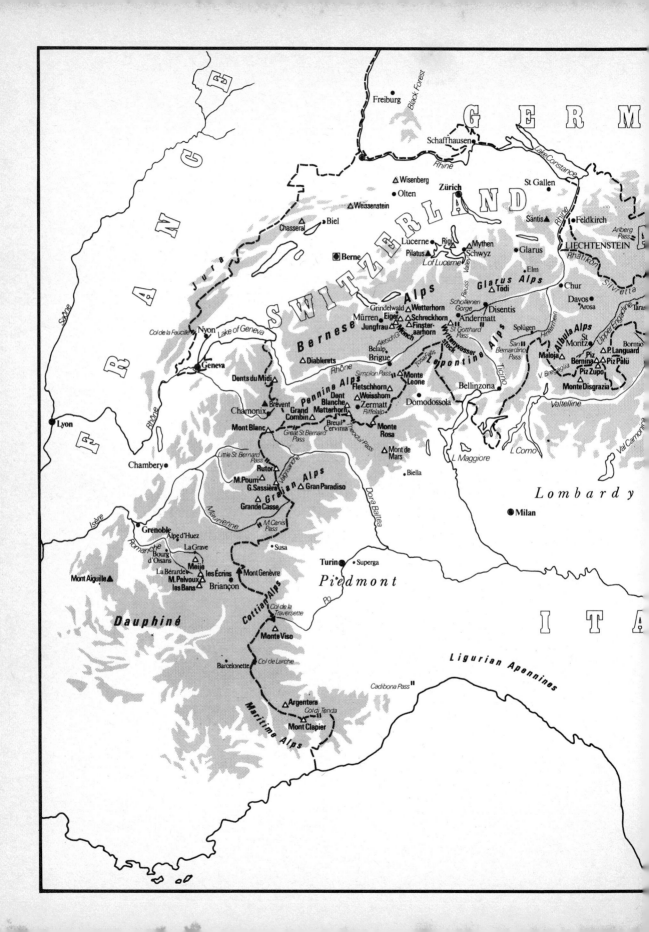

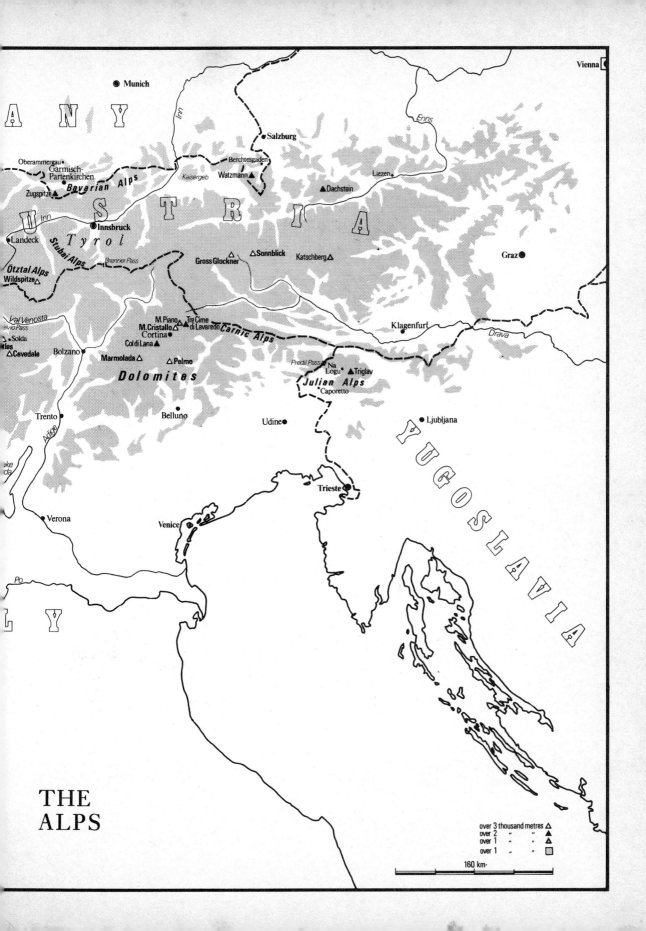

Vienna

Munich

Enns

Salzburg

Oberammergau
Garmisch-
Partenkirchen
Berchtesgaden
Kaisergeb
Watzmann
Liezen
Zugspitze
Bavarian Alps
Dachstein

A U S T R I A

Inn

Graz

Innsbruck

Landeck

Tyrol

Stubai Alps
Brenner Pass
Gross Glockner
Sonnblick
Katschberg

Ötztal Alps
Wildspitze

Klagenfurt

Drava

Val Venosta
elvio Pass
M.Piano
M.Cristallo
Cortina
Col di Lana
Tre Cime
di Lavaredo
Carnic Alps

Solda
Cevedale
Bolzano
Marmolada
Pelmo

Dolomites

Predil Pass
Na
Logu
Triglav
Julian Alps
Caporetto

Trento
Belluno
Udine
Ljubljana

Adige

Trieste

Y U G O S L A V I A

Verona

Venice

Po

L Y

THE
ALPS

over 3 thousand metres △
over 2   "   "   ▲
over 1   "   "   △
over 1   "   "   ▢

160 km

CHAPTER ONE

Bigger than Frontiers

Whether the Alps will have kept much of their natural beauty by the end of the century is a very moot point. 'Each man kills ...', and those who claim to love them are hard at work lacing the slopes with networks of télésièges, electric-fencing the pastures, turning mule-tracks into motorways and, as a shadow of things to come, servicing the first revolving restaurant on a 10,000-foot summit. Man's museum instinct and preservation consciousness fight a tough battle, and the ribbon-development of *chalets-à-vendre* creeping up the Guisane from Briançon will soon be within smell of the industrial smog of the Romanche Valley, where water power still feeds the earliest electro-chemical plants of the Alps.

Such pessimism is not new. To many the rot set in when Pococke and Wyndham visited the almost unknown Chamonix Valley with their fashionable party in the first half of the eighteenth century. A hundred years later, as the post-Napoleonic peace settled over Europe, too many scientific travellers began to follow de Saussure's footsteps above the snowline. As early as 1856 Ruskin was noting that 'the valley of Chamouni .... unique in its way, is rapidly being turned into a kind of Cremorne Gardens.' The railways, which had barely entered the mountain zone when the Alpine Club was formed in 1857, merely expedited the Gadarene rush. The railways had a lot to answer for. So had Mr Cook whose party of sixty-four ladies and gentlemen left London Bridge in June 1863 for his first organised tour of Switzerland.

It was not only travellers below the snowline who were becoming too numerous and having things made too easy. In 1875 A. W. Moore, a leading mountaineer, expressed his regret, with that of several other members of the Alpine Club, 'that the great peaks should be vulgarised by means of mechanical appliances, and the multiplication of resting places. He would', a report went on, 'like to see all huts destroyed and all ropes and chains cut down.'

Yet the growth of huts above the snowline and the fixing of ropes in difficult places was only beginning. Indeed the avalanche of development after the First World War made men think of Moore's times as 'the good old days' when it was easy to have a mountain to oneself, when the funicular still served only a few vulgar tourist spots and the cable-car was little more than a thought at the back of an engineer's mind. Then, after 1945, the deluge.

Sir Martin Conway
(second from left)
in the Alps.

25

Each generation has deplored its predecessors before carrying on with the work. Thus the ruination of the Alps has been a subject for impassioned remorse since men first took its scenery to heart. Yet the most regular cries of 'Wolf' do not prevent the animal itself from turning up one day; constant warnings about the petrol leave unaltered the fact that on an Atlantic flight there is a point beyond which it is impossible to turn back. And it seems sombrely indisputable that the Alpine point of no return is about to be reached: that there is a limit to the number of people this particular range can carry, just as a Highland deer forest can carry only so many animals if it is to survive, and that the maximum in the Alps is only a few seasons away.

There are still many pastures, and more peaks, where people are thin on the ground. There are still valleys where the only permitted petrol engine is that of the mini-bus taking visitors to the hotel. There are still views which catch the breath with their beauty rather than their network of overhead wires. The danger is that within a generation such places will become self-conscious sanctuaries, a series of Central Parks or Hyde Parks hemmed in not by sky-scrapers but by téléphériques and the discothèques of custom-built ski-resorts offering what is advertised as a new way of Alpine life.

Realisation that the Alps represent a finite capital asset, the individual items of which can be ruined only once, is certainly growing. So is an awareness that the Alps of tomorrow are the creation of today – just as today's environment is a legacy from the men before yesterday. As far back as 1907 the Swiss Alpine Club added conservation to its aims; other clubs have done the same, and each Alpine country is taking a longer-term look at the profit-and-loss account of development. At the last minute of the last hour there is a remote sporting chance that they may be in time. There is, moreover, one factor which is some consolation for the traveller of the 1970s as he realises, perhaps with surprise, how the contemporary Alpine environment is so largely the result of what has happened in the last hundred years and almost entirely the result of what has happened within the last two hundred. This factor, which should not be used as a conscience-salver when supporting one's own quota of Alpine ruination, is that progress lurches on unevenly. The range stretches for more than six hundred miles and traverses half a dozen countries, where commerce and conservation, industry and aesthetics, the demands of tourism and of history, are given different priorities. There are also the contrasted qualities of the groups themselves, some wide open to exploitation, some the despair of engineer and local tourist board, some already handed over as burnt offerings to the travel industry.

The boundaries of these groups, whose individuality is likely to govern Alpine development in the future as much as in the past, have been bones of argument since men first began to rationalise their geographical thoughts about the assortment of peaks and passes that stand in a great crescent between the Mediterranean and the Bohemian rectangle. The place at which the Alps begin in the west has been subtly debated; so has the point at which a pin should be stuck in a map to mark their eastern end. Whether they should be sliced simply into Western and Eastern or should include a Central section, thus being divided like Gaul into three, is a question which has driven wise men almost to tears and honest men almost to blows. Alpine academics have discussed the divisions and demi-semi-subdivisions with a raw fanaticism which will shock those unaware of the mountain scholar's ferocity.

However, even the casual traveller, with little thought of photographing a peak and even less of climbing one, will benefit from a mental ground-plan, a basic map on which to pin his impressions of up hill and down dale, of interminable hairpin bends and of paths on which he will echo that immortal pedestrian on the track to the Riffelalp: 'No matter where it leadeth, the downward path for me.'

The Alps can today be seen as a single entity on the one-shot views from the satellites, a long white half-moon separating the Italian plains from central and northern Europe. Its creation is, like most geological stories, hedged round with qualifications, limitations, special cases and exceptions. Yet it is not too inaccurate to say that many millions of years ago the area was covered by a sea, and on the generally crystalline sea-floor there was laid down a thick layer of what became sedimentary rocks. This sea-floor was then subjected to pressures, roughly from north and south, which pushed up three tablecloth folds running approximately east and west. The central fold was the highest and before long – a mere few million years – much of the sedimentary layer was eroded away to reveal the crystalline layer beneath. To the north, and separated from the central fold by the embryonic Rhône, Rhine and Inn, rose what were to become the Bernese Oberland and the limestone mountains of Tyrol. To the south, beyond the Dora Baltea, the Adda and the Drava, lay such groups as the Dolomites and the Carnic Alps. This relatively simple picture was then confused by a second bout of pressure – not from straight north and south this time but from west-north-west and east-south-east. The second upheaval had particular effect in the Bernese Oberland and to the west on the Mont Blanc area and the Dauphiné.

Despite its contrasts, the range of the Alps can therefore be considered all of a piece. Few, however, have considered it thus since Martin Conway, more than three quarters of a century ago, decided in his lordly way to stroll it from end to end. It was possible, he decided, 'taking the whole range of the Alps, to devise a route, or rather a combination of climbs, the descent from each ending at the starting point for the next, so that a climber might begin at one extremity of the snowy range and walk up and down through its midst to the other extremity over a continuous series of peaks and passes'. He did it in three months in 1894, climbing most of the time with one or two English companions and all of the time with two Gurkhas he had brought from the Himalayas to train in snow-and-ice craft. The geographer's eye could 'see' an area as a whole, without benefit of satellite. Lesser mortals will need first to decide on their Alpine boundaries.

There is no difficulty on the south, for the huge Italian plain, flat as a billiard table for mile after mile, leaves no doubt in either atlas or mind. On the north and west the mountains sink more slowly into France or the central Swiss plain – which in a homely way is sometimes described as the Midlands –

or into the hills of southern Germany, and it becomes more difficult to know where the line should be drawn. In some ways the Rigi and Pilatus, gazing at one another across the Lake of Lucerne, have almost as little right to be called Alpine as Constitution or Capitol Hills have to be called mountainous; yet they cannot be left out. From the Tödi, whose first ascent fulfilled the life-long ambition of the eighteenth-century monk Placidus à Spescha, it is possible to trace mountains and hills in ever-diminishing height almost to the outskirts of Zurich itself, and further east the problem is worse. Hitler, brewing trouble in the Eagle's Nest above Berchtesgaden, was in the range, if only just. The northern boundary is therefore capable of being lifted back or forth according to the demands of history or scenic magnificence. But there is one rule it is unwise to ignore: if the country goes green on the map for more than a valley-crossing you are out of the mountains.

It is west and east, where the Alps curve down to the Mediterranean or lose themselves in the outliers of the Carpathians, that the real trouble starts. On the west geography makes its own private joke by twisting back the end of the crescent as it approaches the coast, so that the range begins to turn back on itself like a puppy's disobedient tail instead of neatly dropping into the sea. To the south-east the Apennines, almost at the end of their journey from central Italy, try to meet their Alpine counterparts and the scrub-covered ridges in between, bounded on the east by the Cadibona Pass and on the west by the Col di Tenda, are known variously as the Ligurian Apennines or the Ligurian Alps. The former seems marginally better since, if 'the Alps' means any one thing to both scholars and laymen, it means the 'higher or snowy portion of the great mountain range that shelters Italy from the outer world'. Thus the Alps, for us, start at the Col di Tenda.

In the east the situation is a geographer's delight, and a quick glance at the map will suggest an almost infinite number of lines that could be drawn to divide the Alps from the rest. Here, as elsewhere, the 'higher or snowy portion' is a good yardstick. Using it, one draws the eastern boundary south from Vienna to Liezen in the Enns Valley, across the Radstädter Tauern and the Katschberg into the Drava Valley and then, on a long eastern circuit, round the Julian Alps and back to the sea at Trieste. The boundary, compli-cated as it is, has much virtue; drawn on purely topographical principles at the start of the present century, it is roughly the line proposed by formal Italian recommendations in 1926.

The modern traveller has a comparatively easy time in moving anywhere throughout the mountain area within these north-south, east-west boundaries, and not only because frontier rules and regulations have been largely thawed out of existence during the last few years. Today the international frontier is a simple affair which in general follows the watershed: Italy to the south and, on the west, north and east, France, Switzerland, Germany, Austria and Yugoslavia in succession. There are minor exceptions. With this in mind the armchair traveller, map on knee, can leave the Col di Tenda for a brief look at the ground to be covered.

First come the Maritime Alps. They have a number of distinctions, not

'Mountain Chain' by Leonardo da Vinci, from the Royal Collection at Windsor. Reproduced by gracious permission of H. M. the Queen.

least being that from the summits it is possible to see the Mediterranean and a dim outline of Corsica, as well as a splendid selection of peaks inland. Like all mountains at a distance, these are smaller than the hopes aroused. The photographer, appetite whetted, needs the painter's transformation of scale (the longest telephoto will hardly do) before the summits become more than pin-points along the horizon. Nevertheless they are there. They summon up experience through memory or anticipation by hope, and Coolidge, the expatriate American who became the greatest, if occasionally the most insufferable, Alpine historian of all time, has given one account of his vision from Mont Clapier which moved even his pedantic mind towards poetry. The plain of Lombardy was veiled in mist, but above there sailed out 'the great glory of the panorama ... the great chain of the Alps right round from Monte Viso and the higher Dauphin peaks to the Grande Casse, Mont Blanc, the Matterhorn, the Weisshorn and Monte Rosa'.

Rising to only 10,794 feet in the Punta dell' Argentera, less intensively vulgarised than most of the chain, comparatively free of humans when these are apt to be thick on the ground elsewhere, the Maritime Alps meander up to the Col de l'Argentière, above which the Batterie de Viraysée once had the reputation of being the highest building in Europe inhabited all the year round. As elsewhere, a diversity of names can confuse the unwary : the Col de l'Argentière, French-named from the first village in Italy, is known to the Italians as the Col de Larche from the first village on the French side, while a chapel near its summit has also given it the name of the Col de la Madeleine.

The Franco-Italian frontier follows the crest of the Maritime Alps and has done so with a few minor exceptions since 1860, when the area around Nice was transferred from Sardinia to France. One exception was made south of Mercantour, where it was agreed that King Victor-Emmanuel II should keep his sub-Alpine hunting grounds. The frontier therefore bulged round them and was redrawn only by the Treaty of Paris in September 1947. Then the French, remembering 1940, successfully claimed minor alterations on the Mont Cenis and on the Montgenèvre, which gave them the tactical advantage should they once again be attacked from the east.

To the north of the Maritimes, a fine *hors d'oeuvres*, lie the Cottian Alps. This is Hannibal country and almost every pass between the Col de l'Argentière and the Mont Cenis, which bounds the Cottians on the north, has at one time been claimed as the route by which the famous commander and his elephants entered Italy. The Col de la Traversette, slightly to the north of Monte Viso, its upper slopes pierced by a tunnel driven in 1480 to aid the salt-for-oil trade between Provence and Turin, is the most favoured current contender. The Viso, which now seems rather more likely than Monte Rosa to have been Leonardo's Monboso, dominates the northern end of the Cottians; a complicated network of narrow valleys and gorges spreads from the broad base of the mountain, and on its southern-eastern flanks rise the head-waters of the Po, that splendid river of the north-Italian plain.

From the slopes of Monte Viso, on whose summit British and Italian flags were planted in 1961 to commemorate its first ascent a hundred years previously, the view westwards lies across a dark sea of foothills towards what can seem, in the right light and the right mood, almost a separate range. This is the Dauphiné with more than one claim to fame. Its huge rock peak of the Meije, towering over La Grave in a way that no other peak towers above any other Alpine village, was the last great summit of the Alps to be climbed. In the Écrins, Les Bans, the Pelvoux and half-a-dozen other peaks the Dauphiné has classic specimens of mountain architecture that can hardly be matched elsewhere. The almost self-contained knot of peaks which forms its heart was the last in the Alps to be surveyed, explored or climbed, and long after the rest of the range had been opened up, touristed and made comfortable for the masses, the Dauphiné remained what it had been for centuries, an area of literally lousy inns, poor food and a lack of all the facilities that the sophisticated mountain traveller had come to regard as his due. Today the Pelvoux Nature Reserve has its own attractions. And to the west lies what is in some ways the most extraordinary of any peak in the Alpine foothills, Mont Aiguille; extraordinary both in the isolation of its huge rocky walls, in the pure spectacle of its shape and in the fact that its ascent was first made in 1492 on the orders of Charles VII, and was not repeated for more than three hundred years.

History and geography have combined to ensure that the Dauphiné today rubs the most extreme contrasts shoulder to shoulder. Above Bourg d'Oisans, 6,000 feet up at Alpe d'Huez, where there was little but meadows a few years ago, there is now the ultimate in tailor-made ski-resorts with, in Michelin's words, 'the huge hotels and chalets of the most important built-up area in the neighbourhood of the first platform, submerging the barns of the ancient alp.' Only a few miles away the single-track road up the Vénéon Valley to La Bérarde is much as it was half a century ago, frequently cut by avalanches in winter, with the upper valley almost isolated for many months of the year.

Returning to the main watershed via the Upper Maurienne valley, an Alpine Black Country in the quality of its industrialisation, the traveller reaches the Graians which straddle the frontier and divide their major peaks between France and Italy. On the watershed lie the Rutor and the Grande Sassière; in France the western Graians contribute the Grande Casse and

Mont Pourri. Across the Italian frontier lies the lonely trough of the Valgrisanche, its upper reaches flooded for a so far abortive hydro-electric scheme; and, further east still, the Gran Paradiso forms the highlight of a glorious national park. While the Graians' Val d'Isère is a leading ski-resort the Graians themselves are still less disrupted by the coach trade than the high-spots of the Alps. The Vanoise National Park may have, in the words of its propaganda, 'many marked mountain tracks to lakes, chalets, alpine refuges and over fifty summits'. There are, it is true, 'trained instructor-keepers at tourists' disposal'. Yet the traffic is still bearable.

All this changes at the Little St Bernard Pass. Beyond lies the big stuff; beyond lie the postcards *en masse*, the téléphériques, the hard core of the Alpine tourist trade; beyond it lie the most spectacular sights of the Alps and the buzz of activity which such honey-pots attract.

First comes the range of Mont Blanc, once known as the Western Pennines, bounded by the Little St Bernard on the south-west and the Great St Bernard on the north-east. Mont Blanc is not only the highest peak of the Alps; on that score alone it wins by only a comparatively short head with its 15,872 feet against Monte Rosa's 15,217. Here it is necessary to drop a word of warning about heights. No one is likely to challenge Mont Blanc's primacy. But exact heights have been the subject of endless controversy, the result of improvements in technique, differing snow-depths from year to year, slow geological movement and, near the frontier zones, different figures provided by different national surveys. During the first half of the present century, moreover, it was discovered that the Pierre à Niton, a huge granite block in the Lake of Geneva which had been the basis of Swiss altimetry since General Dufour first mapped the country in 1820, was between ten and eleven feet lower than had been thought. The altitude of the Pierre à Niton was challenged on a number of occasions and corrections to mountain heights made on new editions of the Swiss maps; but only in 1957 were the majority of Alpine heights modernised and brought into line on the large-scale map sheets. On these the Matterhorn was reduced by 108 feet to 14,678, the Grand Combin by 20 feet to 14,144 and the Weisshorn by 34 feet to 14,770, although the Combin de Valsorey was given an added 122 feet. Of more interest to mountaineering tigers, the Fletschhorn in the Simplon area and the Piz Zupo in the Engadine were for the first time brought below 13,111 feet, the magic 4,000 metres, thus losing Switzerland two of her forty *Viertausender*.

Mount Blanc presents in almost unique degree both scenic splendour and an exceptionally wide range of human and historical interest. Its great south face, a complex of steep walls, hanging glaciers, rock ridge and arête, is one of the sights of Europe while the Crammont and the Mont della Saxe provide at right height and distance the most convenient of grandstands. On the north nature has done her job just as well. Here the flanks of the mountain, thick with topographical features which are landmarks in mountaineering history, can be seen across the Chamonix valley from any number of points reached by foot or by téléphérique according to taste. The local Syndicat d'Initiative could hardly have landscaped the place more efficiently.

Relatives of Sir Alfred Wills
(1828–1912), whose ascent
of the Wetterhorn in 1854
opened the Golden Age of
Alpine climbing, looking
towards Mont Blanc from
the Col d'Anterne.

They Abbey Church of
Disentis where Father
Placidus à Spescha lived
for many years.

The Mer de Glace, most famous of Mont Blanc glaciers, is surpassed in Alpine length only by three in the Bernese Oberland and by the Gorner Glacier above Zermatt. Here James David Forbes began his vital investigations into glacier movement in the 1840s and here John Tyndall took up the work a decade later, soberly planting his lines of stakes across the ice and arranging for their changing patterns to be recorded at regular intervals. On the surrounding rock spires of the Aiguilles there climbed the mountaineers of the Silver Age, which began after the first ascent of the Matterhorn and lasted for two or three decades according to definition.

Around Mont Blanc geography tends to divide the delights into north and south, French and Italian, but even this minor inconvenience has been removed by the road tunnel linking Chamonix and Courmayeur – and by the umbilical cord of the Aiguille du Midi téléphérique system which in ninety minutes takes a passenger from the streets of Chamonix, up to the Aiguille du Midi (and up the interior of the metal piton-viewpoint built on the long-suffering summit), across the Vallée Blanche and down to the outskirts of Courmayeur. As a contrast there is the Tour of Mont Blanc, a ten-day circum-ambulation which follows a hundred miles of well-marked footpaths sign-posted by two white stripes bounding a red one. Chamonix and Courmayeur have everything; including the crowds.

The division of Europe's highest mountain ridge between France and Italy – with the Swiss commanding the easternmost sliver of the massif – is little more than a hundred years old. For only in 1860 was Savoy ceded to France, thus pushing the French frontier forward to the watershed to include not only the entire northern slopes of the group but also the summit of Mont Blanc itself, where a group of Chamonix guides planted the Tricoleur on 5 July.

To the east of Mont Blanc – technically from the trade route of the Great St Bernard highway with its road tunnel, customs posts, zig-zag of avalanche-protecting *gallerie*, its hospice and its dogs traditionally ready with a flask of the hard stuff – there stretch the Pennines. Here the heroic names lie thickest on the ground. Here there is the Dent Blanche, its summit first reached by Thomas Kennedy in 1862, in a great gale, more than thirty degrees of frost, and so much driven snow that one of the party's hair 'unprotected by his hat, became a mass of white icicles'. Here is the Weisshorn, perhaps the ultimate in beautiful mountains, the peaks of Monte Rosa, each with its own story of personal endeavour, and the memory of Tyndall climbing one of them alone, on a sandwich and a thermos flask of weak tea. Above all, here is the Matterhorn above Zermatt, with the long-drawn-out story of conquest that has all the ingredients of genuine tragedy.

Today the ski-tows clank upwards from the Gornergrat, that natural Royal Box from which to survey, in comfort with the crowd, not only the Matterhorn but a great segment of the Pennine glacier complex. Over the frontier to the south the Breuil of Carrel the Bersagliere, the man dedicated to making the first ascent of the Matterhorn from his native valley, has become the fashionable resort of Breuil-Cervinia. Cable-cars link the agglomeration

The plaque commemorating Sherlock Holmes below the Reichenbach Falls near Meiringen; erected by the Norwegian Explorers of Minnesota and the Sherlock Holmes Society of London.

Father Placidus à Spescha, the Benedictine monk who explored the Tödi. The French allowed him to climb mountains even while they held him prisoner-of-war.

with the Plan Rosa, from which one can ski even in the height of summer. In fact the Pennines have with railway, bulldozer and téléphérique been given the mass-requirements of the twentieth century quite as ruthlessly as anywhere in the Alps. Despite it they have just managed to retain some echo of the mountains as Whymper knew them when the Matterhorn still had 'a *cordon* drawn round it, up to which one might go, but no farther'.

The group itself is divided somewhat arbitrarily into Central and Eastern Pennines by the Théodule, the glacier pass from Zermatt to Breuil that has been used by local people for at least four centuries. They continue east to the Simplon, running from Brigue in the Rhône Valley on the north to Domodossola in Italy, and marking the eastern end not only of the Pennines but of the Western Alps.

Now come the Central Alps. And now, to provide further topographical confusion, which only careful study of a large-scale map will remove, comes a geographical crossroads. West and east run the deep valley trenches of the Rhône and the Rhine, the first flowing to the Mediterranean via the Lake of Geneva, the second reaching the North Sea via Chur and Lake Constance. Between the two lies the upland basin in which stands the travel resort and garrison town of Andermatt. Through it, and crossing the east-west route at right-angles runs the St Gotthard highroad, linking the William Tell country of the Lake of Lucerne via the Reuss Valley, the Schöllenen Gorge, the Gotthard Hospice, the snack and souvenir shacks, and the giant car parks, with Switzerland's southern canton of Ticino. A trade route since earliest times, the line of the St Gotthard is today being transformed into N5, an international highway whose bridges, tunnels and viaduct make up a concrete company's dream of delight.

The crossing of the Rhine–Rhône axis by the St Gotthard route creates four mountain segments. To the north-west, across the Rhône Valley, lies the Bernese Oberland, a mountain outlier in much the same way as the Dauphiné, a long chain of peaks which includes much more than the highlands of the canton of Berne. The Oberland runs from the Diablerets, which look down upon the Lake of Geneva, to the peaks that in the east rise above the Lake of Lucerne. Jungfrau, Mönch, Eiger and the nine and a half miles of the Aletsch Glacier are its set-pieces; the glacier village of Grindelwald its tourists' delight and conservationists' nightmare. The Wetterhorn, Finsteraarhorn and Schreckhorn are among the Oberland peaks which provide the stuff of Alpine history. Mürren, set on a shelf above the Lutschine valley, which gives it the picture-postcard view of the Jungfrau, is a home both of skiing and of Alpine ballooning, while to the Jungfraujoch station, some 2,200 feet below the top of the Jungfrau itself and at 11,401 feet the highest station in Europe, there runs the railway that is desecration or delight according to point of view.

Facing the eastern end of the Oberland across the upper Reuss, in the north-eastern of the four segments, lies the Tödi group, famous for its exploration at the end of the eighteenth century by Father Placidus à Spescha, the Benedictine monk from the splendid abbey at Disentis, which closes the view from the Lukmanier pass like an ecclesiastical plug in a topographical bottle.

The packed wall of a souvenir shop in Misurina.

34

North of it, the north-east corner of the north-east segment, rise the isolated foothills of sub-Alpine Switzerland. Some of these peaklets, like the rocky Mythen and the railway-festooned Rigi, hold no permanent snow and thus almost fail to qualify. But to the north-east the grey limestone crags of the Säntis carry snowfields – as well as summit hotel and observatory.

South of the Rhine–Rhône axis lie the Lepontines, their eastern peaks known as the Adula Alps. The Lepontines are highest on their extreme west where Monte Leone towers above the Simplon, seen from some Bernese peaks without too much imagination as a white lion crouching in the sky. Near it lie the Tosa Falls, one of the most famous cascades in the Alps. And from the slopes of the Wyttenwasserstock, a few miles west of the St Gotthard and symbolically enough at the meeting point of three cantons, the waters run to the Mediterranean via the Rhône, to the Adriatic by courtesy of the Tosa and the Ticino and to the North Sea via Reuss and Rhine. ,

It is at the eastern end of the Lepontines that the Alps refuse to be easily categorised, systematised or grouped into simple divisions. But a clear head and an occasional glance at a line-drawing that does not too drastically simplify by error can produce a useful generalised picture.

The Alps of north-east Switzerland, the Tödi group and the Lepontines – counting from north to south – are bounded on their east by the upper Rhine between Lake Constance and Chur, then by the valley of the Hinterrhein as it descends from the Splügen and San Bernardino Passes. It would be convenient to decide that everything east of this fell under the title of Eastern Alps. It would also be inaccurate, for to the east there lie four groups which according to current topographical form must all be included in the Central Alps. The first three are the Rhätikon Alps, the Silvretta group into which they run on the east, and the Albula into which they run on the south-west. In their midst lies Davos, pioneer of Alpine health resorts, where Robert Louis Stevenson completed *Treasure Island*.

To the south lies the beguilingly long valley of the Upper Engadine, rising past a string of centres where the rich can take their illnesses comfortably, through some of the finest Alpine-flower country, towards the crest of the Maloja. South of the Engadine lie the Bernina with, tucked away in their western corner, the Bregaglia Alps, with a spectacle of forest and flower, rock-spire and snow, among the finest in Europe. Nearby rises the Bernina itself; Piz Palü, still famous for Leni Riefenstahl's film, *The White Hell of Piz Palü*; Monte Disgrazia, one of the half-dozen peaks in the Alps that can claim almost absolute perfection of form; and the Piz Languard, on whose summit John Addington Symonds reaffirmed his engagement to Catherine North. Here also rises the Pizzo Bianco, below whose slopes the scholar W. P. Ker turned to his companions one day in 1923; remarked, 'I always thought this to be the most beautiful place in the world, now I know it', then sank down and died. Here, where at times the 'splendid scenery might almost be a part of the vast commercial enterprise that has developed the Upper Engadine', some of the most difficult snow-and-ice climbs in the Alps brush shoulders with the ultimate in sophistication. It is also funicular country.

Hay-making below the white limestone walls of the Julian Alps

37

Memorial in the centre of Cortina to Déodat de Gratet, Marquis de Dolomieu (1750–1801), the geologist who gave his name to the Dolomites.

The line bounding Rhätikon, Silvretta, Albula and Bernina Alps runs south from the eastern end of Lake Constance, turns east down the Arlberg, south at Landeck into the upper Inn Valley and the Val Venosta, then up over the Stelvio to the Valtelline and the Val Camonica.

All beyond is Eastern Alps.

North of the Arlberg and the Upper Inn lie the Alps of Bavaria, best-known for the skiing resort of Garmisch-Partenkirchen. Here also rises the Zugspitze, the highest peak in Germany, replete with every modern device from téléphérique to rock route blasted for the non-climbing mountaineer. Also in the Bavarian Alps, but further east and in form and temper more fitted to the term, there are the ferocious rock-peaks of the Watzmann, the Dachstein, and the walls of the Kaisergebirge. They provide, wrote R. L. G. Irving between the wars, 'some of the highest precipices in Europe and a considerable proportion of the annual death-roll from climbing accidents'. And here also, south of Salzburg, there stood until recent times the ruins of the Eagle's Nest, the eyrie above Berchtesgaden where Hitler came to plan, in his own private Alpine Valhalla, the world hegemony that nearly came off.

South of the Bavarian Alps rise the Ortler, Ötztal and Stubai groups with, below them as it were, the Lombard Alps which lie some way south of the main Alpine watershed. Further east still are the Central Tyrolese Alps and the Dolomites. All have to lesser or greater extent been victims of comparatively recent frontier changes. At the start of this century the frontier of the Austro–Hungarian Empire made a huge sweep southwards to overlook the Italian plain. However, when in 1915 Italy was brought into the First World War by the Treaty of London a secret clause ordained that should the Allies win, then 'the whole Tyrolese salient up to the main watershed, that is to say, as far north as the Brenner Pass', would become Italian. This was an offer easy enough to make; the territory was not the Allies' to give. The Treaty of Versailles thus pushed the frontier northwards to the geographical watershed. It also removed the significance of the Dreisprachenspitze north of the Stelvio Pass, where it had previously been possible to sit on the meeting point of three countries. The change, which brought to Italy five thousand square miles and a population of half a million, involved more than this alone. Sulden not only became Solda. The Drei Zinnen became the Tre Cime de Lavaredo, the Dürrenstein became the Pico di Vallandro, and Kaiser-Franz-Josef-Spitze the Cima Brenta. Despite the formal adoption of the Italian names, the older versions still come first on Austrian maps. Furthermore it is still possible to ask for the Tre Cime, to meet apparent incomprehension, but to find that everything changes when the ancestors are placated and the magic words Drei Zinnen are used.

The first group in this territory is centred on the Ortler, at 12,802 feet the highest summit of the Eastern Alps, a huge peak, almost a massif, into the shadow of which one sinks in descending the fifty-odd numbered horseshoe bends on the eastern side of the Stelvio. With the Königsspitze and the Cevedale, claimed to be 'the highest ski-mountain in the Alps', the Ortler helps close the Sulden valley to the south.

Further east still are the 'real' Eastern Alps – the mountains of the Austrian Tyrol centred on the Gross Glockner, the Dolomites and, almost within sniffing distance of the Carpathians, the Julian Alps, blanched and bare above, greenly forested below.

Named after Déodat de Gratet, Marquis of Dolomieu, a village near Grenoble at the other end of the Alps, the Dolomites have been modelled by wind and weather from the crystalline double carbonate of lime and magnesia. Only because of the modesty of one man are they not called 'the Saussures'. For when Horace Bénedict de Saussure, so largely responsible for the first ascent of Mont Blanc, asked Dolomieu what he was to call the newly analysed rock, Dolomieu said he wanted to call it 'Saussure', but Genevese modesty ruled that out. Instead, 'dolomite' it became, a word first popularised in

The peaks of the Langkofel in the Dolomites.

Britain by *The Dolomite Mountains*, a record of Victorian walking-tours by Josiah Gilbert and J. G. Churchill.

With their rainbow-coloured vertical rock walls, the isolated pinnacles that are the photographer's delight and, in the Pelmo, one of the most imposing peaks anywhere, the Dolomites epitomise the Eastern Alps. The Dolomites of the South Tyrol, as they were known before the frontier change, are today among the most scenically exploited mountains in the world. Where there is no scenic road such as leads to the Tre Cime (1,400 lire for car and three passengers plus 500 lire for each additional passenger) there is usually a téléphérique. Where there is no téléphérique there are parking bays at the best viewpoints, coin-operated telescopes and the assorted paraphernalia that is a combination of *White Horse Inn*, Blackpool at its most exuberant, and the

On top of the Marmolada, the only Dolomite peak with a glacier.

Rigi-Kulm of Alphonse Daudet's *Tartarin in the Alps*, where missing the sunrise was almost a punishable offence. Places where climbers can be seen to fall off are not actually advertised; but well-maintained paths contour easily round the steepest and most difficult of the super-severes.

Eastwards, beyond the edge of what it is now over-dramatic to call the Iron Curtain, lie the Julians. Here, as in the Dolomites themselves, the frontier has been shuttled back and forth by military victories. In 1914 the Austro-Italian frontier ran southwards from near the Predil Pass, leaving most of the Julians as Austrian territory. After 1918 the frontier was shifted eastwards to run across the summit of Triglav, and the other half of the Julians incorporated into Yugoslavia. After the Second World War, a comparable move west was made, so that all the Julians now lie in Yugoslavia.

Triglav is the jewel of the group, a mountain with one huge wall nearly two miles across and 3,000 feet high, rising in light-grey limestone magnificence from the surrounding green of the pine forests. Just as the Matterhorn had its Guido Rey, so Triglav had its Julius Kugy, a scholar-mountaineer who devoted much of his life to the area and whose anthology *Five Hundred Years of Triglav* traces its history since 1452. His *Alpine Pilgrimage* contains some of the most evocative of mountain reminiscence, and a fine monument to him now stands on the southern approaches to the mountain near the village of Na Logu.

While the Dolomites are comparatively free of glaciers – only on the Marmolada (cable-way to the summit) – the Julians have none. Contrariwise the over-exploitation of the Dolomites is counterbalanced here by the charm of a country still in some ways a century behind the times. Sophistication stops at the Yugoslav frontier; the rugged individuality of the Dauphiné at the western end of the Alps in the 1870s is matched by the Julians in the 1970s.

From west to east the Alps thus show differences of topography, development and exploitation, and their political and mountain histories have been as varied. Yet the entire range has for centuries had one thing in common: the annual cycle of life which it has imposed on its inhabitants, a yearly round of routine which has only begun to break down during the last century under progressive development of the mountains as an open-air laboratory, a sporting playground, and a holiday tourist arena.

CHAPTER TWO

The Arcana of Nature

For centuries most men shunned the Alps. Forced to cross them from time to time, they stuck to the easiest passes, kept their eyes well down, crossed fingers and hoped for the best until they were safely out of the foothills and into the comfortable plains once more. Master John de Bremble, the Canterbury monk who crossed the Great Saint Bernard in 1188, prayed: 'Lord, restore me to my brethren, that I may tell them that they come not to this place of torment.' Bishop Berkeley on the Mont Cenis noted how 'every object that here presents itself is excessively miserable'. John Evelyn, crossing the Simplon in 1646, saw only 'horrid and fearful craggs and tracts' and Horace Walpole wrote of the Alps after his visit in 1739: 'I hope I shall never see them again.' There was the occasional eccentric with other reactions; but for most of recorded history the mass of mankind took a poor view.

This attitude persisted through the medieval pilgrimages which took men across the Alps to Rome, and into the mid-eighteenth century when the magic wand of the Romantic Movement transformed mountain terrors into mountain majesty as surely as pumpkin was turned into crystal coach. Yet is was still an awesome majesty, still to be regarded only at a distance and only by a small number of the literate few.

This position remained until two centuries ago, when the Americans were limbering up for the Boston Tea Party and the French getting ready for the first Bastille Day. Within a century all had changed and Leslie Stephen's *The Playground of Europe*, first published in 1871, was a measure of the change. Stephen's Alps, a good place for metaphysical philosophising, and for working out the traumas which the Victorians found they had worked themselves into, was essentially a playground for the hearty intellectuals and the intellectual hearties. Stephen himself, a forty-mile-a-day man who once walked the fifty miles from Cambridge to London in twelve hours to attend an Alpine Club dinner, was typical; so was Whymper who could continue over hill and dale, apparently for ever, at a steady five miles an hour. This essentially conquistadoring approach was later broadened as others came to look when they could not climb; as men began to see in the Alps a new aesthetic attraction as well as a physical challenge; as winter sports began to exercise their own individual appeal; and as the separate attractions were amalgamated and

Opposite
A typical hydro dam near the Italo-Yugoslav border.

Monument in the Haslital, Bernese Oberland, to workers who built the complex of dams and hydro-electric stations in the upper valley.

Chapel and workers' houses beneath the towering wall of the Valgrisanche dam in the Graian Alps.

streamlined so that the range itself became a tourist magnet for the world at large. But the transformation between mid-eighteenth and mid-nineteenth century was the important one, and it was brought about largely through the honest brokering of science. Its practitioners found in the Alps both problems awaiting solution and a laboratory for experiments that could not be carried out at lower altitudes.

Today the impact of science on the Alps is visible in a dozen different ways. The most obvious show up on even a large-scale map: the curved black lines stemming back light blue fingers – the dams with their attendant artificial lakes which have refashioned some upper valleys as the price of making some Alpine countries independent or near-independent of outside fuel supplies. Any who doubt the visual impact of such schemes should drive up the Val d'Heremence from Sion, a journey whose last few miles seem to be menaced by the increasing shadow of the gigantic concrete wall blocking the southern end of the valley. It should be impressive; at 930 feet the highest dam in the world, almost 100 feet higher than the Rockefeller Centre in New York and more than twice as high as the top of St Paul's.

Such intrusions of science and technology, which have often upset the ecological apple-cart, are only partly counter-balanced by the string of national parks in which, from the Dauphiné in the west to the Julians in the east, plants and animals, birds and unique natural features, quite apart from the scenery itself, are protected from the depredations of man. The Vanoise National Park based on Pralognan, the Swiss National Park south of the Engadine, the almost-adjoining Stelvio National Park across the frontier in Italy and the Yugoslav National Park surrounding Triglav are four of the most attractive. In all there are limitations on the use of the motor-car; in all

44

the ubiquitous marked paths of the Alps are more than normally ubiquitous, while in all the collection of specimens and disturbance of flora and fauna is reserved to the experts.

More specialised are the research centres and observatories which for three quarters of a century or longer have been sprouting near Alpine summits. The Vallot Observatory, set up on Mont Blanc in 1890, and the later ill-fated Janssen Observatory, built on a spot near the summit so badly chosen that it had to be dismantled little more than a decade later, were two of the earliest. Today there is the Nuclear Research Centre above Breuil-Cervinia, while thousands of tourists are each year made at least dimly aware of the Jungfraujoch High-Alpine Research Station, with buildings at both the summit and the base of the Sphinx rock which juts from the snow on the col. Since it is 'on a railway', the most complicated machinery and equipment can be installed even at 11,500 feet. Freedom from soot, dust and fog allows unique astronomical work to be carried out here as well as important studies in physics and physiology.

Somewhat comparable work is done in the Swiss Research Institute for High-Alpine Climate and Tuberculosis in Davos, while above Davos stands the Avalanche Research Centre where a small handful of dedicated men analyse the hundreds of avalanches which sweep the Alps each year.

Modern hydro-electric schemes have in many places changed the face of the Alps. But hydro dams need not be ugly; this one is near the summit of the Lukmanier Pass.

Conrad Gesner (1516–1565), who in 1555 climbed Mount Pilatus, and who resolved to 'ascend several mountains, or at least one, every year, when the flowers are in their glory, partly for the sake of examining them and partly for the sake of good bodily exercise and mental delight.'

Josias Simler (1530–1576) whose book '*Concerning the Difficulties of Alpine Travel and the Means by which they may be overcome* was the first practical handbook to movement above the snowline and to the use of rope and alpenstock.

This particular centre, set up by the Swiss Ministry of Forests and Fisheries more than thirty years ago, and today cooperating amiably and usefully with the other national research centres in the Alps studying the same menace, offers a salutary lesson to any Alpine jog-trotter. Here machines measure the deformation of snow under different conditions or provide chapter and verse for the mechanics of particular avalanches. Some physicists make artificial hailstones which simulate the formation of particular conditions and others provide figures for the comparable defence value of concrete and young fir trees. Yet it is quite clear after even the briefest chat with the devoted experts, who talk of avalanches much as zoo-keepers talk of their charges, that while the danger can sometimes be forecast, and while it can sometimes be directed this way or that, it cannot be tamed. This is a world very different from the Alps of restaurants revolving at 10,000 feet, of lorry routes over and under, guaranteed to be motorable all the year round. It is a world in which, every so often, nature hits back with a bad winter, killing with avalanches more than the statistically expected number; holding back the day when cattle can be taken up to the higher pastures and making it quite clear who is still the master.

All this scientific activity, together with the local societies for studying rocks and birds, the disappearing chamois and the periodic advance and retreat of the glaciers, make up the contemporary picture of the Alps as a laboratory. Yet science has done far more than utilise a high-altitude stationary work-bench on to which the worker can peg instruments. During the centuries which saw the transformation of the mountains from nightmare to dream, and particularly during the hundred years that ended in 1871, science was the mainspring of most Alpine activity, and of virtually all serious activity above the snowline.

The roots go deeper still. It seems to have been largely from scientific interest that Leonardo visited his Monboso; drew his *Mountain Chain*, now in the Royal Collection at Windsor; and wrote of finding in the middle of July an 'enormous mass of ice' that was probably a glacier, saw the sky above him quite dark 'and the sun as it fell on the mountain far brighter than here in the plains below, because a smaller extent of atmosphere lay between the summit of the mountain and the sun'.

Conrad Gesner, who in 1555 ascended Pilatus where the railway now runs, – 'we climbed for a long distance up a very difficult hill, where there is no path and in places crawled up it, clutching at the turf' – climbed partly as a botanist, although he makes clear his almost modern delight in mountain scenery. Josias Simler, who followed Gesner into a professorial chair at Zurich, had much the same approach. He also wrote the first practical handbook on movement above the snowline, the *De Alpibus commentarius*, which gave advice on the use of rope, alpenstock, crampons and dark glasses and which would even today save a few deaths a year if read and properly digested.

However, these predecessors of the scientific mountaineer of the late eighteenth and early nineteenth century were isolated examples. They lit no flame of enthusiasm. Most men still kept carefully below the snowline if humanly possible. The high Alps were still beyond that invisible cordon which Whymper as late as 1860 described as surrounding the Matterhorn, within which 'gins and effreets were supposed to exist – the Wandering Jew and the spirits of the damned'.

The real change began during the eighteenth century with the growing scientific desire to explore glaciers and to understand their formation and movement. There are between 800 and 1,000 of them in the Alps. The three longest are the Aletsch ($10\frac{1}{2}$ miles), the Unteraar (10 miles) and the Fiescher (10 miles), all in the Bernese Oberland; the shortest are numbered among the scores of small accumulations of ice and snow, a mere few hundred yards in length, ranking as glaciers only by courtesy of definition. Most of these rivers of ice – a popular but by no means inaccurate description – can be seen at close quarters only by a sharp uphill walk towards the heart of a mountain. But there are exceptions, notably the Upper and Lower Grindelwald Glacier, both popular sights since the mid-eighteenth century. The Rhône Glacier pushes its snout almost on to the highway descending from the Furka Pass towards Gletsch. And many peaks to the north of the Chamonix Valley give a bird's-eye view of the glaciers descending from Mont Blanc. Anyone who

The Lower Grindelwald Glacier, from Merian's *Topographia Helvetiae*, published in 1654.

Abbildung des Gletschers im Grindelwaldt in der Herschafft Bern.

A Das Eyß oder Gletschen so vom Boden auff wachset und alles was sich hefft mit großem Getümmel und vielem Krachen   B der fluß Lütschnen so unter dem Eyß herfür quillet
C Wohnungen mit welchen man dem Gletscher halt weychen mußen   D Hoch gebürge mit Ewigem Schnee bedeckt

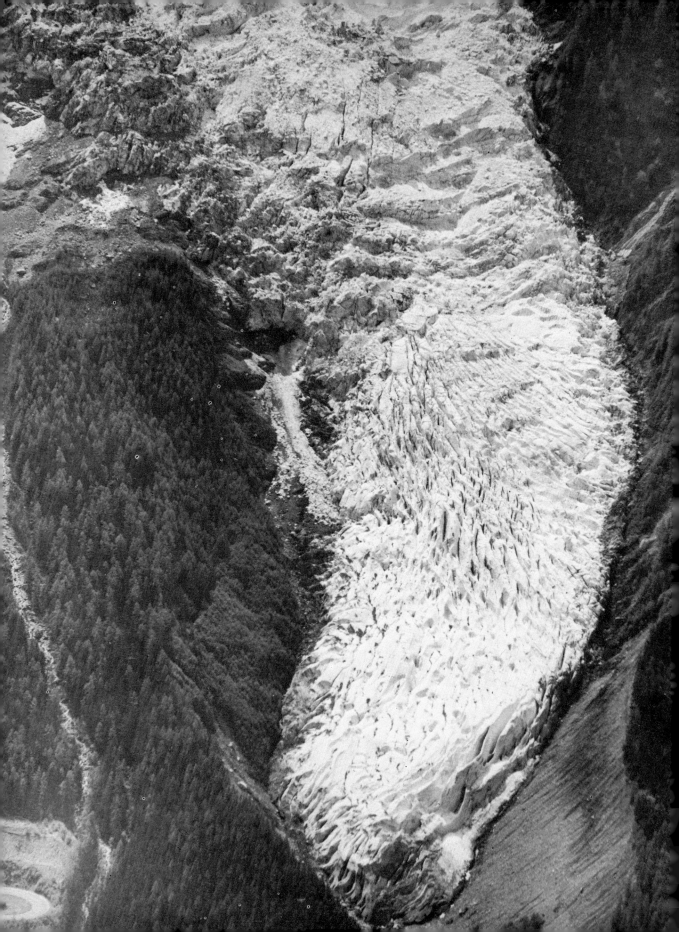

questions the word 'tongue' for their lowest stretch should study the Glacier des Bossons from the Brévent above Chamonix, thrusting down between forested rocky walls to lick the valley floor.

Most famous of all is the Mer de Glace, bending down from the upper slopes of Mont Blanc and the subject of a famous description by the redoubtable William Windham, the Englishman living in Geneva who visited the Chamonix Valley in 1741 and can be credited with starting the mountain movement of his age. 'You must imagine your lake' (the Lake of Geneva), he said, 'put in Agitation by a strong Wind, and frozen all at once; perhaps even that would not produce the same appearance.' The comparison stuck, and the 'mer de glace' became the one particular glacier which needed no further identification – just as there is never a London Alpine Club or a British Alpine Club but only 'the' Alpine Club.

Glaciers are formed by the accumulation and consolidation of snow on the higher slopes of a mountain. Pressure transforms the snow into ice, and gravity draws the resulting mass downhill along the most convenient 'river-bed'. Where there are rocky steps in the river-bed, the glacier falls over them in a cataract of broken ice-blocks or séracs known as an ice-fall. Minor irregularities in the ground, added to quicker movement of the mid-glacier compared with its sides, help to create the deep vertical crevasses which are the main hazard of glacier travel. Rocks and boulders shot on to the glacier by the normal process of erosion from the slopes above, accumulate to form lateral moraines, while the debris carried down on the glacier and deposited when the ice melts at the tip of the tongue, builds up the terminal moraine.

Glaciers are in a constant state of movement, and many have given dramatic proof of the fact by ejecting at tongue the remains of victims who years previously have fallen into crevasses miles higher up. Loss through melting at lower levels is compensated by the annual accumulation of snow at higher levels and the length of a glacier is thus dependent on a balance-and-loss account on which individual items are governed by annual snowfall above and annual average temperature below. For much of the last hundred years the glaciers have been steadily retreating and photographs taken in 1870 and 1950 give in some cases – notably those of the Rhône Glacier – a dramatic illustration of glacier regression. In 1963 a Swiss commission reported that of glaciers studied in the previous year six were stationary, ten advancing and seventy-seven retreating. However, there have been signs during the last thirty years that the retreat is being slowed

Little was known in the eighteenth century about the movement of glaciers. The mountains from which they descended were thought to be not merely snow-covered but ice all through. And the illusion survived more than one description of 'the icy and crystalline mountains of Helvetia called the Gletscher' – mainly the Grindelwald Glaciers – printed in the *Philosophical Transactions of the Royal Society*. After all, it was not long since Scheuchzer had seriously described the various kinds of dragons to be found in the Alps.

The turning point came shortly before mid-century. In 1741 William Windham, his tutor Benjamin Stillingfleet, Dr Pococke the Oriental traveller,

The snout of the Bossons Glacier seen from the the Brévent across the Chamonix Valley.

49

Horace Bénedict de Saussure (1740–1799), the Genevese naturalist whose offer of a reward for discovery of a route to the top of Mont Blanc encouraged exploration of the mountain at the end of the 18th century.

Louis Agassiz (1807–1873), and a companion in his 'Hotel des Neuchâtelois' on the Unteraar Glacier in the Bernese Oberland.

and half a dozen other Englishmen, travelled to Chamonix, walked to where the Montanvert Hotel now stands, and ventured on to the Mer de Glace. The accounts of their expedition, given in Swiss and British papers, described a hitherto unknown mountain world and three years later Windham and Pierre Martel, a Genevese engineer who had followed in his footsteps, wrote for the Royal Society 'An Account of the Glaciers or Ice-Alps of Savoy'. From this time onwards science and adventure tended to travel hand in hand. However, they still travelled slowly.

The year before Windham's adventure there had been born in Geneva Horace Bénedict de Saussure, the epitome of the scientist-mountaineer, who visited the Alps before that historical watershed, the outbreak of the Napoleonic wars. On his first visit to Chamonix at the age of twenty de Saussure offered a reward for the first men who found a route to the top of Mont Blanc. It was a quarter of a century before anyone was able to claim it – the village doctor Michel Paccard and the local crystal-hunter Jacques Balmat.

De Saussure himself climbed Mont Blanc in August 1787, but his interests went beyond the riddles of the glaciers. He checked the boiling point of water at a height where it had not before been checked; he made physiological measurements on himself and his companions; compared the colour of the sky with its colour seen from Chamonix – using paper slips dyed in various shades of blue. He also looked about him and, in an age before the making of adequate maps, realised how great an insight into mountain topography was now possible. 'For what I really saw, and saw as never before', he wrote, 'was the skeleton of all those great peaks whose connection and real structure I had so often wanted to comprehend.'

Encouraged by his success, de Saussure now planned an expedition quite as
daring in its way as the ascent of Mont Blanc. The Chamonix–Courmayeur
cable-way now swings lazily across the Col du Géant, the once desolate and
still impressive ridge-pole between France and Italy, but it had been crossed
for the first time only a week before de Saussure climbed Mont Blanc. Now he
decided to spend fourteen nights there, 11,060 feet up.

He set out on 2 July, 1788. With him went his son Theodor; his valet; a
young painter who accompanied him only far enough to produce two water-
colours of the caravan; and a retinue of guides and porters. At first all went
well. They reached the col, set up two tents, and started work. Then they were
interrupted by the first of a series of storms. De Saussure's letters to his wife,
sent down by hand to Chamonix, went astray more than once. Some of the
guides, apparently not anxious to stay too long, ate more than their share of
the rations. Through it all de Saussure went on with his work, making his
observations, taking his readings, moved by the mountain exhilaration that
was to keep men climbing when the scientific spur no longer remained. 'The
soul is uplifted,' he wrote, 'the powers of intelligence seem to widen, and in
the midst of this majestic silence one seems to hear the voice of Nature and to
become the confidant of its most secret workings.'

De Saussure was a scientific mountain wanderer in much the same way as
Gesner and Simler. But they had lived and worked and wandered in an age
which still regarded the Alps as unfortunate acts of God: de Saussure lived
in the after-glow of Albrecht von Haller's great didactic poem which extolled
their virtues and in the early days of the Romantic revolution epitomised by
Rousseau. No disciples followed Gesner and Simler; but after de Saussure's

death, and as European travel was resumed following the end of the revolutionary wars, a host of men carried on where he had left off, expanding the demand for porters and guides who could be relied on above the snowline, and learning by trial and error the best ways of reducing the dangers of glacier travel. During the first half of the nineteenth century this process developed slowly – and was very largely confined to the Mont Blanc massif and the Bernese Oberland, areas whose impressive glaciers could be reached with comparative ease from the sophisticated centres of Geneva and Berne. As late as 1820 the explorer above the snowline was still basically the scientist turned mountaineer; forty years later he was the mountaineer who might still make scientific observations – but who might just as likely be climbing for the love of it.

It would be wrong to give the scientists all the credit for this new development of mountaineering for its own sake. The first ascent of the Gross Glockner, the highest point in Austria, was organised by the local bishop. Archduke John of Austria commissioned the first ascent of the Ortler. At the other end of the range, the Pelvoux in the Dauphiné was first scaled by a French army captain. Yet these were isolated ascents by men who made few others throughout their lives; by contrast, most of the hard-core mountaineers climbed year in, year out, as part of a scientific programme and carried out their explorations almost incidentally.

Thus the Meyers, sons of an Aarau map-maker who had been consulted by de Saussure, made the first ascent of the Jungfrau in 1811. François Joseph Hügi, who founded the Botanical Gardens in Soleure, climbed with his guides to within two hundred feet of the Finsteraarhorn's summit. Above all there was Louis Agassiz, a geologist from the little town of Orbe at the foot of the Jura, whose early scientific interests were in the direct line of descent from de Saussure and whose followers lead directly into the era of purely sporting mountaineering. Agassiz first evolved his glacier theory and then travelled extensively throughout the Oberland to find supporting evidence. To save time he camped out on the site, thus bringing into existence the Hôtel des Neuchâtelois. This bivouac, created on the Unteraar Glacier that today streams down towards the complex of lakes and reservoirs constructed for the Grimsel hydro-electric scheme, was at first merely a hole under a huge boulder – its entrance screened by a blanket. A rough cabin with wooden frame and canvas covering was added later, and this in turn was developed into a three-room building with a sleeping-place for guides and workmen, a second bedroom for Agassiz and his companions, and a combined dining-room and laboratory. Here Agassiz lived for several summers with a number of Swiss fellow-scientists. And here came distinguished visitors such as James David Forbes, who with Agassiz made the first British ascent of the Jungfrau in 1841.

The following year Forbes himself entered the glacier controversy, using the Mer de Glace as his laboratory. The basis of his observations was the movement of long lines of stakes driven into the ice, a task in which he was helped by Auguste Balmat, whose great uncle had made the first ascent of Mont Blanc, and David Couttet, the lessee of what had by this time become

The dam in the
Valgrisanche, Graian Alps.

52

a small inn at the Montanvert. They formed an interesting trio. Forbes, wearing a suit of chamois leather, long worsted stockings and a pair of double-soled London shoes that had been locally nailed, set up his survey instruments. Balmat chipped observation marks on the most convenient rocks. Couttet acted as general factotum and at times shielded Forbes's instruments from the sun with a large green umbrella. At intervals throughout the following winter, and on the occasions during the following decade when Forbes returned to Chamonix, Balmat inspected the 'stations'.

Three men were typical of this era in which mountain exploration for purely scientific reasons began to merge into mountain climbing for its own sake, and their contributions to science and to the opening-up of the Alps are almost inextricably intermingled. The first was John Ball, who visited Switzerland in 1827 at the age of nine and who later wrote that perhaps nothing had had so great an influence on his entire life as his first view of the Alps from the Col de la Faucille above Geneva. Ball spent much of the summer making new ascents. These were usually fitted into his plan for fresh botanical or geological observations, and he travelled rather than climbed. By 1863, when the first volume of his *Alpine Guide* appeared, he had crossed the main chain no less than forty-eight times by thirty-two different passes, traversed nearly a hundred lateral passes, and made history with his ascent of the Pelmo, the first of the great Dolomite peaks to be climbed. All this experience, and much more, was poured into the *Alpine Guide*. Until its publication information could easily be found about Chamonix, Grindelwald, Zermatt and a handful of other Alpine centres. But the traveller wishing to go elsewhere faced the choice of a long search through specialist – and frequently out-of-date – literature. After Ball all was different; it was no longer only the main centres to which a traveller could go with some knowledge of where to stay, of what would be found on the surrounding slopes.

John Ball himself hoped that the travellers who followed him would contribute to the scientific stock-pot, and when *Peaks, Passes and Glaciers* – records of mountain exploration by members of the Alpine Club – was published in 1860 it contained his advice on how readers could make 'observations connected with general Physics, and with Glacier Phenomena, as well as with Geology and Natural History'. That this would be arduous and complicated is underlined by Ball's own account of how he travelled.

To my knapsack [he wrote] is strapped a stout piece of rope about thirty feet long, with a Scotch plaid and umbrella; the last, though often scoffed at, is an article that hot sunshine, even more than rain, has taught me to appreciate. A couple of thermometers, a pocket clinometer, and a Kater's compass with prismatic eye-piece, may be carried in suitable pockets, along with a note-book and a sketch-book, having a fold for writing-paper, etc.; a good opera-glass, which I find more readily available than a telescope; strong knife, measuring tape, a veil, and spectacles, leather cup, spare cord, and matches. A flask with strong cold tea, to be diluted with water or snow, a tin box for plants, a geological hammer of a form available for occasional use as an ice-axe, with a strap to keep all tight, and prevent anything from swinging loosely in awkward places, complete the accoutrement.

The Alps as seen in the early 19th century. Two prints from the Lloyd Collection in the British Museum, showing the Upper Grindelwald Glacier (above) by Lory and the Mer de Glace (below) by Lamy, with the Dru on the left and the Chamonix Aiguilles on the right.

One reminder still exists of these days when any Alpine traveller worth the description was anxious to be his own scientist. It is provided by the interested flower-lover, the man or woman who would blush at the description of botanist but who will feverishly grub about, scramble up or down, and generally hold up a party as well as any camera enthusiast, in the search for some plant which he is anxious to sketch, to photograph, to collect or possibly only to identify.

Collection can cause trouble. Nowadays all plants are protected in virtually all national parks, while even outside them it is an offence to dig up, or even to pick, nearly fifty protected species. Some of these exist only in places which are dangerous or difficult of access, and C. E. Montague's *In Hanging Garden Gully*, although written of the Welsh hills, also has a lesson for would-be Alpine botanists. Yet many flowers demand perseverance rather than scrambling ability and can be sought with little more in the way of aid than a modern Alpine flora.

Ball's career, which had begun in the days of purely scientific exploration, carried him through the age of the mountain pioneers and into the era of the casual Alpine wanderer. The same was true of the two other scientist-mountaineers who bridge the gap so well – T. G. Bonney and John Tyndall, the latter a giant among Victorian scientists.

Bonney has left a vivid description of what the Alps were like even as late as 1860 when he stayed at La Bérarde at the head of the Vénéon Valley in the Dauphiné.

On the great high road from Grenoble to Briançon there is fair accommodation at one or two places [he wrote]. Off this, everything is of the poorest kind; fresh meat can only be obtained at rare intervals, the bread and wine are equally sour; the auberges filthy, and the beds entomological *vivaria*. It is hardly possible to conceive the squalid misery in which the people live; their dark dismal huts swarming with flies, fleas and other vermin; the broom, the mop and the scrubbing brush are unknown luxuries; the bones and the refuse of a meal are flung upon the floor to be

Forbes's equipment beneath an impressive glacier table on the Mer de Glace.

James David Forbes (1809–1868), and his guide Auguste Balmat (1808–1862) measuring the height of the ice on the Mer de Glace in 1842.

John Barrow (1808–1898), who spent fifteen consecutive summers on the Swiss mountains.

gnawed by dogs, and are left there to form an osseous breccia. The people in many parts are stunted, cowardly and feeble, and appear to be stupid and almost *cretins*. Too often there, as in other parts of the Alps, 'every prospect pleases and only man is vile'.

Born in 1833, when Mont Blanc had been climbed only seventeen times, Bonney lived on into the days of the téléphérique and did not die until 1923. Into thirty-five climbing seasons he packed more than a hundred ascents, sixty-five of them up to or above 10,000 feet, and the crossing of more than 170 passes. As a young man, he tacked on geologising to the making of new ascents; later, as age and ill-health began to catch up, he geologised first and climbed when he could. Yet the change of balance was only relative, and at the age of sixty he walked from his hotel to the top of the Piz Languard, an ascent of about 4,800 feet, 'without a single pause'.

Just as Bonney typifies the amiable, middling scientist, who combined science and exploration, John Tyndall stands out from the roll-call as a dedicated man whose early travels were made exclusively to unravel the glacier riddle but who became, almost despite himself, one of the half-dozen leading climbers of his day. Tyndall followed Forbes on the Mer de Glace; he made a purely scientific ascent of Mont Blanc with Auguste Balmat and spent twenty hours on the top. He climbed the Finsteraarhorn specifically to make observations from the summit while Sir Andrew Ramsay made comparable measurements in the Rhône Valley, thousands of feet lower. The essentially scientific mould of his mind is clear from the bulk of his writings – as when he comments on his six-hour passage of the ridge of the Weisshorn during its first ascent in 1861: 'The fingers, wrist and forearm were my main reliance, and as a mechanical instrument the human hand appeared to me this day in a light which it never assumed before. It is a miracle of constructive art.'

Yet Tyndall was also a most daring mountaineer. He climbed Monte Rosa alone. In 1860 he made an attempt on the Matterhorn with little scientific justification and reached 13,000 feet, higher on the mountain than any man before him. He climbed the Weisshorn mainly because it was 'one of the last great Alpine problems', and his feelings are revealed by his description of how he and his guide trod across a slender snow arête only a few inches wide. 'Right and left the precipices were appalling,' he noted; 'but the sense of power on such occasions is exceedingly sweet.' Tyndall was titillated by the dangers of mountaineering, and his attitude to them is shown by his comment on his guide Johann Bennen as they crossed the Old Weisstor in 1861. 'I followed him while the stones flew thick and fast between us. Once an ugly lump made right at me; I might, perhaps, have dodged it but Bennen saw it coming, turned, caught it on the handle of his axe as a cricketer catches a ball, and thus deflected it from me.'

Tyndall epitomised the scientist who eventually climbed for the 'sporting' appeal of the ascent. But, unlike some of his contemporaries, he still felt it necessary to dissimulate a little, to hide his mountain enthusiasms under a scientific bushel whenever one could be found. He refused an early invitation to join the Alpine Club, founded in 1857, since its primary object was concerned with 'the more difficult mountain excursions', and replied: 'I ask to be excused simply for the sake of my pursuits, and I hope that the scientific side of the Alpine question will not suffer by this arrangement.' However, when the *Alpine Journal* was founded six years later it was – as it still is – 'a Record of Mountain Adventure and Scientific Observation'. Tyndall's touchiness on this issue was illustrated in 1861 when Leslie Stephen, giving a mock-heroic account at the Alpine Club's winter dinner, concluded with what was to become a famous after-dinner paragraph.

'And what philosophical observations did you make?' will be the inquiry of one of those fanatics who, by a reasoning process to me utterly inscrutable, have somehow irrevocably associated Alpine travel with science. To them I answer, that the temperature was approximately (I had no thermometer) 212 degrees Fahrenheit below freezing point. As for ozone, if any existed in the atmosphere, it was a greater fool than I take it for.

Tyndall, incensed, resigned from the club in a huff. The image of de Saussure lingered on; but it was fading quickly and before the end of the decade had virtually been replaced. By 1871 the laboratory had become 'the playground'.

Passing a crevasse on the Glacier des Bossons. From a sketch by William Howard who, with J. van Rensselaer, made the first American ascent of Mont Blanc in 1819.

The peaks of the Graian Alps from the Aiguille du Midi.

CHAPTER THREE
Trans-Atlantic Visitors

While the mountaineers were taking over from the scientists in their exploration of the high Alps, a new sort of traveller was coming in steadily increasing numbers to the valleys. This was the man, often the family man, for whom a trip in the mountains was a pleasant change from the journey to the coast, a purely holiday excursion during which he could gaze and wonder before returning home to recount the extraordinary sights he had seen. He came with many of the same intentions as had earlier visitors but was different in two respects. As travel had become easier and less costly it had attracted in growing numbers those who had little or no interest in the intellectual or aesthetic background of the Alps; the mountains were indeed a spectacle, but a spectacle provided by a celestial showman. The 'playground of Europe' was still being discovered when it showed the first traces of becoming a fairground as well.

However, these travellers were not yet the tourists of the Victorian packaged tour. They were still individuals, often professional men even though lacking the specialised interest which had drawn their predecessors to the mountains. Typical of this intermediate brand of traveller, neither serious scientist nor artless rubber-neck, were the Americans who from the early decades of the nineteenth century not only put the Alps high on their visiting list but also insisted on seeing them above the snowline. Many had a freshness of viewpoint and a lack of inhibition in expressing it which make the accounts of their mountain adventures more lively affairs than those of Europeans for whom the writing of a Mont Blanc pamphlet was a chore expected and duly carried out. The Americans not only had the innocent curiosity of tourists from another continent but came from a country where the craft of mountaineering had grown from the pioneer need to push westwards across unsurveyed territory. To the American doctors and clergymen, getting up mountains was not a sport but a work-a-day job.

Anyone who writes about these early American climbers in the Alps owes an unrepayable debt to Dr Monroe Thorington, a past-president of the American Alpine Club, who has brought to the subject a combination of scholarship and detective work which his compatriots the Rev. W. A. B. Coolidge and Henri Montagnier brought earlier to the more general study of

Alpine history. What is known today of early American ascents is due almost entirely to his perseverance and skill.

The first American ascent of Mont Blanc was made in 1819 by William Howard and Jeremiah van Rensselaer, two young graduates who crossed the Atlantic in 1818 to visit medical centres in Europe. From Geneva they drove to Chamonix, talked with Dr Paccard and with Jacques Balmat, 'The Columbus of Mont Blanc', who had together made the first ascent a third of a century earlier. Only then, when their curiosity had been aroused, did they decide to tackle the mountain.

Both Howard and Rensselaer wrote accounts of the climb. The more vivid comes in Howard's notes which Monroe Thorington unearthed in the 1930s.

Set out from Chamouny Sunday, July 11, at 5 o'clock [these start]. At 10 began to cross the glacier of Boisson – danger – cracks – cross ladder – narrow ridges – cracks deep – stone long time falling – arrive 5 o'clock grand mulet – surrounded by ice – 9 guides – found water – cold 4° above freezing Réaumur.

Monday, 3 o'clock, left grand mulet – ascent difficult – grand plateau – breakfast – snow good – steepest ascent – steep slopes along side of which we walked on footsteps cut with axe – ended in a precipice – so that a slip would have brought us bottom – extremely fatiguing – gasping for breath, relief from vinegar and water – last only 10 or 12 steps without halting to gasp – rock – reach top – extremely cold in wind – sheltered warm – sun bright excessively – sky dark indigo blue – thermometer at freezing in sun.

Arrived at top $12\frac{1}{2}$ – view around injured by clouds – all the highest alps at our feet – staid top $1\frac{1}{2}$ – descent much easier though full as dangerous – sank up to thighs every 2 or 3 steps – descent to grand mulet extremely fatiguing – reaching it, however, at $5\frac{1}{2}$ – rest – arranged our tent – charcoal fire – not so cold as last night.

Twenty years after Howard and Rensselaer had put their mark in the history books another American doctor, Harry Allen Grant, made an attempt on Mont Blanc but was brought to a halt by bad weather. Grant is of interest since he placed lines of stones on the Glacier de Bossons and inspected them some hours afterwards to discover the extent of glacier movement, an experiment carried out long before first Forbes and then Tyndall did much the same on the Mer de Glace. Grant assiduously took the pulse of the members of his party, measured the depth of crevasses by a simple device rigged up on the spot, and generally behaved like one of the professional scientists who followed in the steps of de Saussure. However, his attempt was made on the spur of the moment, he was tourist more than serious investigator, and like others of his kind he complains about the laws which compelled a traveller to take so many guides – who all, he adds, had to attend mass at a special service before they set out for the mountain. An additional six guides, he notes without comment, 'after seeing the preparation of eatables and drinkables the landlord had prepared for our journey, volunteered to accompany us, for the privilege of free access to our haversacks'.

The Americans had a habit of protesting about the Chamonix regulations with a frankness not equalled until the Alpine Club took the matter in hand. Thus Dr Talbot, who made the second American ascent of Mont Blanc in

1854, complained bitterly that: 'Government compels every traveller to have no less than four guides: and each of these, as well as the traveller, must have a porter to accompany him as far as the Grands Mulets.' His ascent was completed without incident, and he reached the summit at noon on a day so crystal-clear that the guides claimed that a little line of blue, 'differing from the horizon', was the Mediterranean. 'I had a pebble in my pocket, which, the summer previous, I had taken from the extreme summit of Mount Washington,' Talbot later wrote. 'I broke it at this place and left it, as a first greeting from the White Mountains – the Mont Blanc of America – to the Mont Blanc of Europe.'

The next two American ascents both generated vivid accounts. The first was by the eighteen-year-old Augustine Heard, who in 1855 climbed the mountain with a seventeen-year-old Eton boy, K. A. Chapman. Both were good goers – because, explained Chapman, one 'being an American goes ahead and does things quicker than other folks, while the other, being an Englishman, would not be beat by a Yankee!'

Like others among his compatriots, Heard sent a graphic description of his exploit to relatives in the United States.

You leave the little hamlet of Boison with the singing of birds & the hum of insects in your ears, the air around being filled with the odour of the hay and flowers [he says]; as you gradually ascend, these things, one after another all disappear: the plants grow more dwarfish, the pines more stunted, & the whole aspect of nature more sterile, until there is nothing before you but naked rocks & snow & ice, except here & there a tuft of grass or moss shows itself between the rocks, while higher up the arctic lichen is the only thing of vegetation to rest the eyes upon, and all around is a dead silence.

On the top, where both Heard and Chapman at first suffered badly from the altitude, the sky appeared black: 'we had approached, as it seemed to me, so near the outside of atmosphere that envelopes the globe, that we could see through the remainder into the black limitless void beyond'. As was the custom on a good day, one guide swore he could see the Mediterranean.

The party was welcomed back to Chamonix with a twelve-gun salute; and even during dinner cannon continued to roar so that the meal was consumed 'amidst what a Fourth of July orator would call, the "thunder of the artillery & the applause of the surrounding spectators!"'

The following year Charlotte – 'Chatty' – Fairbanks arrived in Chamonix with her brother Henry whom she accompanied to the Grands Mulets. Neither intended to go farther, but after watching an English party of three set out for the top Henry changed his mind. 'Chatty' had not gained her nickname without reason, and the long letter she sent back to America gives a mass of interesting detail. After the ascent brother and sister left the Grands Mulets for Chamonix, hoping to avoid 'the parade' which still accompanied a successful ascent.

But [chatted Charlotte] the other party, who had got down before us, had brought the news of his ascent and just as we reached the village we heard the cannon from

our hotel which announced our arrival. Instantly the streets were filled with the most curious faces – peasants and visitors were all out and such an absurd sight. Henry and I walked first, followed by our guides with their axes and alpenstocks, and the crowd would make way for us to pass just as we came to them. I never was placed in a more ludicrous position, and could not control my laughter at all.

It is significant that American travellers, going for the biggest and best-known, concentrated their attentions almost exclusively on Mont Blanc. Not all of them, however, thought the effort worth while; Monroe Thorington, studying the Grands Mulets visitors' book, unearthed one comment comparable to John Murray's famous remark that all who wished to climb the

An American party at the Grands Mulets on Mont Blanc in September 1866.

mountain were of unsound mind. 'Taking into consideration the liability to serious annoyances and danger attending the trip and the small chance for a view,' wrote a Mr Johnson of Philadelphia 'the ascent of Mont Blanc is registered as one of the most foolishly spent days of my life.' Mr Johnson was a rarity. His dislike of the mountains was counter-balanced by James Kent Stone. A Boston man, he was in 1860 elected the first American member of the Alpine Club after a whirlwind record of formidable ascents; a harbinger of Gareth Hemming and John Harlin, who a century later were to bring a whiff of twentieth century trans-Atlantic energy to the Alps.

Sir Alfred Wills (far left)
and a family group at his
chalet, 'The Eagle's Nest',
in the valley of Sixt.

CHAPTER FOUR

The Coming of the Climber

From the beginning of the nineteenth century the Alps were increasingly explored, opened up and transformed by scientists, by tourists, by the occasional wealthy party making the Grand Tour as its fathers had done a generation before. There was even the solitary fellow who liked the mountains for themselves. But at first exploration above the snowline was still traditionally carried out mainly by scientists or by wealthy men with an interest in science. Agassiz camping out with his friends on the Unteraar glacier might enjoy the adventure of the exploit. Forbes, footing it up the wild Vénéon Valley to La Bérarde, was touched by the magic of discovery felt by Baker in his search for the White Nile. The men of Mont Blanc who followed de Saussure not only made their own observations but also drew a whiff of enjoyment from the thin summit atmosphere. From the earliest days all but the most *lumpen* and unimaginative scientists responded to the difficulties and the dangers of moving about in the new world of glacier and rock-rib, ice-wall and crevasse. Nevertheless in 1835 most men who climbed above the snowline still did so very genuinely for some scientific reason. A generation later people climbed because they enjoyed it, because they wanted to get to the top, because they were participants in a new and comparatively non-competitive sport which chimed in well with the mid-century spirit. Some, such as Tyndall, had been driven to climb by a spirit of scientific inquiry but soon found enjoyment of the mountains creeping in. Francis Fox Tuckett often carried when he was on the mountains 'besides such commonplace things as a great axe-head and a huge rope and thermometers ... two barometers, a sypsieometer, and a wonderful apparatus, pot within pot, for boiling water at great haights, first for scientific and then for culinary purposes'; but Tuckett had taken to mountaineering after a lone rambling tour of the Alps, and the earnest spirit of Quaker inquiry which he turned to his mountaineering could not conceal the fact that he liked it. Even so, by the later 1850s the Tyndalls and the Tucketts were being swamped by men such as the Smyth brothers, Alfred Wills, the Walker brothers, Hereford Brooke George, William Mathews and a score of other prosperous British professional men who climbed instead of hunting or shooting. The age of purely 'sporting' mountaineering had arrived.

A group taken in the 1860s showing Miss Straton (centre) and Miss Emmeline Lewis-Lloyd (far left), two of the first British women mountaineers.

The Golden Age lasted for little more than a decade, and although it can be repeated elsewhere – in the Himalayas and Andes today and in more inaccessible ranges later on – it is over and done with as far as Europe is concerned. Yet the Alps still bask in the after-glow. The ascent of the Wetterhorn by Wills in 1854 – not the first ascent of the mountain as we shall see – which is generally, and not too inaccurately, taken as marking the start of the Golden Age, was the event which really made Grindelwald. Whymper's ascent of the Matterhorn, which in 1865 brought the period to an end, is the one single event which still makes Zermatt a shrine and a gawper's delight.

In between the two dates the summits of the Alps fell like ninepins on a day when the bowling goes well – some sixty major peaks, from Monte Viso in the Cottians to the Pelmo in the Dolomites, from the Écrins in the Dauphiné to Piz Roseg in the Bernina. As Whymper and the two Taugwalders descended the Swiss ridge on that fateful afternoon in July 1865, only the Meije had not been climbed to the top.

Credit for the huge achievement of this single decade is often given to the English, wholly and uncritically. In more general terms, exploration of the entire range is sometimes described as though it was carried out by the Island Race, single-handed, in a wait between innings. Yet before 1854 almost all the firsts had in fact been achieved by Continental climbers – who had not only Mont Blanc and the Jungfrau to their credit but the Finsteraarhorn, the Ortler, the Tödi, the Gross Glockner, the Bernina, most of the summits of Monte Rosa, and many others. Then, as though the Great Exhibition had suddenly sparked awake among the British a realisation of their sporting duties, the lawyers from Birmingham and the dons from Oxbridge, the gentlemen-philosophers and doctors and Civil Servants, took

the job in hand. The Swiss, the French, Germans and Austrians continued to climb, of course. But it is difficult to study the records of the times without feeling that they were rather brusquely shuffled aside; that the English, almost as a matter of course, began to monopolise the best guides, to take over the leadership now that they had, at last, found the game worth playing.

Just why the British took over at this particular moment is beyond the scope of these pages. But Tuckett, describing his ascent of the Aletschhorn, the fine peak seen across the Aletsch Glacier by those who téléphérique to the top of the Aeggishorn, had one chauvinistic answer: 'I unhesitatingly maintain that there is a joy in these measurings of strength with Nature in her wildest moods, a quiet sense of work done, and success won in the teeth of opposition … whether we owe it to our Anglo-Saxon blood, as some may hold, or whether it be only one of the modes in which the "contrariness" of human nature crops out in certain individuals.' The influence of which this feeling was the unconscious expression gave to the conquest of the Alps an aura of off-putting Victorian conventionality; it began to disperse only between the two World Wars and disappeared only after 1945 when British climbers, impoverished but impenitent, set a new pattern of climbing not on a financial rope but a financial shoe-string.

Few mountaineers of the Golden Age were impoverished. Arnold Lunn, who has analysed the first volume of Mumm's Alpine Club Register, which

A typical mountaineering group of 1865. Melchior Anderegg, one of the most famous guides of the time, is seen far left, back row; 'young' Peter Taugwalder, one of the three survivors of the Matterhorn accident, is far right, back row. Leslie Stephen is seen seated, far left.

The dramatic statue of
Balmat and de Saussure in
the main square of
Chamonix.

details the climbing achievements of members, has provided some illuminating figures. Of the 281 who joined before 1864, some eighty were practising barristers or solicitors, thirty-four were clergymen, twenty-two were dons or schoolmasters, nineteen were landed gentry and twelve were Civil Servants. Almost all the rest could have been described as professional or business men. These gentlemen conquered the Alps in a leisurely but confident way, not quite, as Frank Smythe wrote of the next generation, 'popping their bottles of Bouvier on every summit', but with something only a little less exuberant. Their enjoyment, they freely admitted, was the main reason for the expenditure of so much energy for so little visible result; their observation was the vestigial remnant of their scientific inheritance; and the almost proselyte fervour with which they acclaimed the virtues of their new pastime sprang from a national pride that the last outposts of Europe were falling to the British.

Comparing these Alpine pioneers with modern mountaineers provides some startling contrasts. They were men with long holidays. There was no hurried rushing out and back in two or three weeks, straight from office desk to summit. Instead at least five or six weeks would be assigned to the serious occupation of climbing; an additional week or so was usually available at the end if the weather was particularly good.

Today the motorist with a schedule has something in common with the mountain enthusiast, determined to pack as many peaks as possible into two or three weeks, Britain back to Britain: for both, bad weather upsets time-tables, ruins tight schedules, tends to turn mountain enjoyment into an obstacle race. The Victorians were able to look at things differently, and at least one of them almost lamented the three months of unbroken sunshine that poured down on the Central Alps throughout July, August and September of 1859. Reasonable enough, no doubt. But with a place booked on the Channel ferry and part of the programme scrubbed out by rain, the consolations of catching up with the diary are slight.

Chamonix group taken in August, 1863 showing (left to right): the Rev. J.J. Hornby, later Head Master of Eton; the famous guides Christian Almer and Christian Lauener; and the Rev. T.E. Philpott.

For the Victorians time could be made to linger a little even if it could not be brought to a halt. However, when the clouds cleared there was always much to do – much more, rated in energy-output per foot of ascent, than there is today – including the long trudge from valley floor to snowline or above, an hours-long upward plod now often represented by a ticket on the téléphérique to a high hut. Examples abound. Thus from Solda, lying beneath its semi-circle of the Cevedale and the Ortler, an Austrian village which no boundary changes will ever really alter, it is possible to do a large slice of upping by chair-lift *en route* to the Payer hut before an ascent of the Ortler; or at least to walk up and spend a leisurely night before the ascent. But in the Visitors' Book of the Post Hotel there are two revealing entries. One, signed by Douglas Freshfield, his wife and two companions, reads: 'Ascended the Ortler Spitz from this inn. Started at 5.30. Reached the top at 11.20. Started to descend 11.40 am and reached the inn at 3.20 pm'. The second is signed by the re-doubtable Mrs Burnaby, the much-married lady who confusingly appears in Alpine literature also as Mrs Le Blond and Mrs Le Main. She had left Bormio at 6.30 am on Thursday, 31 August 1882, and her brief note in the book, after recording this fact, continues: 'Arrived here 6 pm. Leave at midnight for Ortler, descend to Trafoi and return to Bormio on Saturday. Inn comfort-able'.

This quick shuttling to and fro, the ease with which they traversed the range if not from end to end at least from district to district with a lordly dis-interest in elementary logistics, was made possible by the relative size of their purses. They could whistle up as many porters as they required, hire and fire horse-drawn transport as needed, and in many cases had merely to state what they wanted and leave all detail to their chief guide who often exercised the additional duties of master of the caravanserai.

Even so, the pioneers had to be tough, and not only in their ability to cover the long approach routes which led to where the serious business began. A rough hut was built on the Grands Mulets on Mont Blanc in 1853. But it was only in 1868 that Alexander Seiler, the hotelier-king of Zermatt, helped pay for the first rude shelter on the Swiss ridge of the Matterhorn, later replaced first by the Hörnli hut and then by today's luxurious quarters. Before the end of the 'sixties, there was a shelter at the foot of the Grand Combin, and the Gleck-stein gîte on the approach to the Wetterhorn, little more than an adapted cave, had been replaced by a hut. Within the next decade the Swiss Alpine Club alone had sponsored no less than thirty-four huts.

But the men who first climbed most of the major Alpine peaks usually lacked these rough aids to survival. Their pre-ascent bivouac was made either under the stars – although often with the comfort of straw or pine-needles carried up or gathered by porters – or under the scant protection of overhanging rocks. On a typical expedition the bivouac would be just below the permanent snowline. Varying from place to place, and from season to season, this would be from a few hundred feet below 8,000 on the north side of the range to a few hundred feet above 9,000 on the south.

A fire would be built for the night to supplement the warmth of blankets

Peaks seen from la Flégère, above Chamonix.

73

The great slopes of the Fiescherwand seen across the valley from above Grindelwald.

carried up by the porters, needed in the days before windproof materials, and when clothing for a 14,000-foot peak hardly differed from that on a winter walk in Britain. Equipment was rudimentary and country boots fitted with rough hobs by the local cobbler were usual. The ice-axe was still being developed and the headless alpenstock, little more than a long stick with ferrule and point, was still used. Wood-choppers for cutting steps in the ice were not unknown. The special grappling-iron devised by Whymper, which could be slung high above the climber in a difficult place in the hope that it would catch on some unseen protruberance, was considered by most climbers not only unsafe but unsporting. Ladders carried to help cross crevasses were heavy wooden affairs rather than the light alloy contraptions devised a century later. The rope was in use, but its quality often questionable and many guides still regarded it with suspicion. Modern principles of belaying, which can safeguard members of a party, were virtually unknown. Thus there was much on the debit side for the climbers of the 1850s. They had their porters and their guides as well as the cash to pay them; but they had to rough

74

it and they would have eyed with envy – possibly qualified by distaste – most contemporary aids to camping in comfort.

The party would set out in the small hours, helped by the jerking gleams from that permanent prop, the glacier lantern. With first light there would be spread out, at comparatively close range, the scene that non-mountaineers know only at second remove. Roads, railways and the huge variety of mechanical mountain transport do, it is true, bring the non-climbing traveller nearer than ever before to rubbing his nose on the rocks. The light plane and the helicopter, buzzing about the upper snowfields and sometimes creating in the passenger the feeling that he can stretch out and touch the crags, give an illusion of intimate contact with mountain structure. Yet illusion it is. The Alpine world seen from an accessible viewpoint is not the world in which the climber grapples with individual problems of rock and ice. Scale is only one important factor for the non-climber to grasp. The 'little notch' may be a rock wall a hundred or more feet high; the 'little cloud on the mountain', the substance of a raging storm in which men are fighting for their lives.

On many peaks the approach is across a glacier. At its head there runs the bergschrund, the deep crevasse separating glacier from parent mountain. From the far distance, even through binoculars, this will probably be seen only as a thin line where the uppermost snow and ice of the glacier butts up against the rock of the mountain itself. It may be many feet wide and hundreds of feet deep; its features will change from season to season, even from week to week, and crossing it on the ascent can present the first problem of the day.

Above the bergschrund rises the body of the mountain. The briefest inspection is enough to show that it may be made up of almost any permutation or combination of rocky forms; even so, a peak will often have three or four ridges, or arêtes, meeting at the summit, and with the necessary qualifications these arêtes offer the most encouraging routes to the top. Between the ridges are the faces, tackled only in the later stages of exploration, since they are often swept by stones, avalanches, and other mountain debris which bring dangers no skill can be certain of evading. Short cuts to the upper parts of a ridge can sometimes be made by using couloirs – steep wide gulleys of rock, snow or ice. But couloirs, in the nature of things, are also highroads for debris; and the pages of mountain literature are cluttered with warnings of how to escape from couloirs before the rising sun begins to melt the night-frozen snow and ice, to unleash the fusillade.

Ideally the Victorian climber was as high as possible by sun-up and was on the summit by mid-morning. The easiest path was chosen and difficulties were avoided, the aim of the exercise being to get to the top rather than to make a new route. Another contrast with current fashion was that snow and ice were preferred to rocks – and it is significant that while Mont Blanc was ascended for the first time, and for many times afterwards, almost exclusively across snow and ice, the Meije, the last great peak of the Alps to be conquered, is essentially a rock climb.

One result of this preference was the speed with which the great peaks of the Pennines and the Graians fell during the Golden Age, and the com-

Douglas Freshfield (1845–1934) with companions and guide.

Primitive ladder in use for crossing a bergschrund.

Early mountaineering equipment.

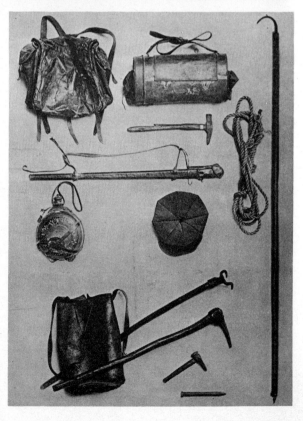

parative lack of attention given to such groups as the Dolomites where glaciers are virtually non-existent and where, during the climbing season, snow and ice are relatively rare. In 1854 the Ostspitze of Monte Rosa was climbed by the Smyth brothers, two of them clergymen and the third an Army officer, and the following year another British party climbed the highest of the peaks which rise from the mountain's summit ridge. The Allalinhorn and the Laquinhorn in the Eastern Pennines were climbed in 1856 and the nearby Dom in 1858, a year in which the Eiger, the great Oberland peak whose north wall is today the most notorious face in the Alps, was also climbed for the first time.

The Eiger ascent was remarkable. It was made by Charles Barrington, an amateur rider who had won the Irish Grand National and had never before visited Switzerland. He climbed the Jungfrau, was unimpressed and said so to two British mountaineers in the Bear Hotel at Grindelwald. 'Try the Eiger or the Matterhorn,' he was advised: Not having time or money for the latter, he set out the following evening for the Eiger.

With two guides he spent the night at the hotel on the Wengern Alp. They left at 3.30, Barrington carrying a flag to plant on the summit. When he tackled the rocks directly ahead, the two guides refused to follow.

So I went off for about 300 or 400 yards over some smooth rocks to the part which was almost perpendicular [he wrote to his brother]. I then waved the flag for them to come on, and after five minutes they followed and came up to me. They said it was impossible; I said, 'I will try'. So, with the rope coiled over my shoulders, I scrambled up, sticking like a cat to the rocks, which cut my fingers, and at last got up say fifty to sixty feet. I then lowered the rope and the guides followed with its assistance.

By midday they were on the top. They stayed for only ten minutes, fearing bad weather, then descended by a couloir. Barrington notes without comment that they saved themselves 'by a few seconds from an avalanche'.

On the Wengern Alp the party was met by about thirty visitors. 'They doubted if we had been on the top until the telescope disclosed the flag there,' Barrington reported. 'The hotel proprietor had a large gun fired off, and I seemed for the evening to be a "lion". Thus ended my first and only visit to Switzerland.'

Few ascents were made as casually as this. More frequently they were first mulled over in Britain as small groups of friends planned which unclimbed peaks to make their own. 'Unclimbed' was what mattered, and as such peaks continued to diminish around the more popular centres, mountaineers turned elsewhere – to the Graians where the Gran Paradiso and the Grande Casse fell in 1860, to the Cottians, where the stately Monte Viso was climbed by William Mathews in 1861, and to the Dauphiné where in 1864 Whymper, A. W. Moore and Horace Walker climbed the Écrins, the highest peak in the group.

All this enterprise was greatly encouraged by the formation of the Alpine Club in 1857, a typically British institution which brought together a small

A.W. Moore (1841–1887), whose party made the first ascent of Mont Blanc by the Brenva in 1865.

number of like-minded men who dined at regular intervals to discuss their mutual problems and experiences. From the first the club demanded that members should have a mountaineering qualification – or, later on, that they should have contributed in some special way to the understanding of mountains, by writing, painting or photography for instance.

This example was rarely followed on the Continent. The Italian club included many first-class mountaineers, as well as the fine writers and artists, but it had no strict qualification gate like the London club. The Swiss club, moreover, aimed to attract all those who were interested in the Alps. In 1869 there came the German and Austrian clubs – united in 1929 – which followed Swiss rather than British pattern. Five years later the French Alpine Club came into existence with an innovation: it admitted women, a move that confirmed many mountaineers in their belief that the French, after their defeat by the Prussians three years previously, could no longer be taken seriously. One French reaction to the Prussian defeat of 1871 was shown, rather ironically in the light of later history, in the wording of the club's motto: '*Pour la patrie par la montagne*'. Thus nationalism in climbing, apparent so far in little more than the friendly rivalry between Swiss and British, and to earn such a black mark between the two World Wars, was nearly made respectable. With the growth of the clubs there came, also, an extension of mountaineering possibilities, brought about in a variety of ways, one of which was provided by a natural characteristic of the Alpine chain.

In most mountain areas valleys stretching out from the main chain are divided by subsidiary chains or ridges and the journey from one valley to the next involves, for the non-mountaineer, a long trudge downhill, a journey round the end of the ridge, and an even more depressing plod back uphill which may land him only a mile or so from the place he left hours before. The motorist has to do this today if he wants to get from the Saastal to the Nikolaital at whose head Zermatt lies; from the Nikolaital to the Val d'Hérens; or from the Val d'Hérens to the Val de Bagnes. The inconvenience was very odious to the early mountaineers, and the first series of papers produced by the members of the Alpine Club appeared under the title of *Peaks, Passes and Glaciers*. The passes were in most cases high ones, made for the first time, and combining a time-saving route with what were very often the severest of mountaineering difficulties.

An indication of how new problems could be found, a search made more difficult by the conquest of the Matterhorn in 1865, was by a tidy coincidence suggested on the day following the disaster. This solution lay in finding entirely new routes up old mountains.

Emerging into bright sunlight from the Italian end of the Mont Blanc tunnel it is possible today to turn either east or west along the deep valley trench that cuts off the massif from the ridge of lower hills to the south – the Monte della Saxe, the Monte Chetif and the Tête d'Arp, from which are seen the cascade of glacier and rock-rib and snowface that make up the huge southern wall of Mont Blanc and its attendant summits.

On the far west, to the left when facing the mountain, there rise the Brouill-ard and Peteret arêtes; further round, almost under the lee of Mont Blanc, is the Brenva face, up whose vertical buttresses Graham Brown and Frank Smythe forced a series of extraordinary routes during the later 1930s; to the east, and bounding the far side of the Brenva Glacier, is the Brenva arête, a ridge of rock, snow and ice rising towards the frontier ridge, which leads to the final slopes of Mont Blanc itself.

This ridge was to be the scene for what is still, after more than half a century, one of the best mountain novels written in English, A. E. W. Mason's *Running Water*. In 1865 it was of importance not because it led to the top of an un-climbed mountain but because it offered a difficult and exciting climb. It is true that the route, if it could be followed, would allow mountaineers in

Courmayeur to ascend Mont Blanc and descend to Chamonix. Yet the ascent of Mont Blanc by the Brenva arête was also typical of the search for 'new' routes on old mountains' to be carried out increasingly during the years that followed.

It was made by Francis Walker, a fifty-seven-year-old Liverpool merchant who had been climbing in the Alps since 1825; his son Horace Walker; G. S. Mathews, who had helped to found the Alpine Club eight years previously; and A. W. Moore, a Senior Clerk in the India Office who had been with Whymper in the Dauphiné the previous year and already had a number of fine ascents to his credit. Their guides, from the Bernese Oberland, were Melchior Anderegg, who the previous year had ruled out the route as being 'a miserable piece of folly', and his cousin Jakob.

The bivouac site was typical of the period, a small rocky platform, which they had levelled as best they could. Here, at about 9,000 feet, roughly on a level with the top of the Tête d'Arp they slept until about 2.30, waking to sip a mixture of hot wine and coffee in the dark before sending the porters back to Courmayeur and setting out across the glacier. By 5.30 they were over the bergschrund and on the long rocky ridge which led up to a little snow peak. Beyond that they would have to force a way through a complicated ice-tangle before reaching the upper slopes of Mont Blanc. They foresaw no other difficulty.

They breakfasted at 7.30, halting for half an hour as the light crept down to meet them and illuminate the Italian plain to the south. Away to the west, ridge upon ridge of the Graian and Cottian Alps shone in the sun. Then they reached the little snow peak that from below had seemed to crown the ridge. What they saw beyond was the horizontal ridge-pole of the Brenva ice-ridge.

On most arêtes, however narrow the actual crest may be [Moore wrote], it is generally possible to get a certain amount of support by driving the pole into the slope below on either side. But this was not the case here. We were on the top of a wall, the ice on the right falling vertically (I use the word advisedly) and on the left nearly so. On neither side was it possible to obtain the slightest hold with the alpenstock. I believe also that an arête of pure ice is more often encountered in description than in reality, that term being generally applied to hard snow. But here, for once, we had the genuine article – blue ice without a speck of snow on it. The space for walking was at first about the breadth of the top of an ordinary wall, in which Jakob cut holes for the feet. Being last in the line, I could see little of what was coming until I was close upon it, and was therefore considerably startled on seeing the men in front suddenly abandon the upright position, which, in spite of the insecurity of the steps and difficulty of preserving the balance, had been hitherto maintained, and sit down *à cheval*. The ridge had narrowed to a knife-edge, and for a few yards it was utterly impossible to advance in any other way. The foremost men stood up again, but when I was about to follow their example, Melchior insisted emphatically on my not doing so, but remaining seated. Regular steps could no longer be cut, but Jakob, as he went along, simply sliced off the top of the ridge, making thus a slippery pathway, along which those behind crept, moving one foot carefully after the other. As for me, I worked myself along with my hands, in an attitude safe, perhaps, but considerably more uncomfortable, and, as I went, I could not help occasionally speculating, with an odd feeling of amusement, as to what would be the result if any of the party should chance to slip over on either side – what the rest would do – and if so, what would happen then.

The question did not arise. The party completed the traverse and found a way up and through the wall of ice towering above – even though the four amateurs were carrying only the long alpenstocks of little use in such difficult places.

The Brenva ridge was not climbed again until 1870 when the twenty-year-old W. A. B. Coolidge made the ascent. A variation was made eleven years after that, but the whole route was followed for the third time, by the German climber Paul Gussfeldt, only in 1893; and forty years after the first ascent it had been climbed by only nine parties. Before this, A. E. W. Mason, himself a competent mountaineer, used the Brenva ridge for the crux of *Running Water*. In it he described the second ascent as carried out by a man of very dubious background. This was too much for the ever-quarrelsome Coolidge, who on publication of the book threatened to bring a libel action against Mason.

The trend of which the Brenva ascent was such a dramatic illustration – that of finding new routes up old mountains from fresh places – has during the last century done much to even out the human load across the Alps. For it was not only the main centres which began to grow more quickly after 1865. In minor side valleys, at the ends of the long depressions which wind up among the main ridges of the Alpine chain, in hamlets and groups of chalets which for centuries had seen only the occasional visitor from the outside world, small groups of mountaineers now began to appear with their questions about neighbouring ridges, with guides from districts that seemed to local people as distant as far Cathay. The huts of chamois-hunters – or sometimes the home of the *curé* – which did service for the odd night's shelter, soon gave way to the humble inn, and this in turn, as the fame of an area grew, gave way to something more elaborate. Trade followed the climbing rope. Within a few days of Whymper's conquest of the Matterhorn, Jean-Antoine Carrel at last climbed the peak from the Italian side, thus helping the process by which through an almost infinite series of adjustments and transformations, Breuil, with the cows slopping through the dung beneath the broad eaves of its wooden houses, has become the trendy ski-resort of Breuil–Cervinia. The Bagni del Masino, an almost idyllic paradise when the neighbouring Monte Disgrazia was first climbed, developed almost imperceptibly into a fashionable spa. The history in which, after the first Brenva climb, the Dora Baltea as well as Chamonix became a possible starting-point for the ascent of Mont Blanc, was repeated throughout the Alps.

This evolution had of course been going on since the start of the Romantic revolution with its acknowledgment that the Alps should be subjects for admiration rather than horror. But it was now quickening in pace, and to the dismay not only of Ruskin. Mr Cook brought his first party to the Alps in 1863, a year from which the tourist industry never looked back. The influx soon began to rise above the snowline, and what many men felt in the late nineteenth century was expressed by Conway in the twentieth. 'The activities of the German and Austrian Alpine Club have no doubt opened the mountains to a number of persons who otherwise would not have visited them, and who profit greatly by the exercise, the fine air, the noble views, that Nature provides for all alike,' he noted; 'but in so doing, it has made parts of the country unpleasant to travel in.' Those who have suffered from the contemporary cattle-crowding of Alpine huts are likely to breathe 'Amen' even if their social consciences object.

Here it is necessary to distinguish two attitudes to the growth of the tourist trade which took place during the last quarter of the last century, which prepared the way for developments after 1945, and which led to the state of the Alps today. To start with, snobbery tended to rule the roost. Mountaineers questioned the invasion of those who remained below the snowline; mere walkers resented the filling up of the valleys by the even commoner herd. All voted for the exclusion of those below them in the open-air pecking order. Only later did there arise a more respectable reason for querying the unlimited inflow of visitors: the growing realisation that in the not so distant future the

Monte Disgrazia, first ascended by Sir Leslie Stephen in 1862. Drawn by Edward Whymper.

Alps might have been developed out of existence. However, in the decades which immediately followed the Matterhorn accident, all this was no more than a minor puff of cloud on the horizon.

The extension and aggrandisement of simple villages to accommodate scramblers and walkers, and tourists who merely wanted to stand and stare, was not accompanied by a withering-away of genuine mountaineering once the great peaks had all been climbed, a very real fear a century ago. Whymper himself confided to an acquaintance in the summer of 1865 that after the ascent of the Matterhorn he would give up mountaineering, since there would be 'no great new mountains' to be climbed. In 1883 Bonney, then president of the Alpine Club, foresaw one difficulty: 'that of providing papers for our evening meetings, and of filling our Journal'.

Yet following the conquest of the more difficult peaks, which with the exception of the Meije was completed in the 1860s, three main developments helped to keep alive a zest for mountaineering which was quite distinct from the repetition of climbs already made by other people. One was the climbing of old mountains by new routes such as the Brenva arête. There was also mountaineering in winter. T. S. Kennedy had in 1862 made a January attempt on the Swiss side of the Matterhorn. But he had found Zermatt shuttered up for the winter, obtained shelter with the *curé* only with difficulty, and was beaten back from the mountain. It was not a good augury for such unconventional efforts, and although A. W. Moore of Brenva fame carried out a number of winter expeditions in the Oberland and the Dauphiné during the early 1860s, Kennedy had few followers. Their attempts were isolated exceptions, rare expeditions which in the view of local people – and of most other mountaineers – were tolerated as an eccentricity which should not be pushed too far.

Winter sports were unknown, and when the last of the visitors left during mid-Autumn the inhabitants resumed their normal occupations, compared with which the guiding and touristing of the summer months was only a passing if profitable side-line. All this began to change during the early 1870s, partly due to the influence of W. A. B. Coolidge. In 1873, greatly daring, Coolidge and his aunt, the intrepid Meta Brevoort, planned a winter ascent of Mont Blanc, but got no further than the shuttered Montanvert where they left their names in a bottle as the last visitors of the old year. But in Grindelwald, a few weeks later, they persuaded the owner of the little inn on the Faulhorn to open up specially for them and, looking across to the Wetterhorn, decided to make what was shortly afterwards the first winter ascent.

The idea of climbing in winter caught on. The shortness of the day was a disadvantage, but snow conditions were not as difficult as expected, and the beauty of winter landscapes seen from above was rewarding. At first only the easiest mountains and best-known routes were tackled. And only in the present century was it considered practicable to attempt severe rock routes in winter. But the point had been made. One after another hotels throughout the Alps began to open for the Christmas season. When, later on, a variety of circumstances suddenly produced the first great boom in winter sports, the ground had been prepared.

Climbing in winter peaks that had until recently been considered un-climbable even in summer was one way of clocking up fresh mountaineering achievements, just as climbing old mountains by new routes was another. But there was a third possibility: that of tackling, as new 'peaks', separate subsidiary summits, towers or pinnacles which had always been considered mere outriders of a mountain.

Just as the Brenva arête on the south side of Mont Blanc provides a good example of a new route up an old mountain, so do the Aiguilles on the north illustrate this other development. From the Brévent, the Flégère or any of the other viewpoints which rise to the north of the Chamonix valley, Mont Blanc is the centre-piece of the scene to the south. But across the valley, bounded on the east by the Mer de Glace and on the west by the Glacier des Bossons, there rise the Chamonix Aiguilles, a long line of granite summits meriting the des-cription of Stac Polly in Scotland – 'a porcupine in a state of annoyance'. The Petis Charmoz, the prominent Aiguille de la République, the Grands Charmoz, the Grépon and the Aiguille du Fou, the Caiman and the Aiguille du Plan, are only some of the needles, most of which had fallen before the end of the century to the determined attack of first-class rock climbers.

A.F. Mummery (1855–1895), climbing the Mummery crack on the Grépon in 1881.

These pinnacles, many christened with a separate name only after they had been climbed, drew from the men who scaled them quite as much enthusiasm as their predecessors had lavished on the great peaks of an earlier age. Thus Clinton Dent made no less than eighteen attempts on the Dru, the huge rocky peak rising across the Mer de Glace from the Montanvert, before finally reaching its small sloping summit. 'There for a moment I stood alone gazing down on Chamonix,' he wrote. 'The holiday dream of five years was accom-plished; the Aiguille du Dru was climbed. Where in the world will you find a sport able to yield pleasure like this?'

Dent's siege of the Dru also exemplified another process that had been continuing since men began climbing mountains for the challenge they offered, but which speeded up during the last quarter of the nineteenth century. It was first described by Leslie Stephen as early as 1871. Since he had first come to the Alps, Stephen wrote, many mountains had 'passed through the successive stages denoted by the terms "inaccessible", "the most difficult point in the Alps", "a good hard climb, but nothing out of the way", "a perfectly straightforward bit of work", and, finally, "an easy day for a lady"'.

'Lady' – or rather 'women' – mountaineers had become a normal feature of the Alpine scene well before the end of the century. Their acceptance, to-gether with the growth of winter mountaineering, the making of new routes, and the subdivision of great peaks to provide 'first ascents' of what had pre-viously been considered no more than pinnacles, created a scene that changed comparatively little during the quarter-century that ended with the outbreak of the First World War. More people were climbing, of course, and some of the older-stagers at the Alpine Club might complain that there were far too many. And if the petrol engine really caught on the result might be disastrous.

The Dru and the Aiguille Verte, photographed by the Bisson brothers in 1860.

CHAPTER FIVE
The Thunder of the Guns

The First World War created a watershed between the old and new Alpine worlds quite as prominent as those it created elsewhere. A massive frontier realignment, the transfer of half a million people from one country to another and the Italianisation of the most famous names in the Dolomites were only the most obvious results. The new nationalisms which followed the Treaty of Versailles played their part in bringing a brutalising spirit into mountaineering and in transforming it from a sport into a quasi-military occupation. A more democratic European society – which would have come into existence in any case but whose strengths were increased by the war – brought to the mountains after 1918 a flood of recruits who would not otherwise have visited them. And for the first time the question of how many humans the Alpine environment could absorb became more than academic.

These developments helped to make the war of 1914–18 more important than any that had gone before. Yet it was, after all, merely the latest of many which the mountains had seen. The Alps had for centuries amassed their own crop of military legends, as well as a patina of memorials, cairns and monuments quite as moving as the plaques to guides which adorn the walls of churches and Alpine museums.

For more than two thousand years actions have been fought out across the passes, and in the upper valleys, in an effort to control the routes linking the plains of Italy with Central Europe. The signs are everywhere: the simple white cross beneath the Meije with its name and the legend 'Front des Alpes, 1940–45), the astonishing Suvorov monument in the Schöllenen Gorge on the St Gotthard route, the gigantic piton replica beneath the rocks of Triglav in the Julian Alps, a tribute to the Yugoslav partisans that is perhaps the most remarkable of all the world's war memorials.

The first recorded example of war in the Alps has caused more controversy than most and can still, some 2,000 years later, trigger off an excuse for military detective work and a journey into the less publicised upper valleys. The question is where did Hannibal actually take his elephants, a conundrum that has raised tempers, produced opposing schools of thought, and created a good example of the Alpine controversy that splits families down the middle. The climate of the argument is well illustrated by Sir Gavin de Beer, who

The Devil's Bridge near Andermatt, above which General Suvorov fought his battle with the French in 1799.

86

prefaces one of his books on Hannibal with the cautionary quotation from Mark Twain: 'The researches of many antiquarians have already thrown much darkness on the subject, and it is probable, if they continue, that we shall soon know nothing at all.'

In the late summer of 218 BC Hannibal crossed the Pyrenees from Spain with a considerable army – and with the elephants; marched to the Rhône; travelled up it some way before making a contested crossing; and then marched east for Italy. Before the year was out he was successfully over the Alps and creating mayhem with an army which was later to win a classic victory at Lake Trasimene. But where did Hannibal cross the Alps? How did he succeed in forcing his African elephants – numbers unknown – over what must in any case have been a formidable pass, at the end of October, and almost certainly after the first of the early winter snowfalls?

The evidence is confused and sometimes contradictory. According to various authorities, Hannibal crossed the Montgenèvre, the Mont Cenis, the Little St Bernard, the Col de Larche, the Col de Mary, the Col Clapier or the Col de la Traversette. Respectable, if not entirely convincing, arguments can be made for most of them. Recently a much firmer case has been made by Sir Gavin who with his unique combination of scientific background, military experience and Alpine knowledge has used weather data and logistical analysis to show that 'all things considered, the Col de la Traversette is the one pass which best satisfies all the requirements'.

The Traversette lies high up on the Franco-Italian frontier ridge below Monte Viso. It has the distinction of being the first Alpine pass pierced by a tunnel, and is reached by the long Guil Valley, which debouches into the Durance at Mont Dauphin where Vauban's huge fortress still stands on its rocky promontory. Hannibal appears to have reached this vantage-point after crossing the Rhône north of Donzère, where the French have built their massive hydro-electric and irrigation system, marching up the Drôme Valley, and then taking to the Durance south of Gap.

Standing at Mont Dauphin today it is easy to understand why the Carthaginians turned out of the Durance Valley, even though it in fact leads up past Briançon whence the comparatively easy Mongenèvre gives access to the plains of Italy via the Dora Riparia and Susa. For north of Mont Dauphin, a circlet of mountains appears to bar the way. Yet a sharp right turn reveals to the east an apparently easy route past the plug of Mont Dauphin itself and into the temporarily broad area in which Guillestre lies. Beyond, a simple way seems to lead even further east. It is possible that the local men deliberately tempted Hannibal up into this valley from which there is no exit to Italy half as convenient as the Montgenèvre; if so, the lie of the land helped their deception. For whatever reason, Hannibal turned east, marched up the Guil to Guillestre and only then, when it was too late to countermand orders, realised what faced him.

Even today, the narrowing Guil valley above Guillestre suggests – for a moment at least – that the road is leaving the lusher haunts of civilisation. The rock-walls close in. The road has a minor bout of tunnelling as it is carried

Château-Queyras, standing on the rock that bars entrance to the Guil gorges – probably the 'bare rock' on which Hannibal bivouacked before crossing the Alps in 218 BC.

hundreds of feet above the river. At places it is difficult to see where an exit can possibly be discovered, and it is chastening to think of Hannibal and his men making the same passage without benefit of modern roads and in the face of a native population rolling down boulders from the heights.

Beyond the defile lies Château-Queyras, probably the 'bare rock' on which Hannibal bivouacked in comparative safety with the advance guard while waiting for his main body of troops to emerge from the gorge. Also fortified by Vauban it is, even more than Mont Dauphin, the epitome of the military bastion built on topography, covering the exit from the gorge. Behind it there stretches out the widening upper valley of the Guil. Here, where the Carthaginian troops prepared for the even tougher test ahead, there lies today the village of Aiguilles and higher up the smaller township of Abriès, both decently fashionable skiing centres. Above Abriès the rough road leads to the edge of the Belvédère du Cirque, the huge corrie above which rise the ribs and ridges of Monte Viso. To the north-east, over steepening grass slopes, lies the Col de la Traversette, a narrow ridge from which there spreads out with unexpected suddenness a view of the Piedmont plain that takes in the hills above Genoa and stretches as far as Milan. Here Hannibal gave his men their first glimpse of the promised land.

Snow and ice made the passage of the col difficult, and the Carthaginian method of splitting the rocks with fire below and vinegar above has become famous. But it was quite possibly the last hundred feet or so which alone caused serious trouble, and nearly 1,700 years after Hannibal these difficulties were removed by a 250-foot tunnel driven between the French and Italian slopes. Nearly seven feet high, with iron rings in the roof, thought to have been used for hanging lanterns, and hollows in the sides believed to have been lay-bys for mule-trains, the tunnel became part of a minor trade route after its completion about 1480. Fourteen years later part of Charles VII's army passed through, en route to the conquest of Naples, and in later years the track up the more difficult Italian slopes was, as a military defence measure, allowed to disappear. More than once in the following centuries the tunnel was blocked by debris; more than once it was re-opened, notably, and rather ceremoniously, in 1907.

Forcing a way across the Alps onto an enemy who believed himself protected by impassable mountains was a common ploy from Roman times onwards. Towards the end of the sixth century the Lombards surged over the Montgenèvre to conquer Gaul and soon afterwards surged back with the Franks hard behind. In 1515 Francis I took an army of 20,000 men and seventy-five cannon from Grenoble over the Col de Vars and the Col de l'Argentière and fell upon the papal army at Marignano so suddenly that its leader asked if the enemy had dropped from the clouds. Little more than a century ago the French crossed the Montgenèvre to fight the battles of Magenta and Solferino. Solferino.

Between these almost random examples, a host of minor armies marched and counter-marched over the more practicable passes to support the fortunes of the duchies, dynasties, houses and city states that for something

The summit-plateau of Monte Piano in the Dolomites, bitterly fought for by Austrians and Italians during the First World War.

like 1,500 years jostled for existence in the sub-Alpine areas north and south of the range. The remains of a stone redoubt built by the Duke of Savoy's troops in the seventeenth century still showed on the Théodule when Whymper and Lord Francis Douglas crossed the pass in 1865 for their fateful appointment with the Matterhorn. And on the Col du Mont, which offers the easiest passage on foot between the ski-resorts of the Val d'Isère and the Italian Valgrisanche, it is still possible to discover the remains of stone fortifications. They were set up at nearly 8,700 feet during desperate fighting between Piedmontese and French in the revolutionary wars at the end of the eighteenth century. Below, in the Valgrisanche itself, more recent fortifications still look up-valley towards the frontier.

Only with the advent of Napoleon and his vision of a united Europe – dream or nightmare – did military reminders start to litter the landscape. And with Napoleon, or rather his opponents, comes the classic example of a mountain engagement, the forcing of the Schöllenen Gorge and the St Gotthard route by General Suvorov.

In 1799 Suvorov was seventy, in retirement in Moscow after a lifetime of military victories which had earned him the reputation of a 'soldier's soldier', an army eccentric who lived with his men and slept on a truss of hay. In the summer of that year he was recalled to the colours by the Russian Emperor and sent to Italy charged with helping the Austrians oppose the French. Suvorov maintained his reputation, winning in quick succession battles against General Moreau on the Adda, General Macdonald at the Trebbia, and General Joubert at Novi. That task done, he was ordered north to join forces with General Korsakoff, known to be operating in central Switzerland, and to support him in the campaign to drive out the French.

It was September before Suvorov set off with 21,000 men, passing through Bellinzona and Airolo before starting the ascent of the St Gotthard. Centuries earlier Charlemagne had made the track fit for pack animals, and for some decades it had been a carriageway of sorts. Almost a quarter of a century before Suvorov, the enterprising British mineralogist Mr Greville had taken a light chaise across the route without dismantling it, as was then normally done. However, it was only in the 1820s that the route was turned into what would now be called a road, and Suvorov had considerable problems even in the narrows of the Ticino Valley below Airolo, by no means the worst of the difficulties.

Above the town there began the steep zig-zag of ascent which a century later was to include the most photographed hairpin bends in Europe, modified only after the Second World War into the better-engineered and less formidable road of today. In 1799 the old hospice at the top of the pass – the only building which remained after the rest had been wiped out by an avalanche twenty-four years earlier – was occupied by French troops. These withdrew and Suvorov advanced without undue opposition on to the broad plateau where Andermatt stands.

The French retreat had been purely tactical, for Suvorov's route now lay down through the Schöllenen Gorge into the Reuss Valley leading to Altdorf.

The crux lay first in the rocky slopes stretching down from the pastures round Andermatt, then in the gorge, a combination which for centuries had impeded even unopposed travellers. For many years a narrow wooden terrace, 200 feet long and suspended by chains from iron stanchions above the foaming River Reuss, had been the only means of negotiating the most difficult stretch. This had been superseded by a short tunnel, and the terrace itself had fallen into decay. There was also the first version of the Devil's Bridge – so named because, in local legend, the Devil had allowed its construction only in return for the soul of the first living being to cross it. The Swiss, quite up to tricks of this sort, built the bridge and sent across a billy-goat. When the most recent bridge was opened they sent across another goat just to make sure.

The French manned the position with great confidence. Suvorov attacked on 24 September, made little impression, and was forced to adopt the desperate expedient of trying to outflank his enemy. Fighting went on for three days, and at one point the French began to advance. When he heard the news, Suvorov lay down in a freshly dug grave, saying he would die where his troops first retreated. The rot was stopped and on the night of the twenty-seventh the French began to move back down the gorge, destroying the bridge on their way. Even today, walking up the abandoned motor road, it is possible to gain at least some feeling of the engagement now commemorated by the thirty-six-foot granite cross and inscription on the eastern face of the gorge.

The battle was only a foretaste of things to come. Suvorov marched down the valley to Altdorf near the head of Lake Lucerne, then on to Flüelen beyond which the Axenstrasse today burrows through the cliffs that fall to the lake. But until the Axenstrasse was built in the early 1860s the only direct route onwards was by water. But the French had seized all the boats. The Russians were therefore forced into making a smart right-hand turn, up over the 6,800-foot Kinzigkulm Pass and then down into the Muotatal which leads to Schwyz. Here, unexpectedly, Suvorov found a strong French force barring the way. For the Army under Korsakoff which he had made such great efforts to join had by now been defeated by the French under Masséna. Suvorov, no longer strong enough to face the French, was compelled to make his way east as best he could.

During the last days of October the Russians therefore turned back up the Muotatal and, strongly harassed by the French, fought their way over the 5,100-foot Pragel Pass to Glarus. Once again, they found their passage blocked by the enemy. Now Suvorov was forced to turn south, up the little side valley at whose end lies the village of Elm, and then over the 7,900 foot Panixer Pass into the Rhine Valley above Chur. Only then could he turn east to reach the remnants of Korsakoff's army at Feldkirch.

For the first time in his career Suvorov had not won all his battles. But he had retained an army in the face of strong forces operating on internal lines and holding strong defensive positions. Anyone who doubts his achievement should first trace out the route on a large-scale map, then pad it out on foot through the little-frequented valleys north of the Tödi.

Less than a year after Suvorov's Alpine campaign, Napoleon arrived at the northern approaches to the Great St Bernard, in charge of the Reserve Army which had been massed in secret and whose existence was doubted even in France. Learning that the Austrian General Melas still thought it impossible for him to put a fighting force across the Alps, he embarked on one of his earliest gambles.

From Martigny Napoleon first sent General Berthier across the frontier. Then he ordered off the advance guard, six regiments which left between midnight and two in the morning, reached the crest of the pass in eight hours, and descended in another two. This precaution taken, one division was sent across the pass each day, the provisions and ammunition being despatched first, followed by infantry and cavalry who led their horses over the most difficult stretches. As much as possible was put on mules, even the gun-carriages and ammunition waggons being taken to pieces and packed onto them.

The cannon themselves were still left, and their weight could not be reduced by the division of the load [wrote Thiers]. With the twelve-pounders in particular, and with the howitzers, the difficulty was greater than had at first been expected. The sledges on wheels, constructed in the arsenals, could not be used. A method was contrived, tried immediately, and found to answer: this was to split the trunks of fir trees in two, to hollow them out, to encase each piece of artillery within two of these half-trunks, and to drag it thus covered along the ravines. Owing to these precautions no collision could damage it.

At first the mules were used to drag the pieces. But both mules and mule-teers were soon exhausted. Then the local peasants were offered 1,000 francs for every cannon they manhandled across the pass. Working a hundred men at a time, they found that each gun took one day to get up and another to get down. Soon the locals would have no more of it, and the artillerymen themselves had to take on the task.

To encourage them, they were promised the money which the disheartened peasants would not earn [says Thiers]; but they refused it, saying that it was a point of honour for a body of troops to save their cannon, and they laid hold of the forsaken pieces. Parties of one hundred men, successively quitting the ranks, dragged them, each in its turn. The band played enlivening airs at difficult points of the passage and encouraged them to surmount obstacles of so novel a nature.

Thus, with band playing, the cannons reached the summit where the monks were feeding all comers.

Napoleon himself crossed the pass on 20 May, wearing his famous grey coat, mounted on a mule, and personally accompanied by a local guide. After a short halt at the hospice, he descended 'suffering himself, according to the custom of the country, to glide down upon the snow' – probably the future emperor performing a sitting glissade.

Napoleon's success after this swift invasion of northern Italy enabled him to exact the peace treaties of 1800. It also impressed on him the value of being able to cross the Alps without undue trouble. The passage of the St Bernard had been an exceptional affair, not to be repeated lightly and within three months of Marengo Napoleon decided that the road from Brigue to Domodossola across the Simplon must be made passable for artillery. Absolute priority was given to the work, which was finished in 1805.

Suvorov and Napoleon lie back beyond the line which divides modern history from the rest. So do many of the memorials, ceremonial cairns and stones carved, marking small individual tragedies which lie scattered across the Eastern Alps. But many others are the legacy of the First World War. At its outbreak the frontier – settled by the Austro-Italian war of 1866, which itself had brought fighting to parts of the Dolomites – started at the Dreisprachenspitze above the Stelvio Pass and ran in a 350-mile 'S' to the Adriatic west of Trieste. As Cruttwell emphasises in his splendid history of the First World War: 'This curved line strongly favoured Austria, whose boundaries in the Alpine regions stretched far down the southern slopes, with pillar upon pillar of ascending rock behind them, menacing the Italian plain.'

Most of the fighting took place on the eastern stretches of this front, and the word Caporetto still hangs miserably over Italian history. Along the rest of the line mountain troops manned positions blasted from the Dolomite rock, ingeniously reinforced and vulnerable only to attack that combined mountain and military craft in equal proportion. The war along this front was in strong contrast not only to the fighting on the Western Front, with its im-

Lake Misurina from the memorial chapel near the summit of Monte Piano.

personal mass assaults and huge casualties, but to warfare as it had developed during the previous half century. Battle here was rather the struggle of small unit against small unit or of man against man, with the situation sometimes further personalised by troops being local men who knew their opponents. It would not be fair to romanticise too far; but just as fighter duels in the air produced pilots a little different from the normal run of men, so is this war in the Alps remembered as less horrible than Flanders fields. It was not only the landscape. Here, where warfare returned to the days of individual combat, it had features that were ameliorating if not redeeming.

Much of the Dolomite frontier had been fortified before the war; any gaps were quickly filled. At places the troops retreated to better positions, as when the Austrians fired the indefensible village of San Martino and pulled back. Along the front itself sappers cut an extensive system of communication tunnels and ammunition caves in the Marmolada glacier, fortified couloirs, and transformed mountain features into defensive positions. There was a premium on mining, the most famous example – later to form the spectacular highlight of Luis Trenker's film, *The Doomed Battalion* – being the sapping of the Col di Lana. Here the Austrians held strong positions from which they repulsed the most desperate Italian attacks. Towards the end of December 1915 the Italians secretly began boring a gallery which led under the Austrians. Beneath these positions they constructed a transverse tunnel which ended in two mine chambers. The work was only completed in April. Two tons of explosive were taken to one chamber and three tons to the other. On the eighteenth all was ready. The two mines were exploded simultaneously, blowing to pieces the entire crest of the mountain.

Even more dramatic was the situation on the Castolletto, also occupied by the Austrians. Here a 700-foot gallery was cut from the living rock by men who could reach its entrance only under fire. Nearly thirty-five tons of explosive finally destroyed the whole mountain top.

There are many places in the Dolomites where this war of more than half a century ago still obtrudes its ghostly presence. Few are more evocative of men dead and gone than the summit plateau of Monte Piano three miles north of the tourist shops of Lake Misurina. Near the end of the lake the road forks, the eastern branch leading up across a little neck of land on to the recently-built panoramic road which ends at the foot of the Tre Cime di Lavaredo – the Drei Zinnen of 1914. The western branch runs over another low pass, between slopes still riddled with the remains of gun emplacements, then down the Val Poppena across the former Austro-Italian frontier. Between the two depressions rises Monte Piano, a bastion of a mountain surrounded by nearly vertical cliffs soaring upwards some 1,600 feet to the summit plateau, a limestone pavement reminiscent of the Yorkshire moors sloping gradually upwards to the west.

The top of Monte Piano can be reached by road, until recently of the class usually signposted as impassable for motors. Zig-zagging up the southern cliffs, the track had an unmetalled surface, a rock-face on one hand and an unprotected vertical drop on the other. Some corners could only be taken by reversing, when the view down and back towards the blue rectangle of Lake Misurina gave a profound impression of height. Here was the classic position defensible if not by a man and a boy, at least by a very small handful of men.

At the end of the road there is the Rifugio Bosi and a small chapel with a book containing the name of every man who died on Monte Piano. The situation is impressive. But it is even more so above the chapel, on the spreading green table-top, through which the limestone pushes up bare bones. Here are emplacements and trenches, fashioned from the limestone, weathered by only half a century but strangely reminiscent of prehistoric artefacts from a different millenium. Here, among the blue gentians and white anemones which line the crumbling trenches, there are still to be found stray bullet-case and battered mess-tin, relics of the companies who for more than three years held the summit of Monte Piano against all comers.

Just what this meant is clear from the briefest glance around. A few miles to the east the Drei Zinnen rear up, grotesque and formidable, and to the south-west the northernmost summit of Monte Cristallino. Both were in enemy hands and the impression of openness and of vulnerability is overwhelming. Yet here the defenders withstood bombardment and more than one suicidal attack mounted up the cliffs by the enemy.

Near the upper western end of the summit plateau there are small memorials to individual men, and, on the highest slope, a giant cross. The scene is

The cross on the summit plateau of Monte Piano.

97

extraordinarily evocative, especially in the lonely silence of a still afternoon with an ominous cloud front approaching, covering fresh ground yard by yard, growing in an almost cellular way, falling at the bottom, rising at the top, and steadily obscuring the view with the tenacity of the tide coming in. Did the men on Monte Piano ever consider poison gas? Or would it, perhaps, have been against the unwritten rules of mountain warfare, which could accept more easily the horrors of the bayonet? Yet the long-drawn-out siege of Monte Piano was merely one incident in the struggle between the Italian Alpini and the Austrian Alpenjäger, whose dead are commemorated by a huge granite tower outside Cortina. Here, fittingly enough, are recorded the names of the men from both armies.

During the First World War the only two parts of the Alps where serious fighting took place were the Dolomites and the Julians, where Julius Kugy wrote his magnificent autobiography in the trenches. On the west the frontier ran between France and Italy while neither Central Powers nor Allies contemplated the invasion of neutral Switzerland whose bulk filled the centre of the Alpine line.

A quarter of a century later the Alps saw some of the most bitter encounters of the Second World War. Of this, the bulk took place between regular forces and resistance fighters, guerillas or partisans, a type of warfare in which customary rules tend to get neglected. Once again Switzerland remained neutral in the centre; the obvious advantages to Germany of having more direct physical contact with her Italian allies was more than counter-balanced by Swiss determination to destroy the trans-Alpine road and rail links if necessary.

On the east the Germans, after the *Anschluss* with Austria in March 1938, were physically in contact with the Italians along the entire frontier which had divided the two countries twenty-five years earlier, notably via the Brenner Pass. At first Italy remained technically neutral. Only in May 1940, anxious to share the loot of an apparently victorious Germany, did she begin operations in the Maritime Alps and the Mont Blanc massif. In both areas the French positions were formidable and although France had sent most of her Chasseurs Alpins to Narvik in northern Norway, the Italians made little progress in the desultory operations that alone were possible before the French Armistice of June 1940.

Two years later, resistance to the Germans was already in progress at both ends of the Alps. To the west of Mont Aiguille on the outskirts of the Dauphiné, the first Maquis camp was already being set up in the Vercors, the rugged plateau south-west of Grenoble, an inhospitable country seamed by gorges and for long rigorously avoided by the occupying troops. Many hundreds of miles to the east the Julian Alps were already being used as a base by the Yugoslav partisans.

Comparatively little has been put on record about either of these two mountain campaigns although the French fighting, which from early 1944 onwards was increasingly supported by regular officers parachuted in from Britain, has been magnificiently described in 'SES' (Section d'Éclaireurs

The giant piton memorial to the partisans, below the slopes of Triglav in the Julian Alps of Yugoslavia.

Skieurs) by Jacques Boell, who before the war put up a remarkable set of new climbs in the Dauphiné and recorded them in an equally remarkable book, *High Heaven*.

In the Vercors intensified attacks on the Germans planned to coincide with the Allied invasion of 1944, got off to a disastrous start. At Vassieux-en-Vercors the Maquis prepared a landing strip for Allied planes and on the day it was completed aircraft appeared in the sky. They were German planes, towing gliders packed with SS troops who crash-landed around the village. They razed the whole area, killing scores of Maquis and civilians, the first of many such operations in which they systematically cleared the Vercors.

Meanwhile events had been going more favourably for the French in many parts of the Mont Blanc area, where Resistance forces were soon in control of Chamonix. Here a bitter if small-scale campaign continued against the Germans, increasingly isolated as their communications were cut by the Allied advance and by Allied bombing. At times one force would hold the lower station of a téléphérique and the enemy would hold the upper. Confusion was increased by the fact that Germans manning the Italian frontier came under one command and those next door, in southern France, under another. The French suffered differently from the legacy of the Resistance forces only now, and largely in theory, forged into one. Thus there continued for months a series of isolated and at times almost incoherent mountain battles, waged above 10,000 feet between the French, who had endured the risk of summary execution throughout four years of occupation, and the Germans, whose hope of survival lay in surrender orders that never came.

At the other end of the Alps Yugoslav partisans had already taken over from the occupying forces throughout most of the Julians. Here small wayside plaques, bearing the names or numbers of partisans shot by the Germans, began to spring up among the monuments and cairns of earlier wars. And here, under the north face of Triglav, there was later built the most breath-taking of all European war memorials.

Today Triglav stands in a Yugoslav national park, an area of white limestone peaks set against green pines and running water. To the west of the mountain, outside Na Logu – whose Alpine Museum is a model of what small museums should be – stands the powerful and lonely statue of Julius Kugy. Born Austrian in Trieste, transformed into an Italian by the Versailles Treaty, the high-priest of the Julians now honoured by the Yugoslavs, he remains forever gazing chin in hand at the mountains he loved. Six miles away, on the other side of Triglav and reached circuitously by road over the Vršič Pass, lies Alijavez Dom, inn and rest-house at the end of the road leading up under the huge north face of the mountain. A mile or more on, the pine trees begin to thin, and one of the highest single rock-faces in the Alps gradually comes into view between the upper branches. Then in a clearing made by the windings of the mountain stream there appears an astonishing sight. In dreams, and in Alice, there is a monstrosity of size that appears normal. Here too, after realisation sinks in, the giant metal piton appears normal: some sixteen feet high, thirty times larger than life, rising from a rudely-fashioned rock-plinth and carrying an equally huge metal karabiner or snap-ring that can just be swung against its support to produce a dull bell-like booming heard far down the valley. Quite solitary, a memorial to the partisans, and movingly impressive.

Whether or not any part of the Alps will in the forseeable future again become a battlefield is a very moot point. The tradition of the hardy mountain people fighting for their rights against the invader dies hard. Yet a generation after the Second World War, well into the last third of the twentieth century, the military importance of the Alps is less than it has ever been. They would of course be defended in any attack across them from north or south, but this eventuality seems even less likely than invasion by Lichtenstein of the United States. Road and rail links over and under the passes could be destroyed at the touch of a button. And to the countries which share the range, its main military benefit is not as geographical defence but as training ground for specialist troops more likely to be used in military tournaments than in battle.

In many places between the Maritimes and the Julians well-engineered paths still lead beguilingly uphill to what are finally revealed as gun emplace-

Swiss troops on manoeuvres
near the summit of the
Furka Pass.

ments. Around the St Gotthard it is possible to discern camouflaged ammunition dumps and metal 'rock-faces' which swing open on heavy hinges. Elsewhere, there are notices which warn: 'Shooting! Bangs to be expected' and the even more alarming: *'On tire! Attention! Détonations!'*

The military in no sense occupy the mountains, but between them the Alpini, the Chasseurs Alpins, the German mountain troops and the Swiss, who are trained to fight in the mountains as naturally as most troops fight on flat land, have between them a fair section of the Alps corralled off in the exercise season. Few experiences can make one more aware of this than to traverse the central knot of the Furka and Grimsel while military manoeuvres are in progress. The summit of the pass can well be occupied by anti-aircraft detachments who are surprisingly willing to display their equipment. Military convoys provide an additional hazard in the game of pass-crossing without trouble. And there is something invigorating in finding one of the minor roads blocked by an elderly man who holds back the occasional car with hand-signals while jet-aircraft flash past only a few feet up, taking off from the improvised airfield which straddles the road.

As polluters of the Alps the Services have always made only a small mark; nevertheless it is one more mark on an environment already smudged with them.

CHAPTER SIX

A Bed-and a Ski-in the Sun

Long before the growth of Alpine travel was halted by the outbreak of the First World War, two other influences were becoming almost as important as the interest in mountains evoked by the Romantic Movement, extended by the demands of science and vigorously exploited into a sport by the Victorian professional classes. One was the discovery of the Alps as a six-hundred-mile health resort, a discovery which was soon attracting a new class of wealthy and leisured travellers who within a century were to transform many valleys. The other was the birth of winter sports which began as a spare-time recreation among those recovering their health between autumn and spring; which prepared the ground for the practice of skiing, the new method of moving over snow imported from Scandinavia; and which was to lead to the revolutionary developments now taking place as big business moves in above the snowline.

Many Alpine villages had retained since Roman times a reputation for the curative properties of their springs and many had developed into 'baths' where one took the waters, perhaps even wallowed in them, and made pleasant conversation with the other usually wealthy unfortunates. This was particularly so in the Grisons, or Graubünden, Switzerland's easternmost canton which occupies a sixth of the whole country. So much was this so that Dr Yeo, an English doctor who helped jolt the Swiss cure system into Victorian prominence, noted: 'The canton ... is par excellence the canton for cures; and nearly every third village is a "Kurort", and has its "Kurhaus", its "Kurliste", its "Kurarzt", its "Kurmusik" and finally its "Kuristen" as those are termed who come to be cured.'

Among these villages was St Moritz in the Engadine. Its springs had been famous for centuries but only in 1817 had a small pavilion been built over them. There was no shelter for drinkers and it was not until 1854 that the local commune leased the springs to a company which built a large bathing establishment and hotel.

The Swiss had acted at the right moment. Quite apart from invalids, many other travellers, including some mountaineers, were for the first time beginning to visit this backwater of the Alps. The sheets of the great Dufour map covering the Grisons were published towards the end of the 1850s, and in

Twin ski-lifts at the winter sports resort of Alpe-d'Huez in the Dauphiné.

1861 two members of the Alpine Club climbed the Piz Bernina, 'the Queen of the Engadine', ascended for the first time a decade earlier. Climbers as well as invalids were looking towards the Grisons and were further encouraged to do so by Mrs Freshfield, who toured the area in 1861 and wrote her influential *A Summer Tour in the Grisons*.

By Mrs Freshfield's day the invalid industry was already under way. It was necessary to book rooms in the bathing establishment before the start of the season, even wise to book a year in advance. St Moritz continued to flourish and expand during the 1860s, supported by the hearty as well as the ill. Numerous visitors, including many British, were now coming to the embryonic spa not merely to take the waters but to spend there a greater part of the winter months. Their life, which was to lead naturally into the winter sports scene, can be judged from one entry in the St Moritz Kulm visitors' book:

A pan of water kept on the stove is also indispensable to prevent the already dry air of St Moritz becoming over-dried [it runs]. On an average, we were out four hours daily, walking, skating, sleighing, or sitting on the terrace reading – this latter two or three hours at a time; twice in January we dined out on the terrace, and on other days had picnics in our sledges: far from finding it cold, the heat of the sun was so intense at times that sun shades were indispensable, one of the party even skating with one. The brilliancy of the sun, the blueness of the sky, and the clearness of the atmosphere quite surprised us. The lake affords the opportunity, to those who love the art, of skating without interruption for five months. The ice has, to a certain extent, to be artificially maintained. To do this, we, with other English friends, formed a small club – first, for keeping a circle clear of snow; second, for renewing the surface whenever it became impaired by turning a stream on it.

If this is not a sufficient shadow of things to come, it is provided by a letter in *The Times* of 21 February 1870, signed by the 'President of the St Moritz Sporting Club'. After dealing with skating he continues: 'Another favourite entertainment of the English, as well as natives (and one also practised in Canada and Russia), is sliding down steep inclines on sledges constructed for this purpose. The speed attainable is almost incredible.' Similar goings-on took place elsewhere in the Upper Engadine where a long string of smaller health resorts began to spring up, and further down the valley at Tarasp no less than twenty medical springs were soon in use.

Thus by 1870 a sizeable slice of Switzerland, occupied a decade earlier only by the Swiss and the occasional mountaineer, was becoming a regular winter resort for those with an illness and the money to cure or indulge it. However, baths and spas existed in many parts of Europe, and those in the Engadine were merely one variety. It would be unfair to claim that taking the waters at such places was always essential: in fact one doctor went so far as to say that flushing out the system with large draughts of water, whatever its health-giving impurities, would have a good effect on those who habitually wined and dined too well. But what the enthusiasts in the Engadine were really enjoying was a cure in an Alpine setting rather than an Alpine cure. Many were, moreover, out-of-condition rather than ill, poorly rather than dying, and took enthusiastically to snow-sports much as visitors to fashionable Brighton took to sea-bathing. Meanwhile only a few miles away something more important was developing.

North-west of the middle Engadine, slightly lower but lying in an extraordinarily sheltered and wide pleasant valley, is Davos. In 1862 its Dr Alexander Spengler wrote a paper for the *Deutsche Klinik* which discussed the problem of pulmonary complaints and pointed out that Davos people never contracted them while they lived in the valley. Furthermore, if they settled abroad and became consumptive, they usually recovered when they returned home.

A Herr Richter, suffering from consumption, decided to give Davos a chance and survived to become the village bookseller. A Herr Coster, also in a bad way, came to Davos, recovered, and subsequently became landlord of the Belvedere Hotel, where several of his servants in later years were men and women who had also struggled back to health in the village. Within a few years two hundred people were coming each winter to Davos, where, as a British doctor put it, 'meat when hung up does not putrefy, but is thus dried and kept for use ... nor do the lungs rot in the living man'. By the mid-seventies the number had doubled again, although most visitors were still Germans or Austrians. This situation was radically altered in 1877 by two events which succeeded in putting Davos on the British medical map.

The first of these was a visit by Dr, later Sir Clifford, Allbutt, who had specialised in the study of consumption and went to Davos mainly to discover whether the claims made for it could be justified. The result of Allbutt's visit was two articles in the *Lancet*: 'On Davos as a Health Resort'. There is no doubt that the good doctor had been genuinely astonished. There was Herr Coster at the Belvedere, by now 'stout-looking and energetic'. Herr Richter was in the best of health. Moreover there was, he went on, little 'medical machinery' in the place. There even appeared to be few invalids. 'Where are the patients?' he asked.

One visitor whose arrival in Davos that summer did as much as any other event to bring it fame and fortune was John Addington Symonds who had set out with his family from London for Egypt where he expected to die. His sister was staying for the summer in Davos, 'a little-known village of the Alps', and the Symonds' cavalcade broke the overland journey there. They got as far as Chur. 'I could scarcely crawl up to my bedroom, and had fever and profuse sweats,' Symonds told Allbutt. 'I remember', his daughter later wrote, 'the sickening horror with which, childlike, I suspected something; Death indeed was very near.'

But Symonds reached Davos. A month later he told Allbutt: 'I now never perspire, I can eat fairly well, and I can walk up above the pine trees – i.e. somewhere about 600 feet to 800 feet high.' A few weeks later he was able to climb 1,000 feet 'without pain and without fear of haemorrhage'.

The Symonds family stayed in Davos until the following spring, and Mrs Symonds described how they all drove in sledges down the zig-zags of the Maloja Pass – 'Such a journey was never performed by a respectable English family before, and though the wind and blinding snow drove in our faces and dripped from our hats, J. was none the worse. It speaks well for the hardening cure of Davos.' They later returned, settled in the village permanently, and quickly became the centre of a growing English community.

Whether there is any real connection between consumption and the so-called literary 'temperament' is still debatable. Nevertheless, a century ago, when the Symonds were discovering the Engadine, numerous writers did find it useful, for genuine health reasons, to spend a winter in Switzerland. Mrs Gaskell wrote *Wives and Daughters* while staying at Pontresina. Robert Louis Stevenson, Conan Doyle and later Saki all lived in Davos during periods of literary activity. This helped. And just as Queen Victoria at Balmoral gave a new impetus to all things Highland, encouraging there people who would never before have dreamed of crossing the Border except by accident, so did the literary community draw to the Grisons a new and larger public.

Sils and Pontresina in the Engadine, as well as the baths at Tarasp, which quickly grew into the Scuol–Tarasp–Vulpera complex, later glutinous with the really rich, all began to cater for various kinds of ailments. Elsewhere in the Grisons Lenzerheide and Arosa did the same. At the other end of Switzerland, above the Rhône where it enters the Lake of Geneva, there was Leysin, lying on a broad shelf of country high above the lake and looking out on to the glorious prospect of the Dents du Midi. Leysin soon became a resort that, like Davos and Arosa and like Montana on the southern slopes of the Bernese Oberland, specialised in the treatment of consumption. Elsewhere in Switzerland the very real and hitherto unexpected benefits of mountain air were soon being used to attract a new sort of visitor. The change was evident even on the Rigi where Rigi–Kaltbad sprang up 1,200 feet below the summit.

Symonds was eventually alarmed by the numbers crowding into what had previously been his own almost personal retreat, just as the early climbers who wrote of the glories of the sport were irritated when they later found more people on the mountains. The crisis was overcome, as it was elsewhere. Proper sanatoria were built for those who were really ill, and the long lines of beds in the sun became a familiar sight throughout the Alps. At the same time the recognition that merely living among mountains could cure intractable disease completed the transformation begun a century or more earlier. The 'horrid' mountains of the pre-Romantic era had changed first for the scientists and then for the intellectuals who made up the climbing community. The growth of tourism, which came as the railways pushed up to and under the Alps, had brought at least acquaintance with the mountains to ever greater numbers of ever more ordinary people. Now there came this realisation of the Alps as a perfectly respectable place to visit on doctors' orders. In the nature of things, this tended to attract the rich and the doctors were thus responsible for bringing to the Alpine scene a potent injection of money. As a by-product they attracted many who had little to do, a process which reached its apogee during the inter-war years when the main resorts would post daily lists of the notables – monarchs and tycoons, film stars, athletes and the merely notorious – who were honouring such humble and gratified resorts by their presence.

Skiers on the slopes above Chamonix, with the aiguilles on the skyline above the valley.

Ladies on the St Moritz curling rink, early 20th century.

The process was well under way by the start of the twentieth century. So was the parallel by-product of the doctors' discovery. For well before the old century was out the winter skating and sledging of the not-so-invalid had been enlivened by the arrival of skis from Scandinavia. By the early 1900s men and women were beginning to enjoy in numbers this new and revolutionary method of getting across country in winter, harbingers of the multi-million-dollar consortia that within seven decades were to move in on the world above the snowline.

Every winter day some thousands of visitors set out from the huge chalet-hotels, which within the last few years have been built to create a new township on the pastures above one particular Alpine valley. They queue at the lower station for the cable-cars in which they stand for the journey to the upper station. From there a fan-like metal tracery of ski-tows is available to haul them to the higher slopes; and from these slopes, as criss-crossed with ski-tracks as Hyde Park Corner with vehicles, the runs converge downhill. As long as the sun shines, and it usually does, the scene is a perpetual busy rush-hour, tribute to a participator sport with an Alpine history of little more than three-quarters of a century. From spring to autumn the scene is a little different. Bulldozers thresh along new roads to expand what the French percipiently call the *agglomération*; maintenance men work hard on the cable-way systems; a splatter of advertisements for *chalets-à-vendre* expands an atmosphere of budding property investment.

Less than a generation ago the same hillside was useless to the developers even though a small handful of men and women took a tough agricultural living from it. Today the wooden houses of this older generation, mostly empty, can be seen with their near-deserted church a few hundred feet below the new centre, lonely beside the curves of the skilfully engineered concrete road which leads from valley-floor to the huge parking lots which the new recreational centre demands. What this adds up to is of course mere change of use: a change from growing goats and the occasional catch-crop to growing

The Vajolet Towers, Dolomites.

Medieval bowmen on skis.

winter-sports enthusiasts who offer a better return on capital, have helped raise local living standards and are pleased to pay for the zest for living they have found in their escape from the communal life of cities to the communal rigours of skiing.

All this may seem a healthy entry on the credit side of the ledger, more than balancing the destruction of another piece of natural scenery and the urbanisation of another small corner of the mountains. Certainly not all of the new ski-centres are the horrors suggested by copy-writers. Some capture, by the very arrogance with which they have imposed themselves on the landscape, as well as by their architecture, by their impression of not caring a damn for anyone else, the spirit of an earlier and more aristocratic Alpine world; but others tend to echo either the tweeness of Surrey stockbroker country or the brashness of the people's packaged tour. And even if each were justifiable on its own individual ground, it would still be true that the Alps, like the three-dimensional air-space through which international airlines lace their multiplying routes, is an area of finite size. Like the British countryside, it can stand only a certain amount of erosion if it is not to disappear altogether. Thus the benefits of any new ski-complex should be considered not in isolation but against the background of new and startling developments now altering the face of the mountains as drastically as the petrol engine has altered the face of the lowlands.

In 1945 Austria had twenty-five cable-cars, mountain railways and ski-lifts. By 1970 there were more than 1,800. At the other end of the Alps, where the French five-year plan has allocated £11,500,000 for the building of mechanical lifts and £8,400,000 for giving more roads and power to mountain resorts – and where the Val d'Isère ski-lift system can already handle 50,000 an hour – an additional 100,000 skiers are expected during the first half of the 1970s. They will be catered for in new tailor-made resorts built in places where, as the French travel people put it with a throwaway phrase, there was 'nothing before, nothing but snow and mountains'. This unfriendly environment has now been transformed by 'mammoth undertakings involving the construction of access roads, the installation of all machinery and services and the building of accommodation and shopping complexes, to create self-contained and self-sufficient holiday stations'.

On the Franco–Swiss frontier, where in one area alone it is planned to build three new villages, raising the number of beds available from 4,500 to between 10,000 and 12,000, the two countries' systems of ski-lifts will be linked to provide a network of more than 200 miles of *piste* with 150 lifts. Elsewhere, in the Maritime Alps, one £20,000,000 development scheme is already building in virgin territory a 6,000-bed ski-resort with thirty-three ski-runs to be served by nineteen lifts to take skiers from the doorsteps of their hotels. 'The buildings, including hotels, apartments, shops, discothèques, night clubs, restaurants, bars, form a continuous line of construction on various levels, facing south to catch the maximum sunshine,' it is added. 'The resort will be electrically heated.' Indeed, 'the whole station is connected by a network of heated arcades and galleries making it possible to walk in perfect comfort from one end to the other, even to the departure hall of the télécabine, without having to go out into the snow.'

Elsewhere, the hamlet of Flaine, lying at the head of a byway off the Arve Valley, has been transformed to provide a new way of life in the mountains. It is admitted that 'Marcel Breuer's concrete snowflake-block Condominium here, grafted on to the mountain and giving the impression of a huge wartime fortification, shocks many people who see it for the first time.' However, first impressions can be deceptive, and 'inside is a honeycomb of boutiques, bars, night-clubs, and a supermarket. Galleries lead off to apartment blocks and offices.' However curious an attraction this may sound to those satisfied with nothing but snow and mountains, there is little doubt of its mass-appeal or of its investment value. As the French Tourist Office proudly points out, between 1968 and 1971 the price of apartments in Flaine rose from 1,734 to 2,568 francs per square metre. Nor is overcrowding on the slopes likely to be an insuperable problem. 'Forward-looking Flaine', says an issue of *The Traveller in France*, 'has also asked the French Army if it can borrow a couple of bazookas to change the landscape where necessary for better skiing.'

This metamorphosis of the mountains, sometimes by large groups and property companies on to a good thing – and ostensibly performing a public service by satisfying a demand – is not limited to the levels of winter skiing. As the packaged tour has worn away some of the social gloss that gives a sparkle to winter sports, summer skiing has been exploited to fill its place. Thus the cable-cars have long ago been pushed well up into the permanent snow, and above Breuil at the Plateau Rosa, above Chamonix, and above an increasing number of resorts, it is possible to ski the year round.

There are, moreover, a growing number of smaller new centres, adequately serviced by mechanical aids, so that those allergic to the larger concentrations of humans can still get what they want. As yet, the Alpine ski-world is not quite bursting at the seams.

The very early history of the two wooden boards is a field for argument almost as broad as Hannibal's march. It is not even certain, although it seems likely, that they evolved from the pattens or snow-shoes which date at least from the winter of 401 BC when Xenophon's Ten Thousand used them in traversing the Armenian Highlands. But it is known that the Scandinavians used skis at least from the thirteenth century onwards, both for normal winter travel and for equipping military scouts and reconnoitring groups. There are also isolated references to skis in Europe from the seventeenth century onwards while Arnold Lunn, who in a long and glorious life has forgotten more about the subject than most men will ever know, points out that skis were certainly used in Cumberland during the early nineteenth century and probably in Devon before that. Then there is a gap until, about 1880, skis appear in the Alps.

While the proven links between the introduction of skiing and the start of winter mountaineering are slight, circumstantial evidence is considerable. When, in the mid-1870s, Coolidge was making his first winter ascents in the Oberland, the early British invalids were coming to St Moritz and Davos. In 1877 the first toboggan race was organised in Davos, and within a few years the village had an ice-rink and St Moritz had the Cresta run. At the other end of the Alps, Henri Duhamel in Grenoble had imported a pair of Swedish skis and was experimenting with them for winter ascents in the Dauphiné. In 1883, when winter mountaineering was becoming acceptable if not common, a Dr Herwig of Arosa acquired a pair of skis and in the same year a passing Norwegian traveller presented the monks at the St Bernard Hospice with a pair. Accustomed as they were to moving about during the winter for business rather than pleasure, the monks soon acquired about a dozen pairs, and inaugurated races.

Before the end of the decade the Davos community had been joined for a season by Colonel Napier, an Englishman who took the chalet in which Robert Louis Stevenson had written part of *Treasure Island*. The colonel brought with him a Norwegian manservant and the manservant came with skis. Their use gave rise to many tall legends, including the claim that he would ski down from the chalet to the centre of the town, tea-tray on shoulder. The colonel left at the end of the winter season but bequeathed the skis to the daughter of

John Addington Symonds. Shortly afterwards a local businessman, Tobias Branger, imported a number of skis and began to interest English residents, including Sir Arthur Conan Doyle. These 'modern imported distractions' as Coolidge grumpily called them thus began to make their appearance as more mountaineers were coming to the Alps during the winter; as semi-permanent colonies of expatriates, largely invalids or quasi-invalids, were being founded in and around the Engadine; and as an interest in competitive winter outdoor sports was beginning to grow.

Events crystallised in 1893, a year of critical importance according to Lunn. Branger and his brother travelled on skis from Davos over the Mayenfelder Furka to Arosa – a pass over which they took Conan Doyle some twelve months later; the 5,261-foot Chasseral above Biel was climbed on skis; and the first Swiss Ski Club was founded in Glarus.

During the next few years many other summits were climbed for the first time on ski – the Rauriser-Sonnblick in 1894, the Oberalpstock in 1895, and Monte Rosa in 1898 to mention only three of them. But this was still the activity of the expert; it might have remained so for much longer had it not been for the contemporary growth of winter sports in general. Chamonix was opened for the 1898–9 winter season. Other centres quickly followed so that during the first decade of the twentieth century an increasing number of potential skiers were drawn to the Alps during the winter months, coming for skating or luging or bobbing, but open to suggestions that they might try this new and exciting means of moving about the mountains on wooden boards.

The period up to the outbreak of the First World War saw great advances in equipment and in techniques. What had been merely casual became the object of scientific study, and this was intensified with the outbreak of war; for now, on the Austro-Italian front, the most efficient use of skis was as a weapon of war. From 1918 onwards the development and spread of skiing followed almost naturally along expected lines. Competitive skiing increased, and in the 1920s was given an extra zip by the invention of the slalom course, a downhill race between markers involving many turns.

But for many skiing still remained ski-touring. As the expert has said: 'Downhill is a fine sport, but only a sport. Touring is an education, downhill a sign of the times.' Téléphériques certainly existed and it was always pleasant to escape the uphill plod for the downhill glide. Yet until the outbreak of the Second World War the ski-landscape of the Alps was frequented mainly by those who would at least know how to get there on their skis.

The change came with the post-war travel boom. Just as the Victorian mountaineer's eight-week leisurely campaign had been replaced by the quick out-and-back trip, so were the pleasures of ski-touring increasingly replaced by those of the long downhill runs that the téléphérique and the ski-tow made possible. With yet another injection of humans into the high mountains, the pleasures of the few were made accessible to the many; a fine state of affairs, but one which raised a question it would be cowardly to avoid – for how long can the Alps deal with a traffic of such intensity?

CHAPTER SEVEN

The Three-Ring Circus

As the clouds of the First World War gathered, far more men and women were climbing in the Alps than had climbed half a century earlier. Nevertheless they did so for much the same basic reason as their predecessors. They too regarded mountaineering as a sport, and if the routes they made were more difficult than those of the pioneers, that was simply the result of a natural evolution in which techniques, equipment and the knowledge of individual mountains had improved and increased over the years. Geoffrey Winthrop Young, making a number of classic ascents in the first fourteen years of the century, was a very different man from Whymper on the Matterhorn, yet both saw their activities as a personal tournament between mountain and man; Young's efforts were, as he put it in one famous poem, part of a lifelong effort to 'wrestle one more fall'. In much the same way George Leigh-Mallory, one of Young's companions in that pre-1914 world which seems as distant as the Middle Ages, appears in the direct line from Leslie Stephen, believing that 'a day well spent in the Alps is like some great symphony'. Few mountaineers could express their feelings as well as Young or Mallory, but most still climbed for the relatively light-hearted enjoyment of physical exercise in fine surroundings or for enjoyment of scenery with the heightened appreciation that comes from hard exercise. Contact between man and mountain was personal, and the fewer the pieces of equipment that disrupted it the better. As for a man's experiences, those were essentially his own personal property; he might describe them in a club journal for the understanding few and he might occasionally be bold enough to express them in a book. But, for better or worse, they were part and parcel of a small enclosed world.

All this changed quickly in the half-century that followed 1920. Man alters his habitat and different men make different alterations. A more varied kind of climber was attracted to the Alps and the environment gradually became more gregarious and urban. This was partly an extension of previous developments; larger and more numerous huts, cable-cars that cut out the long afternoon slog from the valley-floor, public interest in the more sensational climbs – these all followed naturally from the first hut on the Grands Mulets, the coming of the railway to Zermatt and the furore about the first ascent of the Matterhorn. Nevertheless, between 1920 and 1970 the character of Alpine

George Leigh-Mallory on the Aiguille Verte.

Opposite The Dru (right) and the Aiguille Verte.

climbing changed in many other ways that did not follow on from the previous half-century. This is not necessarily to be deplored. Too great an affection for the good old days would have mankind still swinging from bough to bough; distance not only lends enchantment to the past but also knocks the sharp corner off unpleasant memories and suffuses the years before yesterday with a golden haze. Nevertheless what is beyond dispute is that the reasons for which men climb, and the type of world they create above the snowline, began after the First World War to undergo a sharp change whose pace has quickened since the Second.

The change most obvious even to the non-mountaineer is epitomised by the contemporary climber approaching his work, clanking with hardware like a local ironmonger's at sale time. This is the result of 'mechanisation', a word used to describe the transformation of the man who climbed with little more than hands and feet into the expansion-bolt specialist for whom movement up a difficult pitch is an engineering as much as a physical exercise. But of course few men did ever climb with hands and feet alone. To begin with there were shoes. Then came artificial aids, the first of which was the medieval crampon or climbing-iron. One of the next was the alpenstock. The ice-axe and the climbing-boot followed in quick succession. All these, it is often pointed out, are very different from contemporary ironmongery. This is so, but although a line must be drawn somewhere there is little agreement about where it should go, and it is the logic behind the development of artificial aids, rather than the aids themselves, which is often claimed to create the watershed between allegedly good past and allegedly bad present.

Among the most usual pieces of contemporary mountaineering equipment is the piton, a metal peg with a hole in one flattened end and pointed at the other. Driven into rock or ice, the piton can provide a missing hand- or foothold; more importantly, with the addition of a snap-link (the French *mousqueton*, the German *Karabiner*) attached via the hole, and into which a climbing rope can be threaded, it can be used to safeguard a climber in a fall. From such simple beginnings there has developed a multitude of devices including slings; étriers or stirrups which can be attached to a piton and in which a climber can stand; expansion-bolts for which a hole must be drilled or hammered in the rock; and various systems of double-ropes with the help of which a climber can utilise pitons to raise himself crab-wise, left foot, right foot, up previously inaccessible places. Crash-helmets as a protection against falling rocks (or dropped equipment), piton hammers, and descendeurs, which can be attached to the waist and used for easy descent down a fixed rope, are other items which the well-equipped climber carries.

It is sometimes claimed that virtually all this paraphernalia developed from the need to safeguard a climber in a solitary difficult place – where driving in a piton would make morally justifiable a climb otherwise too dangerous to be attempted. Almost forty years ago the American climber Rand Herron, who fell to his death during a descent of the Pyramids, described this attitude in an article on the Kaisergebirge, where the hard men of the early 1930s were carrying out extraordinary feats called daring or rash according to viewpoint.

A good climber, of course, will avoid any movement endangering the stability of his position on the rock [he wrote]. However, in passages of extreme difficulty, some risk always exists, and a 'piton' gives a certain guarantee and feeling of safety, without which he could not go to the limit of his physical possibilities. If I wished to compare climbing to the feats of circus acrobats I could say that the 'piton' corresponds to their net. As a means of getting farther where it would not otherwise be possible, the artificial aid also opens up rockfaces with passages of extreme difficulty which would not be known otherwise.

From this it followed that artificial aids were justifiable when used to safeguard a man in a place which he could climb only at great risk, but not necessarily justified if they made climbable an unclimbable pitch on a mountain.

However, history shows that such a maxim is in reality a newcomer. In the fifteenth century Mont Aiguille was climbed only with the most artificial of aids. More than a century ago Whymper devised his grappling-iron, which with the help of a second device enabled him 'to ascend and descend rocks, which otherwise would have been completely impassable'. In the 1880s the Aiguille du Géant was climbed by blatantly artificial means. Until the early 1920s such episodes were rare, usually the subject of comment and often of criticism. But they show that safeguarding was not quite the be-all and end-all of mechanical aids it was sometimes claimed to be during the 1920s and 1930s.

Nevertheless the campaign against their extension was pursued with much vigour and blunt speaking. It was led by the more conservative members of the Alpine Club under command of the redoubtable Colonel Strutt, editor of the *Alpine Journal* from 1927 to 1937. As early as 1928, the *Journal* was commenting of two young Courmayeur men who had climbed Le Père Éternel, a pinnacle at the end of the north-west arête of the Aiguille de la Brenva : 'They are stated to have worked for days with chisels, iron spikes and fixed ropes. This sort of exploit is quite beyond the pale and is a degradation of mountaineering. Any steeple-jack could have done the work better in a tenth of the time.' Quite so. But it could just as easily be claimed that the men were ahead of their time, since within less than a generation such exploits had become mountaineering. 'Further outrages are reported on the long-suffering north face of the Cime di Lavaredo and Langkofel,' it was later claimed, while the same doughty fighter who had also declared all-out war on cable-ways wrote as easily, and without inhibition, of 'two members of the Hammer and Nail Co. Unlimited'. The question is perhaps one of balance ; it is possible to regret the development of mechanical mountaineering, while finding it diffi-cult to take too seriously the objections of those pre-war years. Perhaps time gives them a hint of caricature they do not deserve.

Certainly over-dependence on external aids allowed an occasional air of farce to creep into mountaineering. Thus as early as 1936 there came the first reported 'theft' of a climb. This followed the attempt by an Italian party to make a new route on the Cima Occidentale di Lavaredo in the Dolomites. Nearly two hundred pitons were used before its members realised they had run out of supplies and were still some way from the summit. They therefore retreated and set off for the nearest town to buy more. They had, however, been watched by a second party which was replete with pitons. Party No. 2. waited until Party No. 1 was out of sight, repeated the lower part of the new route using the pitons already in the rocks, and then completed it by making use of their own. Party No. 1 is reported to have brought a legal action, presumably for restitution of priority.

Such episodes did little to deter the spread of mechanisation, and since the end of the Second World War artificial aids have become universally accepted. Pitons for safeguarding have become *de rigueur* while genuinely 'artificial climbing' – the ascent of places which would be quite impossible without mechanical help – has broadened out into a new specialised division of the sport, attracting those for whom engineering technique is of almost as much interest as the mountain.

This is some way from Mallory's 'great symphony'. But had it been all, had the mountaineer merely invoked technology, the aesthetic climate of Alpine climbing might still have deteriorated, but the intellectual climate might have improved as compensation. Neither the piton nor the crash-helmet of itself drove romance from the Alps; if Kipling's McAndrew could see 'predestination in the stride o' yon connectin'-rod' there was nothing to prevent the wielder of the piton hammer from getting his own vision of the mountains just as real, if very different, from Ruskin's or Leslie Stephen's. There can be a magic of ironmongery, however shocking the idea may sound to those who dislike treating mountains as pin-cushions.

But the swing to the mechanical was accompanied by two other developments. One was the classification and grading of climbs on a numerical and quasi-scientific basis which enabled climbers to compare their Alpine exploits with greater accuracy; the other was the re-birth of nationalism in mountaineering in a form which would have been comic had it not been tragic.

Until the 1920s the difficulties and dangers of routes up various Alpine peaks were described in only the most general terms. The Italian ridge of the Matterhorn was known to be more difficult than the Swiss ridge, the Furggen and Zmutt ridges far more so. It was more difficult to get to the top of the famous Chamonix Aiguilles than to the top of the Wetterhorn. But comparisons rarely went much further. More important, there was usually added some vague qualification. Were the rocks snow-covered or ice-covered? If snow-covered, could the snow be easily scraped away from hand and footholds; if ice-covered, was the ice entirely a disadvantage or would it be so thick on the rocks that steps could be cut in it across what might otherwise be an impassable pitch?

Once these factors were recognised it became clear that even when considering rock-peaks it was difficult if not impossible to compare like with like. Two experienced climbers, using the linguistic shorthand of their craft, would convey to one another the comparative problems of two different mountains. But there would be no short cuts in the comparison, and any one-word description would have been as useful as describing a Rubens as good and a Leonardo as better. When it came to snow mountains, or to Alpine peaks which involved the crossing of glaciers or a bergschrund, the traverse of a snow-ridge or even a lengthy plod up snow-slopes, brief descriptions meant even less. Conditions on a great mountain change not merely from season to season but almost from hour to hour and what is 'easy' one day can be impossible the next.

One result of this apparently intractable refusal of routes to be graded was that rivalry between mountaineers was limited. There could be competition between climbers to be first up one particular route, but there was little point in boasting of having done the 'difficult' routes, A, B and C, if under certain circumstances the 'easy' routes D, E and F might present even greater problems. Human vanity could not go very far without looking ridiculous.

This happy state of affairs changed between the wars. The 'playground of Europe' slowly became its pseudo-military sports arena as the first 'grading' system for climbs was evolved by a young Munich climber, Willy Welzenbach. And the worst competitive excesses came from those who diced with death for the greater glory of the Fatherland rather than for love of the mountains. Looking back from the 1970s, the strictures of the times, particularly some of those in the *Alpine Journal*, seem over-condemnatory. However, this is largely a specialist argument of Alpine ethics in which it is possible to make a plausible case for either side; what concerned the future of Alpine climbing was that with Welzenbach's system it was easier to compare – if often misleadingly – the performance of various mountaineers.

The system was announced in 1925. It dealt only with rock mountains and assumed that conditions on these were always basically the same. At the bottom was Grade 1 which included climbs so easy that many mountaineers hardly classed them as climbs at all; at the top was Grade 6, which represented the limit of human capability. The number of grades, which were divided into upper and lower categories, were the same as those used in German and Swiss schools for examination papers. Welzenbach's system had initially been worked out for the comparatively short rock-climbs of the Bavarian Alps but was soon taken up by the Italians who applied it to the Dolomite peaks. But the Italians have more than rock-peaks and the system spread. The French soon came in, and while they acquiesced in Welzenbach's six-fold division their feeling that words were more amenable than figures when applied to infinite gradations, induced them to name them rather than number them – from *facile* through *peu difficile* and *assez difficile* to *extrèmement difficile*. Much as there might be said for this it led, as it did when grading was applied to British mountains, to such descriptions as 'an easy very difficult', the type of phrase which meant something to the specialist but restored confusion for everyone else.

This rivalry would probably have become inevitable anyway, as more and more men and women came to the Alps between the wars, as mechanical aids began to alter more quickly the boundaries of what was considered climbable, and as there arose the possibility of comparing climber A, who was only a Grade 5 man, with climber B who had notched up a Grade 6. However, it was sharpened by the cult of danger, which from the early 1930s onwards was encouraged largely for military purposes by Germany and Italy and by the transformation of first ascents from sporting achievements into national triumphs.

Danger is never very far from a mountaineer on even the easiest of climbs, and of death Geoffrey Young wrote in one of his finer poems,

> I never see him, but his tread
> Sounds just before my own.

Yet for many decades it was an accepted ethic of climbing that while it was right to risk dangers which were largely under the control of a mountaineer's own ability and judgement, it was wrong to court those in which chance alone was the arbiter. To test one's judgement of a snow-slope by cutting steps across it in a potentially lethal situation was justifiable; to climb a gulley known to be swept regularly by stone falls which could not be avoided was to play Russian roulette with the mountain and to degrade the whole art and craft of mountaineering. In practice, of course, there existed no clear-cut line dividing one from the other; neither mountains nor human nature can be compartmentalised as easily as that. A man's judgement of his own ability might be so warped by circumstance that his actions might be difficult to justify; the experience of a party crossing a stone-swept slope could greatly minimise an unpredictable risk. Subjective and objective dangers are in many cases as interlinked as the electron orbits of the atoms making up a molecule. Nevertheless, until a period which can be put at roughly forty years ago, it was generally felt to be bad mountaineering, bad form, and breaking the rules of the game, to let the safety of a party depend on more than the minimum of chance.

The ending of the First World War had something to do with starting a change of emphasis.

On a bright, crisp November morning the cannon that announced the armistice informed us that our bodily safety was assured [Pierre Dalloz has written]. For others, not for us, the boundless relief and happiness it gave! Too much pent up energy and feeling, now useless, was thrown back at us. We had to find some outlet for it. Climbing came as a revelation to us, just when it was needed, and to it we gave ourselves up, body and soul, while others threw themselves into the pursuit of business, politics and pleasure. It gave us the complete fulfilment of our dream, it proved to us our worth, and in spite of the event which had robbed us of war, it allowed us to taste the intoxicating pleasures of the heroic life.

How justifiable it sounds! How grand when coming from a Frenchman, and how different from the young Germans who were willing to die on the north face of the Eiger in the hope of making the first ascent and thus winning, among other things, an interview with Hitler.

Yet there was, in reality, a subtle difference, and one which has rarely been better emphasised than by Othmar Gurtner in his long dissertation on *The Eiger Myth*.

It cannot be denied [he says] that drastic breaks in the way life is lived may be accompanied by changes in the type of man. The more sensitively and suspiciously a race faces its destiny, the more subtle is the intellect in choosing the compensatory aids. It is thus understandable that two natures as different as the French and the German perceived one and the same activity in completely different ways.

However, the rightness or wrongness of individual climbs is not an either/or question. Looking back, it seems clear that the odium with which the Nazi and Fascist regimes were regarded outside Germany and Italy brushed off on to mountaineers who set out to climb the almost unclimbable. Their reasons were sometimes more innocently adventurous than would be suspected from the bombastic patriotism which their countries supplied. When 'the medal for valour in sport, the highest distinction accorded by the Duce to exceptional contests was awarded to climbers who vanquish mountains by new ascents of the sixth standard', it was difficult to believe that the winners might really be climbing for pleasure as well as reward. But could it not be claimed that here, writ large in twentieth-century terms, was only the story of the Swiss guide who reserved one of the Wetterhörner for the Swiss Louis Agassiz rather than present it to the English Mr Speer? Was the Duce doing anything more than up-date the rivalry between Whymper and the Italians on the Matterhorn?

There was one difference, and it was a vital one. The earlier rivalries between British and Swiss, French and Italians, Germans and British, had been purely sporting. If no one consciously claimed 'the game's the thing', there was a generally accepted belief that while it was good to win, mountaineering was worth while for its own sake. From the 1930s onwards the rivalries became less comparable to those of sport and more allied to those of war. Thus a fatality came to be considered less a blunder to be condemned and more a death in battle which brought laurels rather than condemnation. The character of mountaineering in the Alps itself began to change since failure to push on with ever more difficult climbs was to accept shameful military defeat, rather than to see the game as not worth the candle. The transformation was well described by Geoffrey Young. 'If we begin', he wrote, 'to accept an interpretation that justifies young men in wagering duration of life and the duty owed to it upon a haphazard adventure so unchancy that it exacts, sooner or later, the penalty of death from a large proportion of the players, we are outside any definition that seems application to the idea of a game.' During the years before the outbreak of the Second World War mountaineering in fact came dangerously near to being turned from a sport into a bloodsport with all the consequent degrading side-effects on spectators as well as players. Only 'dangerously near', however. Some sections of the leading Alpine clubs warned their members against making the more desperate and potentially suicidal climbs; many mountaineers, foreign and British, who did not go all the way with impassioned condemnation of the 'new Alpinism', yet used their moderating influence.

It was the north face of the Eiger which polarised attitudes in the 1930s. Due to geological and meteorological factors, the north faces generally present the steepest and most dangerous walls in the Alps, routes cold and bleak and usually swept by falling stones, on which intelligent planning and expert technique can minimise dangers but not eliminate them. The most famous of them became, in succession during the 1930s, 'the last great problem of the Alps'. Thus the north face of the Matterhorn, climbed by the Schmid brothers in 1931, was replaced by the Grandes Jorasses. Climbed in 1935, the north face of the Grandes Jorasses was in turn replaced by the Eigerwand, the part of the great north wall of the Eiger which seems to have been created to make the greatest Alpine difficulty, the greatest Alpine danger and the greatest opportunity for Alpine *voyeurism*.

Rising more than 5,000 feet from the screes between the west and east ridges, the north face is split roughly into two by a barely discernible north spur up which Hans Lauper and Alfred Zürcher, with Alexander Graven and Joseph Knubel, in 1932 forced a classic route virtually clear of objective dangers. To one side of the spur lies the Eigerwand, described as recently as 1958 as 'an area of objective danger which, by all the laws of mountaineering should remain untouched'. To most laymen, this might seem a reasonable judgement since the face consists of continuously steep unreliable rock and is regularly exposed to stone-falls. By the summer of 1970 more than 250 people had climbed it and forty had died on it.

The first attempt on the Eigerwand was made in the summer of 1934 when three Germans were rescued from the face by guides who utilised the 'window' in the railway tunnel which takes a wide detour through the bowels of the Eiger on its way to the Jungfraujoch. The following year there came two young climbers from Munich, excellent rock men but apparently quite unaccustomed to snow and ice. They were forced to bivouac on the face, first for one night, then for a second, then a third and finally a fourth, after which bad weather

The Eiger, showing the North Face in shadow on the left.

closed in and no more was seen of them. Days later, when the clouds lifted, a military plane flew as close to the rocks as possible and the pilot identified one of the men standing frozen upright in the snow. The corpse could be seen from several points and the automatic telescopes did a brisk trade.

The following year the attraction of the Eigerwand proved irresistible. The first couple came to grief on a nearby training climb, one man being killed, the other badly injured. Next were two soldiers from the Berchtesgaden Jäger and two men from Innsbruck, four from a party of ten Germans and Austrians who camped below the wall. Soon after their first bivouac one of the four was badly injured by a falling stone, but the climb went on. After a second day and a second bivouac, retreat became inevitable. But the weather had deteriorated, and the rocks were awash with freshly melted new snow. One climber was now killed by falling stones. Then the man who had previously been injured fell and strangled himself while roping down. During the third bivouac one of the two remaining survivors died of exposure.

Meanwhile a desperate rescue operation had been organised by guides, who traversed the face from the Eiger station on the railway, climbing under constant threat of stone fall and avalanche. The survivor was still conscious, but frost-bitten and hanging on the rope between two corpses. He succeeded in cutting himself free and in roping down towards the guides who were unable to move upwards. Then his strength failed. One of the guides, standing on a colleague's shoulders in an acrobatic feat of immense danger, succeeded in reaching the man's crampons. Neither could do more and the survivor died within inches of rescue.

The presence of crowds on the Kleine Scheidegg below the face, combined with the fact that the railway took visitors so close to the scene of the drama, ensured maximum publicity. The Swiss, well aware that it was publicity of the wrong sort, put the north face out of bounds and threatened to fine any party who attempted the climb. If the Eiger needed further advertisement, this provided it.

The following summer no less than seven parties, attracted by the ban as well as the climb, carried out reconnaissances of the north wall. One was impeded by the discovery of a body from the previous year; revealingly a member of the German party wrote that 'the finest day of the season was wasted, bringing it down to the valley'. All attempts either failed or were abandoned, and in England Colonel Strutt, giving his valedictory address as President of the Alpine Club, noted: 'The Eigerwand – still unscaled – continues to be an obsession for the mentally deranged of almost every nation. He who first succeeds may rest assured that he has accomplished the most imbecile variant since mountaineering first began.'

Success came within little more than six months. In July, a few weeks after two Italians had fallen to their deaths, two Germans, Heckmair and Vorg, arrived at the foot of the Eiger in great secrecy. On the mountain they found to their surprise two Austrians, Harrer and Kasparek. In Heckmair's illuminating words, 'We, the sons of the older Reich, united with our countrymen of the Eastern Border to march together in victory.' What he means is that they

The Eiger, Mönch and Jungfrau, seen across a cloud-sea from the Schilthorn.

got up their mountain successfully – a three-day effort of great competence and courage. The *Alpine Journal* paid tribute to the skill, modesty and endurance of the party but saw 'no reason to dissent' from Strutt's earlier verdict, a view that was probably shared by the majority of contemporary mountaineers. But the climb had been worth while for the four men concerned. All were presented to Hitler.

The war put a temporary end to all this, the Germans and Italians being employed elsewhere, and the Swiss discouraging attempts by their own people since mountain-rescue teams were occupied on defence work. However, where one party could succeed, others could follow, and it was inevitable that after the war the Eigerwand should resume its role as testing ground for the up-and-coming mountaineer. Life itself was probably now valued less than it had been before 1939, and it was more generally felt that if young men wished to risk their necks there was little moral reason for stopping them. In addition new equipment, notably improved lightweight clothing and bivouac kit, better ironmongery and rope, and the ability of transistors to relay weather warnings, all tended to bring objective dangers under slightly better control. There was also the new financial stimulus which after the war slowly but steadily prodded on the more spectacular kinds of mountaineering. Accounts of the climb could be sold to the popular papers as well as providing the substance for broadcasts and TV appearances. To many young men, who in a previous era would have been amateurs enjoying their sport, but who were now anxious to make a living from mountaineering, these inducements were not to be ignored. There seems little logical reason why they should have been, even though they tended to introduce a new kind of side-show into the playground.

Rescuing an injured climber by helicopter. (A Shell photograph, Switzerland).

Professional guides naturally enough had a direct interest in what had been accomplished by amateurs, and in July 1947 the second ascent of the Eigerwand was made by Lionel Terray and Louis Lachenal, two of the finest French guides then alive. Two more ascents were made in 1950, and in 1952 no less than thirteen men climbed the mountain between 22 July and 27 July, nine of them in four parties setting out on the same day. Of the nine, two were Austrians, one being the outstanding Hermann Buhl; two were Germans with considerably less experience; five were Frenchmen, only one an amateur. All succeeded, all survived; a new spirit of cooperation animated Austrians, Germans and French. But, in the words of Othmar Gurtner, conditions 'brought a devastating catastrophe very close'.

Catastrophe was in fact rarely very far from the Eigerwand. By the end of 1953 four more ascents had been made – and four more men had died in attempts. In 1955 Gaston Rebuffat and two colleagues made a film emphasising the objective dangers of the wall but the following year there were two more fatalities, and in 1957 three men died in one of the long-drawn-out tragedies which the wall encourages. Two Italians and two Germans had joined forces on the face. One of the Italians died from exhaustion, and his companion was rescued only seven nights later after extraordinary efforts which involved lowering a rescue basket from the summit for hundreds of

feet. French, Dutch, German and Italian climbers tried to coordinate rescue efforts on the summit in darkness and storm, and added one more episode to the story which, as usual with the Eiger, was given worldwide publicity.

The ironic dénouement did not come until four years later. No trace had been found of the two Germans and it was assumed that they had died on the wall after five or six nights of exposure. Then, in 1961, their bodies were found – not on the Eigerwand but on the comparatively easy descent from the summit towards the Eigergletscher station. They had reached the top and died during a last bivouac, only an hour from safety.

In 1961 the first winter ascent was made; two years later, the first solitary ascent. By this time, moreover, John Harlin, an American climber of extra-ordinary ability, had climbed the wall and become obsessed with the idea of making a 'direct' route – like the *direttissime* in the Dolomites which start at the bottom of a cliff and go straight up, allowing diversion neither to left nor to right, 'the ascent of a face by a route following a plumbline falling from its top to its base'.

By 1964, no less than 144 climbers had climbed the wall and twenty-five had died in the attempt. The British, coming in on a new wave of enthusiasm, had already put Chris Bonnington and Ian Clough up the Eigerwand, and in 1966 an Anglo-American team including Dougal Haston, Layton Kor, Chris Bonnington and John Harlin arrived to attempt the *direttissima*. A German team was there already but the outcome was very different from the pre-war international rivalry. British and Germans climbed sometimes together, sometimes independently, sometimes sharing bivouacs. Massive use of pitons demanded that the assault should be spread over many days, and the exercise took on the character of a Himalayan siege. Then, on 22 March, a fixed rope broke and Harlin fell to his death. The climb went on, in the face of much criticism, but in the determined belief that it should be completed as a memorial to Harlin.

The *direttissima*, and the extensive coverage that its ascent was given by press, radio and TV, emphasised that the Eigerwand, an arena so conveniently placed for spectators, was the most newsworthy face in the Alps, and in 1969 no less than seventy-eight men and women climbed it, many of them greatly helped by fixed ropes left by a Japanese party. This party consisting of five men and a woman had spent nearly six weeks on the face.

So far, however, no one had made a film of the climb. This was left to a strong British party which in the late summer of 1970 brought to the drawing-rooms of Europe via ITV and a remarkably efficient ascent, at least an impression of what modern mountaineering is all about.

A few months later between 24 December and 21 March another Japanese party laid siege to the wall. A total of forty-two days was spent on the face and some members of the team spent up to twenty-four days on it without a break, an effort during which they made the second winter ascent of the original route. More than 7,000 feet of rope was taken as well as some 350 pitons. Cost was estimated at £6,000. Alpine climbing had not merely come of age as a spectator sport but had reached the First Division.

The summit of the Stelvio pass, one of the Alp's most miserable eyesores.

Commercial traffic on the
St Gotthard road, Europe's
trans-Alpine through-route.

CHAPTER EIGHT

Over and Under and Through

Marvellous Bends — Easy Ways up — Above the Alps

The opening-up of the Alps during the last century has not been entirely dependent on the ebb and flow of public interest. While better communications often followed public demand, the roads and railways which were pushed over, under and through the range for reasons of war or trade in themselves encouraged tourists to places where tourists had not previously been encouraged. Thus Alpine travellers and Alpine communications have some features comparable to the chicken and the egg.

The creation of roads through successive stages of pack-track, carriage road and motor road, has had the greatest effect, although for a period at the end of the last century it looked as though the railway boom might change the trend. But the motor-car during the first half of the twentieth century, and the coach tour during the second, effectively leapfrogged road transport ahead once again.

Motorists of course depend on machines rather than legs for enjoyment; their highways have helped along the *'vulgarisation des Alpes'* more than any other single factor; and it is certainly true that the commercial development they have brought to certain key points has created unique eyesores. Today the summit of the St Gotthard itself becomes a monument to modern knick-knackery soon after the first snow-ploughs have whirled clear a way across the crest; the summit of the Stelvio, for long the highest motor road in the Alps, is an almost unbelievable illustration of man's capacity to foul his environmental nest.

Despite this it is not easy to feel for the road network the same dislike evoked by the téléphérique and the funicular. For one thing it follows with few exceptions the traditional lines demanded by geography, and thereby retains a historical link with the comfortable human past. Once the confusion of construction is over, most mountain roads tie in with the landscape more naturally than the most cunningly placed téléphérique tower – although the new Brenner autobahn and parts of the Gross Glockner road are glaring exceptions. They keep to their station in life, marking out a new sort of 'line above which one may not go', and to that extent dividing travellers into motorists and others. One may not agree that 'the windings of a ribbon road are beautiful in themselves and marvellously effective in their sinuous curves,

129

Early avalanche tunnels on the carriage-road across the Simplon.

while the boldness of construction of the Stelvio, the Splügen, and others is a source of unfailing admiration for human skill'. Nevertheless the Grimsel, the Pordoi, the Restefond are only three high passes to which it can be claimed without too much special pleading that the engineers have added a new and dramatic quality. There is also the challenge to skill presented by even the least fierce of the mountain roads and the lingering feeling, sometimes justified, that driving here is more adventurous than motoring across Salisbury Plain.

The major wave of building which in the first decade of the nineteenth century began to transform mule-tracks and uncertain carriage roads into the basis of today's highways was largely the work of Napoleon. Just what it meant in terms of engineering can be judged from the fact that between Brigue and Sesto Calende on the Simplon his men built more than six hundred bridges. The Monte Cenis road, as well as those over the Montgenèvre, the Colle di Sestriene and the Col de la Faucille, were all Napoleonic achievements. The point was noted, and after Waterloo many governments began to look to their Alpine highways. The Austrians built the splendidly engineered road across the Splügen, and between 1820 and 1824 completed that over the Stelvio, linking the Tyrol with the plains of Lombardy across a 9,000-foot barrier. Satisfaction at negotiating today the Stelvio's fifty-odd numbered hairpin bends on ascent and then the same number on the other side should be tempered by the knowledge that this was first done in 1900 and that two years later a driver took his car from Milan to the Stelvio and back, 279 miles over mainly Alpine roads, in a single day.

Most early passages by cars are badly documented – as distinct from the later story of the Swiss postal buses which between 1919 and 1927 opened a series of regular services across the Simplon, the Julier and a number of other passes – and it is not at all clear which route first became regularly used by motor-cars. The Simplon itself might well claim the honour but for the ban on mechanical vehicles which kept all cars off some Swiss roads until well into the present century. The Lautaret, linking the Romanche and Guisane Valleys to the east of the Dauphiné, is probably the likeliest candidate.

Swiss suspicion of the car lasted long, particularly in the Grisons, even though it was here that there took place, soon after the Napoleonic Wars, an early example of international cooperation in road building. Switzerland, Austria and Piedmont paid jointly for remaking the Splügen road and for construction of a carriage road across the San Bernardino, the latter operation being financed largely by the King of Sardinia, who was in favour of one trans-Alpine road not controlled by the Habsburgs. The inhabitants of the Grisons nevertheless were slightly chuffed with the coming of the motor-car and for many years, using the local referenda which are still one of the triumphs of Swiss democracy, kept motor-vehicles from the roads of the Grisons. The tourist trade was not so happy, and its pressures eventually forced the cantonal government into a curious compromise, and petrol-driven vehicles were allowed on the roads as long as they were drawn by horses. Some motorists took advantage of the rule and drove their early vehicles with horses trotting alongside.

The burst of road-building in the first half of the nineteenth century which served the carriage trade so well was replaced in the second half by the spread of railways, and as these took over the upkeep of the roads declined. Even so, by the outbreak of the First World War, nearly a hundred Alpine passes were crossed by motorable roads. During the years that preceded it – before roads used what has been called the 'mean modern subterfuge of a tunnel' – these dusty highways provided just the combination of possibility and difficulty which encouraged the pioneer motorist to extraordinary feats of driving and endurance over roads whose unguarded corners would bring many modern motorists to a crawl. Only slowly did the drop to Eternity gain a protection, first of small stones, then of cambered metal corner and finally of stout safety barrier.

In places there also grew up the reprehensible practice of taking cars where cars had no business to be. Just as in Britain a motor-car was taken to the top of Ben Nevis, so in Chamonix Douglas Fawcett, the man of letters who claimed that his 'distinctive mark [was] the discussion of Imagination as the fundamental reality of the Universe', created in 1904 one record that is unlikely to be broken. In the words of his entry in *Who's Who*, he 'made the only recorded ascent to the Mer de Glace, from Chamonix, up the mule-path on a motor-car of ordinary size', an exhibition of vandalism that can be excused only on the grounds that it was hardly likely to be repeated. However, for a man of Fawcett's intrepidity much can be excused – for many years he climbed the Matterhorn annually until a heart attack put an end to the practice at the age of sixty-six; he then took up flying two years later and flew among the mountain tops until shortly before his death at the age of eighty-four.

Between the two world wars there began the somewhat frenetic attempt to win, and keep, the laurels for having 'the highest'. This started with construction of the Col d'Iseran road by the French, a relatively useless route, but one that at 9,088 feet was eight feet higher than the Stelvio. To put the result of the contest beyond doubt the French in 1962 opened the Restefond, with its narrow, rough, unguarded ascent from Jausiers near Barcelonette to its triumphant altitude of 9,193 feet.

During the last two decades the existing Alpine road network has been radically changed by two things. One is the increase of the proletarian motorised tourist, and the amelioration of road conditions to suit him, a process which has transformed the lower stretches of many routes and kept a continuous supply of concrete pouring into the construction of *gallerie*, tunnels, avalanche-protection devices, retaining walls, bridges and viaducts. The other has been the emergence of a more unified industrial Europe, determined to increase internal trade. The result of this can be seen in such projects as the St Gotthard route, part of a highroad from northern Europe to the tip of Italy; in the tunnels beneath the summits of the Great St Bernard and the San Bernardino and through the Felber Tauern, all tending to keep commercial routes open for longer periods during the winter; the new Brenner highway; and the Mont Blanc tunnel which opens up a new route between France and Turin and lops many many miles off the trans-Alpine journey.

The Mont Blanc tunnel which has pushed a line of concrete and a roar of engines into what was the peaceful junction of the Val Veni and the Italian Val Ferret – and as a by-product enables Chamoniards to visit the weekly market in Courmayeur – has aroused more arguments, for and against, than most similar projects. Nevertheless it is the outcome of plans well over a century old. A tunnel was first proposed in 1844. Fourteen years after this scheme collapsed for lack of support a fresh one was drawn up. In 1874, in 1879 and again in 1907 road or rail tunnels were planned, while negotiations between Italy and France for the present road tunnel were nearing completion before the outbreak of the Second World War.

Gallerie on the Italian side of the Montgenèvre.

The latest post-war upsurge of building, renovation and tunnelling has vastly widened the variety of Alpine motoring. Before the Second World War there was of course some difference in roads; yet it was still possible to talk of 'typical' conditions; anyone who had crossed the Galibier, the Furka or the Gross Glockner would have a good idea of what they would meet on most passes. Today the distance between extremes has increased. On the St Gotthard and the Maloja modern engineering has reduced the previous problems to comparative insignificance; what makes driving difficult here for a good part of the year is the traffic – the tourist cars and coaches on both routes plus the heavy commercials on the St Gotthard. Along such main trade routes, once the snow has gone and traffic is no longer squeezed into a narrow channel between the melting white walls carved by the snow-plough, any driver who can negotiate Hyde Park corner in the rush-hour need have few fears; unless he is one of the unlucky few who genuinely suffer from vertigo. In that case the protective edging of *bouteroues*, or small granite pillars, the guard-rails and the other devices that have done so much to alter the character of motoring in the last few decades, may only emphasise the gulf below.

Off the beaten track the story is very different. Here, by contrast, the efforts of local Syndicats d'Initiative have combined with the more adventurous motorist to open up fresh routes which run close to the border separating road from mule-track and provide severe tests of springs, driving ability and nerve. The minor routes of the Alpes Maritimes and such roads as that reaching the top of Monte Piano in the Dolomites presented, until 1970, cart-track surfaces, hairpin bends which demand cautious reversing, and the classic situation of narrow way bounded by vertical rock-wall and unguarded sheer drop. There is still a fair spattering of such places. Thus judgement is all. Each driver has to chart his own course between discretion and biting off more than he and his car can cope with.

Some general rules are still as useful as in the days of constant stops to let the car cool down. These may no longer be frequent or even expected; but note the yellow plastic jugs on such passes as the Umbrail and the Grimsel. Boiling radiators come so rarely to most motorists that two warnings are not superfluous. Use gloves before unscrewing a scorching radiator cap and stand well back as you do so; secondly, let the radiator cool well down before topping up with what will probably be ice-cold water.

Using the same gear on the descent as in coming up is still a good way of keeping the foot off the brakes and of preventing them from overheating. On a steep road it is still wise, when stopping, to leave the car in reverse if descending and in first if ascending – but still with front wheels turned sharply to swing the car in, whatever the trust in brakes and gears. Note also that the number of short road tunnels is constantly increasing; in them dark glasses, useful at all times and essential above the snowline, tend to accentuate the contrast between sunlit exterior and tunnel interior. What happens, until the eyes acclimatise, is that all the lights seem to go out without warning.

Most passes offer fine viewpoints. The camera is usually busy, and on less frequented roads it is easy to forget the precaution of stopping only where no obstruction will be caused. On a lonely road, where vehicles are few and far between, it is easy to take a chance; doing so is certain to whistle up from an empty landscape the biggest trailer combination in Europe, a vigilant road patrol and the man who drives without looking.

In one respect Alpine motorists are lucky. The Michelin 1:200000 maps (one centimetre to two kilometres, which is roughly an inch to $3\frac{1}{4}$ miles and comparable to the Ordnance Survey's old quarter-inch motoring sheets of Britain now re-scaled to 1:250000) are all that motoring maps should be, and sheets cover all except the easternmost parts of the range. The Kümmerly & Frey sheets at 1:500000 are excellent at giving a more bird's-eye view and all the countries involved publish national series on scales such as 1:100000 and 1:50000. The Austrian 1:100000 sheets from Freytag-Berndt, which cover also the Julian Alps of Yugoslavia, are magnificent although of less use to motorist than to walker.

As to choice of season, winter motoring is of course in a class of its own, with many of the main passes blocked from November until May or June. Some are usable by vehicles with chains or snow-tyres, others are normally open all the year round and this fact, together with the new road tunnels, the train ferries through the Mont Cenis and the Lötschberg, allows a good deal of movement. But the months-long closing of the Grimsel and the Furka still makes a journey between east and west unhappily long. No two years are the same, and in spite of the extraordinarily good services of the Swiss Touring Club – news of exceptional weather on the radio and reports on the telephones in three languages – winter touring is a chancy affair. Green and white notices at strategic points state which passes are open, and throughout most of the Alps there is an efficiency in the road system that tradition suggests must be inherited from the Swiss. All the same, motoring between November and April is strictly for the enthusiast.

What remains is the nose-to-tail packed summer season, the late spring when the community is regaining its balance after winter sports as the snows begin to melt, and the autumn weeks sandwiched between the end of the summer and the first winter snows. Here choice depends on temperament, and success depends on luck. The advantage of either spring or autumn is the ease in getting a bed for the night and the comparatively empty roads and tracks are enjoyable to those allergic to large numbers of the human race. In spring the early flowers will be bursting through and with luck there will be that unforgettable sight of nature aping the picture-postcards and pushing up fields of crocuses through the melting snow. In autumn the trees make up for the lack of snow-melt coming down the waterfalls.

Against this, there will in spring be hotels that have not yet opened and in autumn those that have put up the shutters for a few weeks' refurbishing in preparation for the winter-sports season. Accommodation will in general be no problem, but specific accommodation in specific places may well be. Some of the téléphériques may be closed for overhaul and maintenance, and a run of bad luck in either period when the servicing community takes a deep breath can be a disillusioning experience. There is moreover the weather.

There are late seasons as well as early ones, and the dates at which particular passes open vary considerably from year to year. More disturbing, they may be open when plans are made in London and closed once again when the Alps are reached. Even when open, all is not necessarily plain driving; to cross one of the higher passes shortly after the snowploughs have cleared a way, when the wind-driven loose snow becomes an almost impenetrable white curtain and ice-patches still remain on the surface, can be a taxing experience. In the autumn nature can work the other way just as inconveniently, dropping a blanket of early snow to close passes that should be negotiable for many more weeks.

On many Swiss roads the driver will encounter the almost-legendary postal coaches, recognisable by their bright yellow paintwork or by the yellow post-horn on a black ground. The vehicles have absolute right of way on the mountain roads and their drivers, multi-lingual men of unusual ability, at first glance a mixture of Jehu and Ben Hur but in fact the *crème de la crème* of Swiss drivers, can legally order other motorists to back, park or take any other measure necessary to clear the way for the mails. The postal coaches can be heard coming, although their simple three-note motif, taken from the *andante* of the overture to Rossini's *William Tell*, is a pale shadow of the repertoire which the postilions of the horse-coaches once had. One tune then signalled departure of the coach, another its arrival. One extra coach, put on when traffic warranted it, had its own signature tune. There was a special signal for 'caution', and other sounds on the horn revealed the number of coaches in convoy and the number of horses involved. When control of the Swiss posts passed to the Federal State in 1848 carriage of passengers was just as important as carriage of mail. The tradition has continued and the post service today carries passengers on 4,700 miles of road – more than twice the length of the Federal Railway network.

What are the 'musts' among Alpine roads? Every man will have his own list, but the way in which the great Dolomite peaks rise from easy ground makes the road from Bolzano to Cortina one of the few on which the spectacle does equal what the publicity brochures show. So, too, with the diversion

An early postal coach at Gletsch (Switzerland).

over the Sella Pass with its astonishing view of the Langkofel, over the Grödner Pass to Corvara and then back over the Compolongo Pass to the main highway at Arabba. These roads, spectacular as they are, give the drama in the natural course of going from here to there; engineered and surfaced for the motorist, they present the minimum of driving problems for the maximum of visual splendour.

At the other end of the scale, as lonely as the Dolomites are vehicle-packed, there is the by-est of by-roads that turns off east from the Ferra Valley and makes for the Predil Pass into Yugoslavia through miles of deserted forests and sub-Alps within a mile or so of the frontier. There is the 'Panoramastrasse' to the Tre Cime above Misurina, engineered as only the Italian road-builders can engineer such roads, a drive well worth the toll; as long, that is, as the

The 'Fell Railway' on the Mont Cenis with the carriage road in the foreground.

driver can stomach a road being there at all. The Stelvio should be taken, if only as an endurance course, and to see at the summit what a lamentable eyesore man can create if he really tries. A journey through the Mont Blanc tunnel should be made, if only for experiencing that touch of the unseen electronic hand which monitors vehicles by radar and triggers alight a blue warning of '100 metres' if a driver inadvertently gets too close to the car in front. And at the southern exit there is, for those sensitive to such things, the transformation shock caused by the change from north- to south-facing slopes: an effect only felt fully when crossing a pass on foot and striding down into the lusher vegetation of some minor Italian valley. For those who do not go on foot the car can still yield passable consolation prizes – although a large-scale map is often needed to win them.

'Easy Ways Up'

Above Prato, in the Val Leventina, it is possible to look down on the St Gotthard railway as it plunges into one of its *tunnel hélicoidal*, those ingenious engineering brainwaves which allow a train to enter the mountainside, travel in a rising spiral as if the engine were about to swallow the guard's-van, and emerge higher up the slope but not very far away. Somehow the scene fits. The track, even the trains, have become as much a part of the landscape as the English telegraph pole. A century of survival has added a patina of respectability to what was once at best an intrusion, and at worst a development which seemed likely to destroy the peace of the Alps for ever.

The pessimists were probably right. Yet even the line to the Jungfraujoch, a project which in the early years of the century ended romances and divided families, is today a part of the Oberland like the souvenir shops and the larger crowds which collect at the Kleine Scheidegg when there is a fair chance of death or disaster on the Eigerwand. Most skiers would feel lost without the téléphériques, which enable them to make the maximum number of downhill runs in a day. And even the later development of télésiège or chair-lift is sometimes claimed to have a harmless air, hoisting happy, carefree couples in summer up over green slopes to vantage-points they would never otherwise reach. Just as the Grépon was changed over the years from 'the most difficult climb in the Alps', to 'an easy day for a lady', so has protest against the 'iron horse', nuzzling Scheutzer's dragons from the Alpine valleys, lapsed into acceptance.

Infiltration by railway and allied devices has been of three kinds. The first came during the last third of the nineteenth century and the first decade or so of the twentieth, as the Alps were crossed by rail for the first time. Until 1844 the railways had not come even to Switzerland, and thirteen years later they hardly entered the Alpine zone. But within the next half-century lines were driven over the Brenner and under the Mont Cenis, the St Gotthard and the Arlberg – while the Simplon and the Lötschberg tunnels came only a few years later. Overlapping this there came the age of the viewpoint funicular, the cogged-rail lines that took Mr Cook's tourists to such minor but commanding heights as the Rigi, Pilatus, and a score of other summits from which the mountain tops were laid out in convenient array. Later, and first developed between the wars, there came the téléphériques and their progeny, the cable-cars swinging up to unimaginably inaccessible points, the chair-lifts, great in number and some of an almost rural one-off variety, the ski-tows, ski-hauls and télébenne which have only two things in common: the cable clanking over rollers or runners and the pylons, pillars or posts supporting an aerial spider's web prominent enough to reduce any good conservationist to tears.

The British, it must be admitted or claimed according to taste, were the first in the field of trans-Alpine railways for it was the enterprising Mr Fell who used British capital to build a line from Lanslebourg to Susa across the Mont Cenis. Its unique feature – previously utilised on the Cromford and High Peak line in Derbyshire – was a central rail grasped by horizontal wheels to brake the carriages. The track on which these climbed rose in six sweeping zig-zags on the outer edge of Napoleon's road, in extremely tight curves and at a gradient of up to one in twelve and a half. With British capital, British engineers and British drivers, the Fell Railway was a three-years' wonder between 1868 and 1871, and Whymper's description of it leaves little doubt as to why this was so.

'For fifteen miles and three quarters it had steeper gradients than one in fifteen', he said. 'In some places it rose one foot in twelve and a half! An incline of this angle, starting from the base of the Nelson Column in Trafalgar Square, would reach the top of St Paul's Cathedral if it were placed at Temple Bar!' At places the line was boarded in and as much of the route from Lanslebourg to the summit was through forest, watchers were sometimes confused by puffs of steam rising first in one direction and then another as the unseen train zig-zagged up through the trees.

All this excitement ended with the coming of the first railway tunnel through the Alps, for it had been a condition of the Fell Railway concession that its track should then be torn up. This came in 1871 when 'the Mont Cenis tunnel' was opened in a burst of festivities enjoyed by a host of invited guests including Whymper. The quotation marks are necessary, for the new line followed the Arc Valley only as far as Modane, some fifteen miles below the pass. Here it turned away south, burrowing beneath the Pointe de Fréjus, which gives the tunnel its more accurate but less-frequently used name, and emerging at Bardonecchia, whence it runs down into the Dora Riparia and so to Susa where the road over the real Mont Cenis is met.

This is still a railway trade route to northern Italy. It is also useful for the winter or spring motorist anxious to change the Dauphiné for Mont Blanc. The Col du Galibier may still be closed but the Montgenèvre from Briançon to the Dora Riparia is normally open throughout the year, and it is thus possible to drive to Bardonecchia, put the car in the open trucks that run an hourly service through the tunnel, and reach Savoy via the Maurienne Valley taking the long route round through Grenoble.

The Fréjus tunnel had been open for a mere two years when work started on the St Gotthard, a project that involved, quite apart from the driving of the main ten-mile tunnel, the construction of nearly eighty minor tunnels and 324 bridges. As with the Fréjus, opening of the St Gotthard virtually coincided with the start of another line under the Alps. This was the Arlberg which opens a lateral but important route from Switzerland to the Inn Valley and the Eastern Alps. The Simplon and the Lötschberg followed, and by the outbreak of the First World War the current network of trans-Alpine railway lines had been established.

While conventional railways had been spreading, Niklaus Riggenbach had completed a track up the Rigi. He was followed by ever-more audacious schemes which took railways Pilatus, to the Jungfraujoch – still the highest railway in Europe – and to numerous less important summits. Objections were raised against most of them; not only on the ground that it might be dangerous to whisk unacclimatised tourists up a few thousand feet in as many seconds but also because short-term benefits might be outweighed by the expenditure of non-renewable unspoilt scenery. However, most countries acted like men rich enough not to worry about the drain on their capital. The Swiss Alpine Club, and its British equivalent in London, protested vigorously against the short-sighted policy, while the French, Italian and German clubs were not far behind. Yet it was financial rather than scenic cost which prevented some of the more outrageous plans from being carried out.

As early as 1865 the French newspaper *Phare de la Loire* suggested that a railway in the interior of Mont Blanc might take passengers to the summit. Under the headlines 'Observatory on the top of Mont Blanc' and 'The ascent rendered easy for children and for the infirm', the paper claimed that it would be possible to drive a tunnel from the Montanvert, rising so that it would 'open on the actual summit or quite close to it. A tramway being laid down in

The top of the Marmolada cableway in early spring.

140

this gallery and the field engines being erected to work it, a whole caravan of tourists may be transported in a few minutes, without fear or fatigue, and at a comparatively moderate cost, to those regions which cannot now be reached except at the risk of one's life and after enduring infinite hardships'.

However seriously the *Phare de la Loire* expected itself to be taken, specific plans were put forward thirty years later for nothing less than a railway to the top of the Meije in the Dauphiné. There was to be an underground station below the Brèche de la Meije from which a lift was to take travellers to what was described as an 'Hotel Observatoire'. W. A. B. Coolidge, going into the attack with all guns firing, pointed out how obvious it was that none of the sponsors had ever stood on the Meije.

Those who have will, however, try to imagine the Hotel Observatoire filled with guests – say on 1 January – with a snow storm raging furiously around, and will be tempted to believe that though the consumptive patients may get cured in that fine air, yet their nerves will be severely tried by a stay at this new *séjour d'hiver*, and that they will return to their homes no longer sick in body, but very sick in mind indeed.

This scheme was turned down but replaced by a plan for putting a line to the top of the Râteau, on the opposite side of the Brèche from the Meije. Although apparently sanctioned, this also came to nothing and the Meije was not threatened again until 1934. Then, noted the *Alpine Journal*,

having accomplished their utmost to make Chamonix uninhabitable to all but the lowest type of proletarian tripper, the authorities – aiding and abetting, at any rate – are now proposing to erect a *téléphérique* up La Meije. Dauphiné being the last almost completely unspoilt district left in the Alps, it is evidently somebody's aim to eliminate this reproach by the most effective and surest of all methods, entailing, *inter alia*, the 'removal' of 100 feet off the top of the mountain!

A third of a century on, these may seem somewhat extravagant words. But without them, and many like them, the decline from Stephen's 'playground' into fairground would have come even more quickly. The Matterhorn itself was threatened by plans for a nine-mile, partly subterranean railway to its summit, and then for a téléphérique to the top from the Théodule Pass. A railway from Brigue to the Aletsch Glacier in the Oberland, another to the top of the Piz Bernina in the Engadine, and a line across the glaciers from the Riffelberg to Gandegg were other schemes proposed but abandoned before the outbreak of the Second World War. Courmayeur was threatened with the fate of Chamonix by plans for a téléphérique to the Col du Géant. 'We wish the scheme all manner of physical and financial disaster,' noted the *Alpine Journal*.

After 1945 came the deluge, with the téléphérique and its swinging cable-cars a ubiquitous feature of the scene from the Säntis in the north to the Franco-Italian line, the highest in Europe, which links Chamonix and Courmayeur via the Aiguille du Midi and the giant metal piton (*ascenseur*, 3 fr.) on its summit, an example of vandalism unequalled even in the Alps. There are cable-ways to the Aeggishorn and to Belalp from the Rhône valley-floor, to the Diablerets from Reusch above Gstaad as well as from the

Col de Pillon. At all the cashier at the *guichet* tends to sniff the weather and estimate the day's takings like a cinema manager welcoming a wet Saturday evening. The first of the revolving mountain-top restaurants has been built at the top of the Schilthorn cable-way and given the accolade of presentation in a James Bond film. The summit of the Marmolada is reached by a trio of cable-cars in which there is the inevitable jostle for the best photographic viewpoints and in which, during the tramp from one to the other, the first becomes last and the last becomes first again. Even the least distinguished valley has its own selection of snug little fuggeries at the top of the cable-ways, where damp humanity can take refuge in hot drink and hope for a break in the weather. In the district of Bolzano alone uphill transports – including aerial cable-way, cable-way, sleigh-lift and ski-lift – number roughly a couple of hundred, and the memory of present-day authentic Alpine air often includes the whiff of diesel.

'Above the Alps'

All this has the sombre inevitability of ruined coastlines and the concreted English countryside, a progression towards dark Satanic mills and the pit-head apparatus which the cable-ways parallel so efficiently. To it there have recently been added, as convenience or pollution, the facilities of air transport. More than one mountaineer, desperately hanging on to life in the aftermath of an accident, has blessed the phut-phut of the helicopter bringing rescuers to prevent the final slip from this world into the next. Many have benefited from the easier provisioning of high Alpine huts while, in the words of one air-tourist service, 'thanks to the plane, the most prestigious snow-fields are on the skier's doorstep all the year round'. On a different level, used with daring and imagination, the plane has enabled Bradford Washburn to take some of the most extraordinary mountain portraits. Thus aircraft here, like other results of what our wonderful scientists can do, are not entirely a curse.

The predecessor of the aircraft was the balloon, and during the last century many an ingenious proposal was made for utilising it for mountain transport. Thus in 1859 Friedrich Albrecht, architect from Winterthur, published details of an 'aerial railway on the Rigi, with balloons used as locomotives'. The scheme was for a metal track which would guide a series of balloons and gondolas. Once the balloon was released at the foot of the mountain, the gas would make it rise, and the track would guide it to the summit. Here the gas would be siphoned off into heavy containers which would be taken down to Vitznau without difficulty and used to inflate other balloons. Nothing came of the idea.

Nearly half a century later a comparable scheme was planned to take passengers from the Kleine Scheidegg to the top of the Jungfrau. In this the single balloon, with gondola holding fifty, was to be kept if not on the rails at least on its intended route by a chain one and a half miles long running between base and summit. After a stop for passengers to admire the view, the balloon would then be wound down, pulley-wise, and the tourists would de-bus, or de-balloon, to make way for the next load.

Overleaf
The peaks of the Drei Zinnen reflected in the Lake of Misurina.

A cable-car descending from the revolving restaurant on the summit of the Schilthorn towards Mürren and the Lauterbrunnen valley.

142

As these schemes were overtaken by the genius of the Swiss for driving more conventional railways up and through mountains, Alpine ballooning came into its own with the rise of Captain Spelterini – real name Eduard Schweizer. Born in the hamlet of Neuhaus in canton St Gall in 1852 Spelterini, as he was known throughout his colourful career, took up ballooning in the 1880s and logged a series of spectacular flights from many European countries in *Urania*, *Jupiter* and *Stella*. Some years later he discussed flights with Albert Heim, the famous Zurich geologist, and in 1896 a trans-Alpine balloon flight conference took place in the city's Federal Meteorological Institute. One result was that on 3 October Captain Spelterini rose from Sion in the balloon *Wega*, hoping to cross the Alps. The *föhn*, blowing from the south, decided otherwise. Spelterini landed near Besançon after a flight of nearly 150 miles, but still north of the mountains. Two years later he was luckier, crossing the Bernese Alps from the same starting point, and following this with other flights from Zermatt into the Ticino, from Mürren to Turin and from Interlaken to Oberammergau.

The First World War put a temporary end to his ballooning, but in 1926 Spelterini, for whom 'intrepid' seems a mild adjective, made his last flight. He was aged seventy-four but took up three passengers from Zurich on a flight which ended with an emergency landing in the Vorarlberg. He died in 1931, largely responsible for the lead that the Swiss took in ballooning and partly responsible for the International Alpine Balloon Sports Meeting now held every summer in Mürren.

Balloons are not numerous, neither are they noisy. They are colourful, have the attraction of anachronism, and are usually beautiful to behold, so that to object to their sailing in splendid freedom above the mountains implies a curmudgeonly attitude. With aircraft the case is rather different and certainly more complex.

The most important pioneer of flights in, rather than over, the Alps was the legendary Geiger, a native of Sion who between the wars flew a regular rescue service to the site of the Mauvoisin Dam. Geiger became obsessed with the idea of being able to land above the snowline, studied the choughs, which approach their landing site from a position below it, and realised that he needed a sloping surface both for landing and take-off. His small plane was fitted with skis and within a few years 'the glacier pilot' had become one of the most famous characters of the Alps, flying out of Sion airfield and saving countless lives by landing in the most difficult places. However, Geiger – tragically killed in an accident at Sion – was a pilot of exceptional skill. Such men are rare, and while others followed his example their numbers were limited. The arrival of the helicopter revolutionised the possibilities of mountain rescue and today such organisations as the wholly admirable Garde Aérienne Suisse de Sauvetage – which has rescued more than 2,700 accident victims during the last decade – provide an air network which, weather permitting, can reach almost any part of the chain. Thus rescue planes have long become a commonplace of the Alpine scene and as far back as 1961 the roof of the Zermatt hospital was adapted to take helicopters.

Inside the great abbey church at Disentis where Father Placidus à Spescha lived for many years.

But their use, and that of winged planes, has spread far beyond rescue work. In February 1955 a helicopter was used to ferry ninety passengers and seven tons of baggage between Brigue and Zermatt, and in the following months another plane took passengers to the Jungfraujoch and to the top of the Mönch. Provisioning of huts by helicopter – and the landing of troops for mountain exercises – soon followed, while in September 1966 a helicopter lowered a five-foot iron cross to the summit of the Dent Blanche during celebrations marking the hundredth anniversary of its first ascent.

By the early 1960s commercial possibilities were being exploited on some scale. In 1961 the authorities gave permission for passengers to be flown to the Dôme du Goûter and a glacier airport was opened above Diablerets at 10,000 feet. Significantly enough, there were complaints in the same year about excessive use of aircraft in the Engadine, the turbulence from four Swiss fighter planes brought down a snow arête on the Brunegghorn as it was being traversed by climbers, and a civilian plane caused an avalanche which swept two climbers down six hundred feet. Mountaineers on Mont Blanc and elsewhere have been endangered by aircraft, while above Chamonix a French Air Force jet in 1961 severed a cable on the Aiguille du Midi cable-way, releasing three cable-cars in which six passengers fell to their death and immobilising others in which nearly a hundred men and women spent an uncomfortable night suspended 10,000 feet up.

Two developments suggest that the problems created by aircraft in the Alps are unlikely to diminish. One is the growth of mountain parachute-jumping. Started after the First World War largely as a Service venture, it met with only questionable success and was not taken up as a sport until the mid-1950s. But in 1961 three men jumped on to the top of Mont Blanc from a plane some 2,000 feet higher, and progress then became fast and furious. After 1964, in the words of a writer in the *Alpine Journal*, 'each winter-sports resort with an airstrip became a centre for snow-jumping. In the Pyrenees, the Alps and the Vosges the number of enthusiasts multiplied; the skiers of Courcheval, of l'Alpe d'Huez and of la Plagne, grew accustomed to seeing each Sunday multi-coloured cupolas slowly descending, supporting figures who sank gently into the snow.'

Perhaps more important is the growing use made of planes to take skiers not only to ski-resorts, none of which can now really be *à la mode* without its air-strip, but also to the upper snowfields. So much so that in November 1971 an agreement was signed between Air Alpes, which had carried 55,000 skiers in the previous decade, and the Fédération Française du Ski. Members of the federation will get a ten-per-cent reduction in the firm's mountain air-fares, and it is expected that the agreement will 'contribute to rapid progress in the number of passengers transported'.

However, it is not merely the future possibility of too many aircraft circum-navigating too many peaks which has caused questioners to ask whether flying should not be more rigidly controlled. Even to the most sophisticated the mountains are in at least some measure a refuge from the distractions of urban life, a refuge in which air taxis and aerial ski-services have the incongruity of a strip-joint in a sanctuary or a casino in a cathedral. Thus pollution by noise is a factor to be balanced against the ease with which travellers can be given an eagle's-eye close-up of the great peaks, and skiers landed on any glacier that seizes their fancy in the morning. Such services have already passed from the notable to the commonplace. Already the aerial mini-bus and a network of aerodromes in and around the Alps supply a milk-run service for the increasing number who can afford it.

Like the railway and the motor-car, the plane has extended the area above the snowline which can be visited without effort by the ordinary man. Unlike its predecessors, it is still costly enough to be beyond the masses, while flying in the mountains is still too chancy for some tastes. Neither deterrent will last for ever.

PART TWO
Alpine Addicts

It would be unfair to suggest, and difficult to prove, that the Alps attract more than their quota of eccentrics. Yet from the earliest days they have certainly attracted individualists; men – and women – a little out of the ordinary; those who tend to have views of their own, to steer away from the herd, to have only a passing interest in orthodoxy. This is true in almost all those fields where the Alps have offered men a peg for other interests. The most conservative of the Victorian mountaineers were at least slightly different from the mass of middle-class professional men and manufacturers from whom they were largely drawn. Compared with the amateurs, the professionals too were men cast in a rather different mould from their village colleagues. The year's peasant round of sowing and reaping was for most of them sufficient background to a life which was certainly hard but usually tolerable. Was it really common sense for them to risk their lives and possibly – who knew? – the enmity of unknown spirits, merely to reach places where men surely had no right to be? If God had intended man to reach the summits he would have created him more like the chamois. Only a few individuals thought otherwise and became guides.

Thus the exploration of the Alps, and its enjoyment, tended to attract 'characters', intellectual nonconformists who relied on themselves rather than on others, and who brought to photography, to their interpretation of the mountains through history or literature – and even to the creation of the Alps as a field for women's emancipation – a fine streak of human individuality.

Bisson's picture of the
Chamonix Aiguilles taken
in 1860.

CHAPTER NINE
The Splendid Hills

Frank Smythe, the British mountaineer whose photographs between the two World Wars brought the first realisation of the Alps to thousands of English-speaking readers, often used a small *Etui*, which produced pictures $2\frac{1}{2} \times 3\frac{1}{2}$ inches in size. He once found himself near an elderly gentleman using a massive hand-and-stand camera, weighing some thirty pounds and exposing plates $6\frac{1}{2} \times 8\frac{1}{2}$ inches. While Smythe took an instantaneous exposure, his fellow-photographer was enveloped in a black covering, studying a focussing screen and preparing for a time exposure. Then 'the old gentleman popped out from beneath the dark cloth and I heard a single word in which was such an expression of withering contempt that I have never forgotten it', Smythe wrote. 'It was simply "Snapshotter".' Today, some forty years on, the roles are reversed. It is the miniature expert, whose camera plus boxful of accessories only weighs a pound or so, who is the accepted mountain portraitist; the poor fellow with the massive equipment who is out-of-date and out-of-touch.

The contrast between pioneers and contemporaries is greater than even this *bouleversement* would suggest. Auguste Bisson used twenty-five porters to carry his hundredweight of equipment to the top of Mont Blanc in 1861 and was satisfied to have taken three successful pictures during what was a major expedition. Today a pocketful of cassettes can contain many hundreds. Vittorio Sella, and others like him who worked in the later nineteenth century, still had to be their own chemists as well as their own button-pressers. They had, furthermore, to expose without benefit of exposure-meter – compared with the contemporary enthusiast who can post back to home-base a trial run of colour film and be told by return whether he was under- or over-exposed.

Yet although science has revolutionised mountain photography in less than a century and a half, the artistic problems remain. The photographer still searches for a foreground – and still finds wife or girl-friend an invaluable substitute. He still finds that the brain selects and concentrates in a way of which even a Hasselblad is incapable; what the eye sees as a dominant group crowding out the rest of the picture can appear as a small smudge on a film taken with a lens of too short a focus. He still finds that by the time he has estimated exposure the mists have dissolved, the clouds moved to the wrong place, the great shafts of sunlight that gave a visionary quality to the picture have moved on elsewhere and that he is left with the light of common day shining on a mundane scene.

Photography only became a practical proposition in the 1830s, when Nicephore Nièpce and Daguerre produced their pictures and Fox Talbot came up with his own 'Talbot-type' process. A decade later Ruskin, touring the Alps while gathering material for the fourth volume of *Modern Painters*, took the 'first sun-portrait ... of the Matterhorn', a picture used later as a basis for his sketch of the mountain.

Ruskin set the fashion and throughout the 1850s more than one mountain-eer, mountain walker and mere mountain tourist lumbered himself with the necessary paraphernalia. The Smyth brothers who made the first ascent of Monte Rosa and the first guideless ascent of Mont Blanc carried a special photographic tent; George Joad, who accompanied the party most of the way up Mont Blanc, took a number of photographs. An English colonel was in 1858 reported at various places in the Alps with his wife, a mule which carried a developing tent, and other photographic equipment. Friedrich Martens produced a fourteen-section panorama of Mont Blanc. Aimé Civiale, who began work towards the end of the 1850s, made regular expeditions to high viewpoints with more than half a ton of equipment requiring the services of a baggage-train of twenty-five men and mules.

These mountain photographers tended to fall into one of two groups. They either went to the top of one selected mountain after another with the specific aim of taking panoramas which could be used for topographical or scientific purposes. Or, like Hudson and Kennedy, they used the camera as an ancillary during mountaineering expeditions, to record where they had been or what they had seen. The division has tended to widen with the years. At one end of the spectrum there is now the mountain portraitist, willing to spend a day or two selecting the right vantage-point and a week or two waiting for the right conditions of sunlight and cloud; at the other there is the keen rock-climber, Leica strapped close, whose aim is to record the detail of a cliff-face.

During the 1860s, and in fact until the introduction of dry plates in the 1880s, the photographer had to process his glass negatives on the spot, and without too long a time lag. Thus he needed not only a portable dark-room but also quantities of water, a commodity easily obtainable on glaciers but sometimes rare on a rock-peak. How the mountain-portraitist tackled this problem is illustrated by the Bisson brothers, one of whom took in 1861 a classic photograph of men on the Mer de Glace which could hardly be rivalled today. The two Bissons made their first attempt to take pictures from Mont Blanc in 1856, an attempt frustrated by the carelessness of a porter who dropped the heavy box containing the fragile glass plates. Four years later, when the French emperor and empress visited Chamonix, Auguste Bisson accompanied them on the Mer de Glace and later went as high as the Grands Mulets, taking group-portraits of the imperial party.

However, only in 1861 did he make his most successful photographic expedition, to the top of Mont Blanc. Organisation of the party was put in the hands of the guide Auguste Balmat. He had already made eleven ascents of the mountain and was almost dissuaded from making another. 'But', he said, 'I haven't seen the summit since it was French. I want to see it just once more, and who knows but what I shall discover something new there.'

Bisson and Balmat left Chamonix with twenty-five porters and several hundredweight of equipment, including cameras, dark-rooms, chemicals and sixteen-inch by twenty-inch glass negatives fitted into a specially designed carrying case. Bad weather delayed them at the Grands Mulets and another day passed before they reached the summit.

First the dark-room tent had to be put up. Inside it Balmat helped Bisson pour a layer of collodium on a single glass plate and sensitise it in a silver bath. With the plate loaded in the camera, they came into the open, set up the apparatus on a tripod and prepared for the exposure. No record exists of its length, but several minutes was common, even when intense light was reflected back off large areas of snow. In the darkroom the glass negative had to be processed. Water was provided by melting snow. Two hours after setting up shop they had one negative.

Bisson, determined to make the most of the opportunity, carried out the process for a second time, then for a third. At the end he had three pictures, two good and one indifferent. Then he was willing to start the descent – but only to the Grands Mulets where more plates were exposed.

The Dolomites

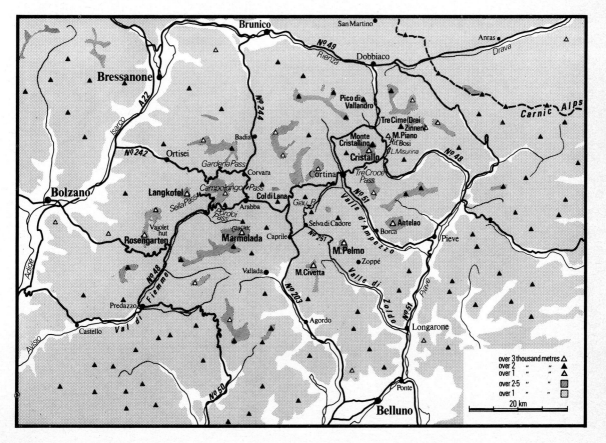

Hereford George's photographic party on an Oberland Glacier, 1865.

During the 1860s many mountaineers, not anxious to be involved in the expense of such massive operations, yet wanting to show the day-to-day detail of glacier travel and mountain exploration, were carrying out time-and-motion studies. They found that both the camera, and the equipment needed for processing, could be lightened in weight and increased in convenience.

Among them was the Rev. Hereford George, first editor of the *Alpine Journal* and an enthusiast who in 1865 decided that a mountaineering season could be combined with a photographic tour. He took E. Edwards as professional expert, a well-known London photographer. Christian Almer was the *guide-chef*, and with him went his son Ulrich, 'a boy of sixteen, whose chief duties were to carry the legs of the camera everywhere, and to keep its master supplied with water'. Three ladies, a male colleague and another guide made up the party of nine who for five or six weeks wandered slowly through the Bernese Oberland. Occasionally George made first ascents but 'the centre around which all else revolved was a photographic camera, and it was understood at starting that all other considerations must yield to the imperative requirements of business'.

His camera was smaller and lighter than most, taking pictures of three sizes, the largest only six inches by eight. It had eight different lenses, plates for three days with the chemicals to process them, and could be stowed in a single small box which, together with a second box containing the tent, could be carried by one man.

Perhaps the core of George's success lay in his design of the tent, an ingenious affair with devices, gadgets and notions worthy of an Alpine Heath Robinson. On being opened up the top of the box containing the tent revealed

Sir William de Wiveleslie Abney's fine portrait of Christian Almer in old age from *Pioneers of the Alps*.

156

a washing tray, on one side of which were separate cells for bottles of chemicals. Below was a cupboard, neatly arranged to hold the plates so that they could be kept damp for hours. This cut out the tribulations of Bisson on Mont Blanc, forced to spend precious time in dark-room processing.

The contrivance was portable, and as George himself later wrote, 'one can have things carried almost anywhere, if one does not mind paying for it'. One major trouble still remaining was the three- or four-minute exposure. During this time clouds would move and branches of trees would wag back and forth to produce what might nowadays be regarded as a fashionable effect but was then the result of defective technique. The exposure itself, produced by removing the cap from the shutter and making a number of mystic passes before returning it, was difficult to estimate, and George himself comments of Ruskin's chapter on 'Mountain Beauty' in *Modern Painters*, that 'the whole chapter is worth attention for the purpose of judging of the exposure required for a photograph'. Second among difficulties was the soot and whitewash appearance of prints, in the days before panchromatic emulsions. Black rocks and white sky were normal; rarely is there a hint of that deepening blue of outer space which comes with altitude.

These were serious limitations, and few early mountain photographs were works of art in the manner of Julia Cameron. Bisson might capture the extraordinary ant-like quality of men moving among the crevasses of the Mer de Glace, but most early pictures taken above the snowline were for use rather than inspiration. However, mountain-top panoramas had topographical value, George's Oberland pictures enabled men who had never been near a mountain to consider details illustrating the rival glacier theories, and photographs began slowly but steadily to replace wood-engravings in books and periodicals. Whymper himself was only one of the mountaineers who by the 1860s was using the camera as notebook, or as it has been called by Douglas Milner, one of today's leading mountain photographers, as a control 'upon artistic licence or defective memory'. At first the problems of reproducing photographs in satisfactory half-tone were themselves too great, and few could afford to emulate the *Alpine Journal* whose second volume carried a frontispiece taken on George's Oberland journey, an actual print of 'Jungfrau from the Steinberg Alp' being neatly pasted into each copy of the journal.

There was one other way in which the camera was significant, if not to the Alps at least to their story. In 1861 the Chamonix guide Jean Tairraz opened a studio where he photographed other guides and their clients, thus preserving some extraordinary portraits of mountaineering Victorians. Quite as important was Captain Abney, a pioneer chemist who in 1886 took the photographs for *Pioneers of the Alps*, a series of essays on famous guides. 'Common sense suggested', he wrote, 'that the *Führer* should not be posed in a drawing-room, nor portrayed in a light in which they were never seen, nor was it desirable that they should be made to appear better-looking than they really were. We were obliged by force of circumstances to secure them as we found them. Some few came in the stiffly starched collar and newly purchased coats of fête-day attire, while others arrived in their ordinary mountaineering dress.'

A superb study of the Aiguille du Géant taken about 1880 by W.F. Donkin, a British pioneer of Alpine photography.

158

The actual sittings were arranged by Melchior Anderegg, leading Oberland guide, and the outcome was a series of portraits in which his colleagues stand from the page with astonishing immediacy – a bearded Christian Almer with rugged independence in his eyes; Jean-Antoine Carrel, waistcoated, pipe in mouth and as ready to start an argument as in the early days of the Matterhorn attempts; Alexander Burgener, chamois-hunting rifle across his knees; and in old age François Couttet, who worked his way from porter to guide to guide-hotelier and then to ownership of the Grand Hotel Couttet on whose lintel there were carved his initials and a couple of crossed ice-axes. What Julia Cameron did for the Great Victorians, Abney did for the guides.

As the photographer was thus beginning to nudge in among the artists there began to take place the first of four technical developments which revolutionised Alpine photography. This was the invention of dry-plate processes, which came into general use only in the 1880s although Hereford George was using them in the late 1860s. With these it was possible to dispense with darkroom tent, chemicals and lamps to produce water. The plates were still of heavy glass; but they could be exposed and then forgotten until they were processed in a proper studio-laboratory.

The dry plate luckily arrived in time for William Donkin, a chemist who when he joined the Alpine Club in 1879, put Alpine photography among his qualifications. With his overlapping contemporary, Vittorio Sella, Donkin was the first of the great artists among mountain photographers. Even in these days it is perhaps necessary to justify the word 'artist' in connection with photography. Those who doubt this should note that even such a percipient man as the late Professor Carr-Saunders, himself a member of the Alpine Club, has gone on record with the opinion that: 'Photography is objective; it tells us what is seen. Painting is subjective; it communicates the artist's vision.' Any who believe this is so should study George Baxter's Mont Blanc print, which shows four mountaineers cavorting on a snow-dumpling of a peak on whose surface there run concentric and completely impossible blue snow circles. But there is also a photograph of the summit by Smythe; on it there can be seen, caught by the 'objective' camera as surely as by Baxter's vision, the same 'impossible' markings, the same fleeting impression which Smythe knew would best suggest the top of Europe.

Smythe's artistic vision was based on a sound technical knowledge – and Donkin's success was also due, at least in part, to much the same thing. His favourite camera took pictures $7\frac{1}{2}$ by 5 inches and though this, with a dozen plates, weighed between fifteen and twenty pounds, he carried it to some of the most inaccessible spots in the Alps. His tripod went with the other gear carried by guide or porter, but he was mobile in a way that his predecessors had not been. Moreover to his specialised knowledge he could add the 'eye for a picture' without which all technique and the best of equipment is a waste of learning and money. The result was that from the end of the 1870s Donkin began to raise mountain photography to a new level. A contributory reason for success was his use of the carbon process, which allows remarkable control over the finished print.

Alexander Burgener: another portrait from 'Pioneers of the Alps'.

Zermatt at the end of the 19th century.

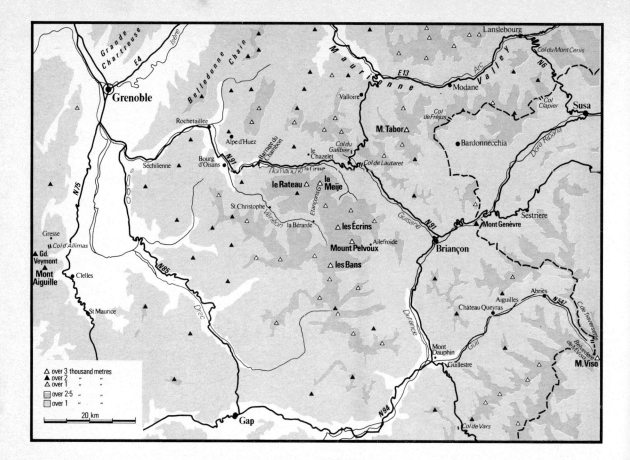

The Dauphiné

The Aletsch glacier, the longest in the Alps, which streams down towards the Rhône Valley from the heights of the Bernese Oberland.

Overleaf
Just a few of the flowers which give colour to the Alpine slopes during the days of early summer.

Killed in the Caucasus in 1888, Donkin did not live long enough to benefit from the three photographic developments which followed one another in quick succession during the last years of the century: panchromatic emulsions, which with colour filters enabled a photographer to create a balance much nearer to that seen by the human eye; the telephoto lens which allows the photographer to 'bring close' distant views; and roll film, which removed the most weighty and fragile part of the photographer's load.

All these advances of course added to the scope of photography in general, but all were particularly important to mountain photography, and all were eventually utilised by Vittorio Sella, who made his first panorama on the Mont de Mars, above his home town of Biella, in 1879, and who lived on into the Second World War. George's account of his photographic journey in *The Oberland and its Glaciers, Explored and Illustrated with Ice-Axe and Camera* had awakened a limited Alpine public to the possibilities of Alpine photography, and Donkin's exhibits at the Alpine Club showed that the photograph could be complementary to the painting. Sella broadened human interest in the Alps rather differently, his finest photographs from the last years of the century onwards being printed in many books of Alpine exploration. Here, in the words of Carlo Ramella, written after Sella's death in 1943, 'one sees skies of gigantic size; silent mountains watching the little man

passing through the snow towards a pale sun ... In his pictures the splendid profiles stand in bold relief. The wide glaciers move like floods across the plain. There are here horizons without end, and one can almost hear the voices of the old climbers in the still air.'

Sella's dictum was 'use a big negative to photograph big things', and his early glass plates were rarely smaller than 10 × 8 inches and sometimes 15 × 12 inches – negatives yielding contact prints with pin-sharp detail. In an earlier age Albert Smith's *Mont Blanc* entertainment in London had lit Alpine enthusiasm; two decades later it was Whymper's *Scrambles*; in the last years of the century it was the mountain portraiture of Vittorio Sella which kept it going.

Donkin and Sella were at the top of the photographic tree. Below them – and in some cases not so very far below – were mountain photographers who were artists in one particular region. Many lived close to the Alps and were able to make maximum use of the weather, the forerunners of those purely local experts who can look from their windows at a mountain 365 days a year and go out on the job only when the perfect picture is possible. With their help, photographing the Alps had become by the turn of the century if not routine at least an additional way of attracting tourists.

Moreover the tourists themselves now had cameras. By the 1900s most of the technical developments now available had come into use, at least in primitive form – a satisfactory colour system being the main exception. Equipment was still comparatively bulky, but the need for the photographic porter had gone and roll films quickly helped to make the camera as common in the rucksack as the spare pullover. Thus the elderly gentleman of Frank Smythe's story, still working with the heavy hand-and-stand camera of an earlier day – had some point in his contempt for the snap, snap, snap brigade. For Smythe was the one in the ten thousand; the vast quantities of 'mountain photographs' that went into the D and P machines were mainly of the 'me and the Jungfrau' variety.

For some years one thing was still lacking. This was the camera ideally suited to the rock-climber and the skier, light, small, and taking many exposures before a change of film was necessary. The answer was the Leica, which arrived in the late 1920s. Today the advantages of its thirty-five millimetre film are taken for granted: thirty-six exposures or more on a single film, easy loading, a wide range of emulsions. The decade that witnessed the arrival of the miniature also witnessed the first photographic flight by Bradford Washburn with his forty-five-pound Fairchild, a jumbo-size apparatus which could take more than a hundred $7\frac{1}{2} \times 9\frac{1}{2}$ inch exposures at a single loading. Washburn, filming the traverse of the Grands Charmoz and the Grépon with his brother, thought that the sequence could be rounded off by a few aerial shots. The flight from Le Fayet in a small monoplane encouraged him to investigate air photography for mountain reconnaissance, subsequently used to good effect in Alaska. Thirty years later he returned to the Alps and with the same camera – plus three decades of experience – produced a series of mountain studies which genuinely merit the description 'incomparable'.

Vittorio Sella (1859–1943), the Italian mountaineer and photographer.

Clockwise from top left: A contemporary guide's grave in the cemetery at Saas Fee; a painted house in the village of Guarda, the Grisons; the wrought-iron inn-sign at Glesch at the head of the Rhône Valley; figure in the church at Solda; the Virgin of the Rocks, Vajolet Valley, Dolomites; the metal Madonna which for years stood on the summit of the Aiguille du Géant, now in the guides' museum, Courmayeur.

From the start the big-format enthusiasts pointed out, as they did in other fields of photography, that miniature work had to be enlarged so greatly that technique had to be perfect. A whole-plate negative, enlarged two times linear, gives a print 13 × 17 inches while a thirty-five-millimetre negative must be enlarged thirteen times to give a print of comparable size. However, on the mountains the advantages of lightness and compactness weighed more than elsewhere, and before the Second World War the miniature had gained a firm hold.

All that remained to bring equipment and materials up to contemporary standards was perfection of a colour process. One of the first, the Autotype, had been available during the early years of the century, but could be used successfully only by an expert; even then results were passable rather than good. Kodachrome in the late 1930s carried colour photography over the hump and wartime research improved it still further. For the last two decades skilful mountain photographers – although few others – have been able to show the Alps in something approximating to their natural colours.

Today the photographer with a variety of lenses and a pocketful of films can go by téléphérique to the top of the Aiguille du Midi in less time than it took Balmat to organise Bisson's porters for the expedition up Mont Blanc. Such opportunities are repeated at a hundred places throughout the Alps. What is the photographer to make of them, at the crowded upper stations, or on the lonely paths that can still be found off the beaten track?

First he should decide what he wants to do. The casual snapshotter, hopefully clicking away with his camera pointed into some gorgeous sunset, does no harm, makes his own pleasure, is unlikely to worry too much about results, and keeps the industry going. The non-casual mountain photographer can have one or more aims and his results will be governed by the care he takes first in thinking about them, then in acquiring the best equipment for the job.

In general, the division still lies between the climber anxious to record the details of an ascent and the man more concerned with the telling mountain portrait. In between stands the photographer who wishes to portray the whole life of a mountain environment. For all size and weight are important factors. The man who wants to show people and things as well as the distant scene will be handicapped by a camera that does not take interchangeable lenses of different focal lengths. So will the man who concentrates on colour, since he lacks the black-and-white photographer's ability to enlarge only a small part of the negative. Anyone who hopes to take good flower photographs must use a camera which can, with the use of supplementary lenses if necessary, be brought to within a foot or so of his subject; if he can reduce the distance to a few inches, so much the better. Those who hope to take both black-and-white and colour must face the choice between perpetually having the 'wrong' film in the camera; carrying two cameras; or investing in one of the comparatively few makes, such as the Hasselblad, the Rolls-Royce of cameras, whose interchangeable backs allow an easy switch from one film to another.

The exceptionally bright light of the world above the snowline makes an exposure-meter essential for anyone whose camera is not as constant a companion as belt or braces; and filters on long-focus lenses can demand exposures long enough to make a tripod preferable if not obligatory. These factors, and many others, are discussed in Douglas Milner's admirable *Mountain Photography*, an inquire-within whose careful study before an Alpine holiday can save much disappointment, gnashing of teeth, and regrets for opportunities not taken.

Even so, the man who records the scenery of his climbs will still need the luck of good weather. André Roch, great mountaineer and great photographer, can take cloud, storm, and mountain and with the touch of genius transform them into an evocation of the Alps as moving as any painter has achieved. For most climbers bad weather not only adds risk to an ascent but increases the chance of the photographic record being little more than a smudge.

The photographer who wants genuine mountain-portraits on the grand scale will need at least three other things: lots of time, lots of patience and lots of luck – as well as the intuition for recognising the right viewpoint when he finds it. Here an advance reading of the map can give some indication of what the sun will be shining on (weather willing) at any hour of the day.

Like the Alps themselves, photographic opportunities are at first glance monopolised by the over-blown and obvious. The Matterhorn with its chalet foreground, the field of crocuses bursting through the snow, and the Jungfrau monopolising the set like a big-bosomed prima donna are the scenes which ape the postcards and the publicity brochures – and are none the less beautiful for that. But this is beginning rather than end. For creative photographers, as for so many others, the Alps offer endless possibilities.

CHAPTER TEN

The Magdalen Hedgehog

Just as some devotees have expressed in photographs what they thought and felt about the mountains, so have others diverted their enthusiasms into different fields. Julius Kugy was more familiar with Triglav, at the eastern end of the Alps, than any man before or since. For Guido Rey the Matterhorn became the subject of exhaustive study and research. C. E. Mathews knew as much about Mont Blanc as the French expert, Charles Durier, and more than most other men; the story of its first ascent was the province of Sir Gavin de Beer, who with Graham Brown produced the definitive account.

Sir Gavin, for whom Hannibal's crossing of the Alps was another *specialité de la maison*, became over half a century one of the leading Alpine historians writing in English, a successor to W. A. B. Coolidge and Henri Montagnier in an earlier age and a contemporary of Arnold Lunn, whose expert knowledge covers not only the history of skiing but the mountain exploits of the later Victorian age. Yet it is the figure of W. A. B. Coolidge who best exemplifies the transformation of the Alps into a field for historical research. In some ways the figure is a caricature, an example in which the idiosyncracies of the textbook historian are so exaggerated as to raise doubts that the genuine article could ever exist. Indeed he did: an Alpine character so rich in eccentricity that his foibles have tended to conceal the very human man who existed beneath.

At the northern end of Grindelwald there still stands Coolidge's home, the Chalet Montana, now engulfed by modern development, a solid four-storey wooden building with wide overhanging eaves and long narrow windows looking out towards the Wetterhorn and the Mittellegi arête of the Eiger. Here lived the scholar who fought with almost indecent stubbornness for his own views on the most academic of points, and whose Oxford Fellowship combined with his literary work, his wisdom and his pugnacity, to nickname him the Magdalen Hedgehog, the Name on the Back of a Guide-Book, the Sage of Grindelwald, and the Fiery Lamb. He was, noted *The Times* obituary when he died in 1926, 'an adept in the gentle art of making enemies and a man who regarded a hatchet as an instrument not for burying but for use'.

As short of breath and of sight as he was of temper, leaning to plumpness even in youth, Coolidge seems an unlikely man to have made more than 1,700

The Rev. W. A. B. Coolidge (1850–1926); his aunt, Miss Meta Brevoort (1825–1876); their guides, 'old' and 'young' Christian Almer; and the dog Tschingel, who made 66 major climbs and 100 minor ones.

mountaineering expeditions including 600 *grandes courses*. An American born in New York in 1850, he was brought to Europe as a boy of fourteen and showed little early sign of the relentless concentration that marks the scholar. Yet before he died it was, as the Alpine authority Captain Farrar once said, 'as ridiculous for a man to speak of Alpine matters without mentioning the name of Coolidge, as it would be to discuss the Bible without mentioning God'.

At that time, when Coolidge was breathing fire and brimstone on anyone daring to quote his name in the *Alpine Journal*, he had been its editor for ten years, a member of the Alpine Club Committee, and honorary member of the club for a decade. He had also edited with Martin Conway the first great series of climbing guides; he had published scores of articles, books, guides and notes in which every aspect of the range was listed, examined, and criticised in detail and with an accuracy that made comment difficult and disagreement dangerous. His standards were inflexible, their enforcement pathological. On one occasion he condemned an entire book because the author had let one wrong accent slip by. When one of his own learned volumes appeared, an editor decided that Coolidge himself was the only man with the knowledge to review it adequately. He did so – and pointed out his own errors with scorn.

He first visited the Alps as a boy of fifteen, arriving in Zermatt with his aunt, Miss Meta Brevoort. The date was significant: August 1865, a few weeks after the disaster on the Matterhorn that ended the Golden Age. On the engraved hotel notepaper showing the mountain he wrote to his mother. 'The two dots you see on the picture represent where they (the victims) fell from, and where they fell. A horrible distance'.

Alpine interest grew. Aunt and nephew were back two years later, and again in 1869, but not before the boy had sought advice on his first literary project. 'A *complete* list of all the first ascents of mountains 10,000 feet and upwards would doubtless be interesting but it would involve immense labour,' replied Francis Fox Tuckett, to whom Coolidge had written for advice. Moreover such an enterprise would 'expose the compiler to the risk of being taken to task for the almost invisible mistakes which questions of priority invariably involve'. The following year Coolidge, his aunt, the guides Christian Almer, his son 'young Christian' and the small dog Tschingel, whom the elder Almer had given Coolidge two years previously, embarked on a major climbing campaign.

They chose the Dauphiné. Its character can be judged from Miss Brevoort. At Valloire, she said, the inn 'was of a primitive character. Only three beds, two in an outer room which the men had, and one large one in an inner room for us.' La Grave was little better.

We arrived soaking at 4.10 after six hours' march from the chalets, and to such an inn. The floor of our room black as the ace of spades, a bag of flour and a sieve in one corner. No means of washing, apparently flowers spread out to dry on the floor, no pillows, sheets like dishcloths! Will went to bed while his clothes were drying and, concluding it was the best place for him, remained there. We made some tea and had boiled eggs, but neither milk nor butter as the cows are away. Fleas without end.

In this primitive environment aunt and nephew strode on to great things. They made the first ascent of the central peak of the Meije, the first ascent of the Ailefroide on the other side of the group, and the third ascent of the Écrins, which Whymper and his party had climbed for the first time six years previously. Then they drove across the frontier to Courmayeur, where Coolidge made the second ascent of Mont Blanc by the Brenva. Aunt and nephew then joined forces again – she had anxiously watched his Brenva ascent through a telescope – made the fifth ascent of the Dent Blanche; attempted the Weisshorn; climbed the Dom; and added lesser climbs to their list before returning to England along a circuitous route necessitated by the Franco-Prussian war.

The 1870 campaign set the pattern. The unusual pair, often accompanied by the dog Tschingel, began to clock up an enviable number of firsts, including in 1871 the first woman's traverse of the Matterhorn. But it was only after Miss Brevoort's death in 1876 – quietly, of illness, at Dorking in England – that her nephew, still only twenty-six, turned himself to the formidable task of putting Alpine history in order.

The previous year he had become a Fellow of Magdalen, allegedly the first 'foreigner' in the college's long history. In 1882 he took Holy Orders, and settled down at South Hinksey on the outskirts of Oxford, devoting to Alpine exploration most of the summer months and, very soon, some of the winter ones too.

However, exploration was subsidiary to Alpine scholarship and academic battle. He had already, with much historical background, described a number of his expeditions. He had contributed learned articles and 'Notes' to the *Alpine Journal.* Then, in 1880, he became its editor, a position from which, keeping his ear close to the ground, he could listen in to the constant rumble of controversy.

Many of the arguments to which Coolidge devoted so much attention had even in those days a touch of the not-really-worth-while. Whether the original route up one particular ridge went left or right of one particular rock pinnacle would engage him for weeks in heated but much relished argument with whoever was so rash as to challenge his views. Anyone unwise enough to get a point wrong about the personal exploits of Miss Brevoort, Tschingel, or Coolidge was putting his head into the lion's mouth on a bad day. One author, writing an inaccurate account of Tschingel's life, received a detailed chronicle of mistakes and, at the end, the comment: '*That* is not the way to write history.'

Coolidge was not only easy to cross, but was often feared. Sir Edward Davidson drew a small sketch for the *Mountaineering* volume of the Badminton Library, which had railway porters handling mountaineers' luggage. Well-known initials showed on each item and flying from a parrot cage was a tag with the initials 'W.A.B.C.' At the special request of the editor, who feared a libel suit, the initials were altered.

The argument with Davidson broke into the open years later when Captain Abney, of *Pioneers of the Alps*, collaborated with another member of the

Alpine Club in publishing a facsimile version of Christian Almer's *Führerbuch*, the record carried by each guide in which employers wrote details of the climbs they made. The book had been borrowed without Almer being told the reason; the contents, furthermore, were the copyright of the writers and Coolidge came in fighting, on Almer's side, and succeeded in suppressing the book after only two hundred copies had been printed.

However, there was a more private argument which had less to commend it. On one page of the *Führerbuch*, revealed with all the horrible clarity of the camera, was a tribute by Coolidge to Almer in which the word 'Schreckhorn' had been written without the first 'c'. The error had been noted and asterisked – by an anonymous climber who added the comment: 'The usual spelling among Germans is *Schreckhorn*.' Coolidge soon identified the writer as Davidson. 'I hunted and hunted,' he said later. 'At last I found that Davidson had put his name to Jungfrau without a "g".' This horrifying mistake he subsequently revealed in the pages of the *Alpine Journal*, and it was of little use for Sir Edward to claim that he had not written the description but only signed it. Fourteen years later Davidson was elected president of the club. Coolidge, who had already resigned once but had subsequently been elected an honorary member, did the only thing possible. He resigned his honorary membership.

Most of the arguments which spatter his controversially satisfying life were ephemeral and parochial, but one had greater and more lasting interest. This was the credibility of Alpine artists in general and of Edward Whymper in particular. Whymper was not only the most thrusting mountaineer of the Golden Age. He was also a draughtsman of very great ability. He illustrated many books describing Alpine scenery, and he is probably more responsible than any other artist for recording what climbers looked like, how they moved, and what sort of clothes and equipment they wore and used between 1860 and 1870.

The label on the parrot-cage in this drawing for the 'Mountaineering' volume in the Badminton series at first bore the initials 'W.A.B.C.'

Sir Edward Davidson (1853–1923) and his guides Andreas Jaun (left) and Hans Jaun, photographed at the Montanvert by W.F. Donkin in 1882.

Whymper's photographic accuracy has been questioned more than once, and sometimes with no ill-intent. No artist, even in Victorian times, was expected to operate like a camera. The best, if sometimes untypical, viewpoint could be chosen; rocks and trees, arêtes and couloirs, could be emphasised, glossed over or even omitted to make the required scene. So could people, and a good example is Whymper's *The Club Room at Zermatt*, an illustration which fortuitously brings together in front of the Monte Rosa Hotel the leading amateurs and guides of the period. But artistic licence can tumble over into something else when incidents form the stuff of history. This was so with the sudden appearance in the sky of the three crosses allegedly seen by Whymper after the dramatic accident on the Matterhorn. The spectacle provided a full-page illustration in Whymper's *Scrambles*, where six years after the accident he described it for the first time. The younger Taugwalder later denied that he had seen any crosses, and while the Brocken spectre has sometimes been invoked, the truth of the incident was probably suggested years later by Captain Farrar, that wise old bird who despite his fulminations against the modernisation of the Alps acted for decades as a ballast of Alpine common sense. 'What more natural than that a clever draughtsman should use some little incident to make a sensational picture and unconsciously exaggerate', he wrote to Coolidge about another Whymper illustration. 'We are all human.'

This verdict was on a controversy which nearly split the Alpine Club down the middle and which brought Coolidge and Whymper to the verge of litigation. It sprang from the obituary notice for the Swiss Alpine Club Yearbook

KEY TO THE CLUB-ROOM OF ZERMATT

1. Mr. F. Craufurd Grove, President of the Alpine Club, 1884–1886. 2. Mr. George E. Foster. 3. Rev. J. Robertson. 4. Mr. Frank Walker. 5. Mr. Leslie Stephen, President of the Alpine Club, 1866–1868. 6. Mr. A. W. Moore. 7. Mr. Reginald S. Macdonald. 8. Mr. John Ball, Original Member, and first President of the Alpine Club. 9. Mr. William Mathews, Original Member, and President of the Alpine Club, 1869–1871. 10. Mr. E. S. Kennedy, Original Member, and President of the Alpine Club, 1861–1863. 11. Prof. T. G. Bonney, President of the Alpine Club, 1881–1883. 12. Ulrich Lauener. 13. Prof. John Tyndall. 14. Mr. (Justice) Alfred Wills, Original Member, and President of the Alpine Club, 1864–1865. 15. J. Joseph Maquignaz. 16. Franz Andermatten. 17. Peter Taugwalder *fils*. 18. Peter Perren.

Edward Whymper's drawing of 'The Club-Room of Zermatt', in which he showed many famous British mountaineers of the 1860s.

which Coolidge wrote after Christian Almer's death in 1898. Inevitably this dealt with Almer's first ascent of the Écrins with Whymper in 1864. In the *Scrambles* Whymper had years earlier described how the party, descending the narrow ridge from the summit, had been brought to a stop by a deep notch. Almer went forward to reconnoitre. 'We learned', wrote Whymper, 'that there was no means of getting down, and that we must, if we wanted to pass the notch, jump across on an unstable block on the other side. It was decided that it should be done and Almer, with a larger extent of rope than usual, jumped. The rocks swayed as he came down on it, but he clutched a large mass with both arms and brought himself to anchor.' With a dramatic full-page illustration the exploit passed into Alpine history.

Coolidge added an explosive footnote to his obituary 'After publication of

this book [*Scrambles*], I immediately showed this picture to Almer who then assured me, in all earnest, that he had never done such a thing and would never have been able to do it.' Coolidge was stating that Edward Whymper was a liar.

Whymper immediately invoked the aid of Horace Walker, a companion on the ascent who claimed to remember the incident, and two of Christian Almer's sons, who said their father had talked to them about it. Then he demanded a special meeting of the Alpine Club at which the whole matter could be thrashed out. The club wisely decided that the subject was outside its jurisdiction, a decision which left the ball in play.

Both sides rejected conciliators. Whymper considered a libel writ. But there was no libel action. Instead Whymper circulated to club members a sixteen-page booklet containing a reproduction of the illustration and a generous selection of the letters dealing with it. Coolidge had meanwhile prepared a long list of what he considered to be inaccuracies in Whymper's *Scrambles*, and would have been delighted to quote them before a quasi-judicial body such as Whymper demanded from the Alpine Club. When the club carefully steered clear of this particular whirlpool, Coolidge did the inevitable thing. He resigned once more.

He had left Britain to live in Grindelwald in the summer of 1896. For a few weeks he stayed at The Bear, witnessing from there Christian Almer's ascent of the Wetterhorn made with his wife to celebrate his golden wedding. Then he moved into Am Sandigenstutz, which was to be his home for more than a decade. The Almer family had the ground floor, Coolidge, the suite above. Here was housed his library of 15,000 books dealing with Alpine history. And here he settled down to work.

By this time he was the undisputed expert. Apart from his learned papers and even more learned books he had contributed more than 200 articles to the *Encyclopaedia Britannica*, seven more to Nelson's encyclopedia. He was being asked by many publishers to bring old Alpine guidebooks up-to-date, and by yet others to write such volumes as a projected *Conquest of the Alps*.

Edward Whymper's 'burying the hatchet' drawing which he sent to the Rev. W. A. B. Coolidge shortly before his death.

However, once he had brought Ball's *Alpine Guide* up to date, he settled down to work on two books more after his own heart. The first, written in French, was *Josias Simler et les origines de l'alpinisme jusqua' – 1600*. Its character can be gauged from the fact that it contained 190 pages of introduction, 307 of text, 130 of notes, 327 of appendices, 62 of notes on the appendices, and a 29-page index. Four years later there came *The Alps in Nature and History*, in which Coolidge for the first time began to interpolate his own reminiscences, a practice continued in his subsequent *Alpine Studies*.

By 1911 he was sixty-one. His old arch-enemy Whymper was seventy-one. And now they came together again. In the summer Coolidge was taken ill and spent some time in the hospital in Interlaken. While there he received from Whymper a letter which contained 'friendly advances' – according to Whymper, the only man who can know, since the original letter has been lost. Apparently enclosed with the letter was a small drawing, possibly the last that Whymper made. It showed a gravestone and the hatchet, initialled 'E. W.', which he wished to bury.

In the summer, Whymper informed Coolidge that he was coming to Grindelwald. 'When I come I shall come in the old style,' he wrote. 'Shall walk up, not order rooms in advance, and take my chance as to finding a room. If none can be had I shall camp out.' On 11 August he wrote that he was 'quite queer from the heat – scarcely able to keep on my legs. I meant to walk across the Gemmi to you, but cannot do it with 110 in the sun.' Instead he went to Zermatt, but it was packed with visitors, and it was only at the Gornergrat above the village that he could find a room.

Finally, between 9.30 am and 9.45 am on the morning of 3 September, Whymper arrived in Grindelwald and walked to the Chalet Montana into which Coolidge had moved a year or so earlier. No doubt they talked about the Matterhorn accident, Almer's leap and the accuracy of *The Scrambles* – which Whymper once admitted to Coolidge required corrections 'too numerous to be pointed out'. But Coolidge kept no record and Whymper made only an uninformative note in his diary. It was early evening before the visitor left. He returned to Zermatt, went down to Geneva, then up to Chamonix. Here he fell ill, refused aid, locked himself in his room and died, alone and friendless.

Whymper's death marked a break with the Alpine past in much the same way that Winston Churchill's drew a line across the aftermath of the Second World War. Something that had been part of life was now subtly transformed into history. Coolidge lived on for another fifteen years. Early in August 1914 he emerged from the Chalet Montana. War had been declared on what he

Coolidge's 'Chalet Montana' with the Wetterhorn in the background.

always described as 'the hated Boche' – the very same who had made so difficult that journey back from the Dauphiné in 1870! Who better than the Rev. W. A. B. Coolidge to open up the English church in the absence of the usual minister?

But now, perhaps for the first time in his life, Coolidge began to feel homesick. He had always put his Alpine history first, just as Einstein put his science first. Now he was coming to regret the lack of time spent in establishing roots, in fostering human relationships. 'Very homesick (as I am every year) for the carols, especially "In Dulce Jubilo",' he wrote to the librarian at Magdalen. And, on another occasion: 'You have no idea how I *long* to be back in England again (even in its present queer state!) but my 23,000 books and my little fox terrier impede my plans much.'

The dog gave a hint of Coolidge's Achilles' heel. Tschingel had been, as he once wrote, 'so much more a companion than a mere dog'. He had never recovered from her death just as he had never recovered from Miss Brevoort's. When he next had a dog he had chosen Nero, a black Labrador as unlike Tschingel as any dog he could find. Then had come Max. Coolidge's human feelings, so unlike those expected in a fiery lamb, are revealed in the letters to England. 'How old do such *small* dogs live on an average?' he asked.

Beneath the hard exterior there breathed the residual humanity of a man who could look back on the creation of a new level of Alpine scholarship, an achievement of dry boniness but one which nevertheless provides an essential skeletal structure for those who lived later. It can hardly be claimed that Coolidge brought new intellectual vigour to the physical sport of mountaineering, or to its historiography. His *forte* was the collection of facts rather than their interpretation. Leslie Stephen and Frederic Harrison in one age, Arnold Lunn and Geoffrey Winthrop Young in a later one, were the Alpine mystics who made mountain climbing more than an exercise. Yet Coolidge's achievement was unique and he could regard it with satisfaction.

And in 1923 Sir Edward Davidson died. At the next meeting of the Alpine Club Committee it was decided that Coolidge should, once again, be offered honorary membership. He gracefully accepted.

By 1925 he was in bad shape. But he could get about and he had one consolation. 'I still have my old dog, Max, who is now *very* old (about 16½) and love him devotedly,' he wrote. Little more than a year later, on 8 May 1926, he died of heart attack at his home. He was buried in the Swiss churchyard after a service in which the Swiss Alpine historian, Dr Dübi, said that but for the occasion he would have been 'tempted to reproach my departed friend for having once again forestalled me, as he did more than sixty years ago when, as a youth of seventeen, he made the ascent of one of the last unconquered summits of the Grisons, upon which I had had my eye'.

As the coffin was lowered into the grave the avalanches from the Mettenberg echoed like a roll of minute guns, which Coolidge would have considered no more than his due. On the gravestone it was noted that 'at his own request he was buried among the mountains he loved so well'; but 'mountains' was spelt without its 'u', a mistake he would have considered unpardonable.

CHAPTER ELEVEN

On All Fours

Even had Coolidge not translated the mountaineering past into a subject for scholarship he would be remembered for one other thing: raising the level of canine alpinism above that of the traditional St Bernard. After the ten glorious seasons during which Coolidge's Tschingel made sixty-six major ascents as well as about a hundred minor ones, the legend of the St Bernard would never be quite the same.

As big as a small pony, shambling through the snow and sniffing out survivors, a keg of the hard stuff dangling from his collar, the kingsize friendly dog from the St Bernard Hospice was long regarded as the only dog in the Alps. In fact, it has always been dogs of the lower-slung breeds, mongrelly and slight, who have accompanied their masters up mountains. It was a fine fellow of indeterminate breed which – at least until recently – made a twice daily return trip from the Vajolet hut in the Dolomites to Gardeccia, 3,000 feet below, where a welcoming bitch awaited him. It is the less weighty animals which can be seen padding after their owners up the Rigi, with never a thought of the leather paw-boots once provided for Tschingel.

However, the St Bernards have their reputation. For centuries they did act as guide-dogs to the monks, who in bad weather made a morning journey down each side of the St Bernard pass from the hospice in search of luckless travellers crossing the Alps between Piedmont and Switzerland. Even so it is for little more than a century and a half that the St Bernard has really been the St Bernard. The dogs used from the Middle Ages onwards were the result of crossing native hill dogs with Danish bull-bitches, a breed kept pure until 1812 when all the bitches succumbed to bad weather. Only after this date did the present St Bernard come into existence, a cross between the Newfoundland and what appears to have been a local variation of the Pyrenean mountain dog. At first they had long hair which hampered them in snow. Eventually the monks succeeded in breeding back to the short-haired strain, and by the mid-nineteenth century the huge animals had become, with the mortuary in which bodies of dead travellers were displayed, one of the sights of the hospice.

Thus the St Bernard became the travel agent's version of canine Alpinism, good in a posed picture, with a sensitivity for smelling out humans that has been developed to an extraordinary degree in the dogs used by modern

The 'historical' St Bernard
dog with one of the
marroniers.

avalanche rescue services, but in no sense a *chien de haute montagne*. For this one must look not to monks but to mountaineers: to de Saussure, who took a dog of undiscovered breed on most of his years-long Alpine wanderings, and to Marc-Théodore Bourrit, who did the same.

Typically enough it was an Englishman who first took a dog on a major Alpine climb. He was Henry Atkinson, who in 1837 climbed Mont Blanc accompanied by a small dog belonging to Michael Balmat, one of the guides. 'It was astonishing to see this little animal which had evidently been trained for the purpose, mounting the steep rocks like a chamois,' Atkinson recorded in his narrative. However, he notes also that the party was 'frequently retarded by the little dog, and heartily wished him at the bottom of the glaciers'. On the ascent, the animal 'was much affected with drowsiness after we quitted the Grand Plateau, and every time we stopped he tried to lie down on our feet, finding the snow cold. He evinced many tokens of surprise by frequently staring about him, and would make an effort to run very fast and then drop. With regard to his appetite, chicken bones disappeared with an amazing rapidity, but he did not appear to suffer from thirst.' According to the account given by François Devoussaud to Douglas Freshfield when they climbed Mont Blanc in 1863, this first canine conqueror of Mont Blanc was a Spitz with very pointed nose and sharp black eyes.

The poor dog was pitched over the crevasses, and helped along by his master, and thus reached in safety the top of the 'mur' [Freshfield recorded]. Hence, he trotted along merrily at the head of the party apparently determined to be the first dog on the top. But, strange to relate, as the dog climbed higher and the air grew colder, his tail which he carried as usual done up in a neat twist on his back, after the fashion of his tribe, was seen slowly to unfold itself till it blew out in a stiff streamer, frozen straight and hard as a poker. The poor beast still trotted bravely on, but frequently turned his head with a thoughtful air as if wondering what could possibly be the matter behind. Happily, as soon as he returned to more genial climes his tail unfroze, and before he reached Chamonix the curly-tailed dog was himself again, and has ever since strutted about with a loftier twist behind than any of his fellows.

The first account of a dog being taken on a genuine rock-climb is given by T. S. Kennedy. In 1865 he had gone to Switzerland on his honeymoon but did not let this interfere with the serious business of mountaineering. He had hoped to make the first ascent of the Verte but arrived in Chamonix only to hear that Whymper was already on the top. A second ascent, by a more difficult route, was fair consolation.

In his account of the climb Kennedy makes only scanty references to his dog. The first comes soon after the party had begun to cut its way up a steep snow couloir. 'My little black dog began, as she always does on hard snow-slopes, to look unhappy,' he comments. 'Although her claws acted in some measure the part of crampons, they were not sufficient to enable her to walk in any but an up-and-down direction, and sitting on her hind legs was manifestly impossible.' The 'as she always does on hard snow-slopes' suggests that she regularly accompanied her master. This would explain how she appears to have been taken as part of the scenery and why she evoked no further

From E. J. Coleman's
Scenes from the Snowfields.

182

comment until the party reached the top, on a day so perfect that 'a lighted candle might have been held in the air'. Here, says Kennedy, 'my little dog was soon fast asleep on a knapsack in the sun'. That is all. No mention of how she tackled the snow on the more difficult descent, nor of whether she was left at the Montanvert, as she probably was, before Kennedy and his companions made a hurried ascent of Mont Blanc before leaving for England.

The honour of the second canine ascent of Mont Blanc almost certainly went to Tschingel – although Sylvain Couttet, one of the Chamonix guides, had a dog which often went with him as far as the Grands Mulets. Tschingel was born in the spring of 1865 in a village in the Bernese Oberland and bought the following September by Christian Almer, the Grindelwald guide who was preparing to join the Reverend Hereford George's photographic expedition. A few days later the party crossed the Tschingel Pass from Kandersteg to the Steinberg Alp, a passage which the young puppy handled with aplomb, even though, in George's words, 'the constant recurrence of narrow crevasses troubled his philosophy considerably, and once or twice he had to be taken up and flung across some chasm rather wider than usual'. On the whole, George continues, 'his performance was highly meritorious, and deserved the recognition it afterwards received, when a committee of the whole party unanimously named him "Tschingel" in honour of his being the only dog in the Oberland known to have made a glacier pass'.

Early in life Tschingel was thus stuck with the 'he' that clung tenaciously even though over the next three years 'he' produced a total of thirty-four puppies in Almer's Grindelwald home. During this period he/she acted as as watchdog, and it was not until the summer of 1868 that she embarked on her renowned career on being given to the young Coolidge. 'I remember well the very cow hut before which we were sitting when this gift was made to me,' he wrote almost half a century later.

Tschingel has been variously described as bull-terrier, a small bloodhound, a large beagle. Judging from surviving photographs, there was probably something of the dachshund in her make-up. She was low-slung, like most climbing dogs, and about nineteen inches high.

She had strong short legs and a tail that ended in a brush [wrote Coolidge]. She was smooth-haired, the colour of her coat being reddish-brown, with white stockings and muzzle. Her body was not handsome, being too thick-set. But she had a very fine head, large and beautiful brown and most expressive eyes, and long dark-brown *very* silky ears – in fact, my mother always said she would have a purse made out of these ears, but she died (1875) before Tschingel (1879). Her voice was deep and musical. She was very intelligent, but too old when we got her to learn new tricks (having only been taught previously to give her paw) save standing occasionally on her hind legs to beg.

Although brought up to respond to Swiss-German, she quickly learned English, but never responded to French, a trait that her master put down to annoyance with the arduous journey across France caused by the outbreak of the Franco-Prussian war.

From 1868 – when she went with Coolidge up the Aletschhorn above the

Tschingel, the greatest-ever canine mountaineer who between 1865 and 1876 made a record number of ascents with her master the Rev. W. A. B. Coolidge.

The monument to Julius Kugy, below the southern slopes of Triglav in the Julian Alps of Jugoslavia.

Aletsch glacier and was 'waved in the air as a sort of red flag' to Miss Brevoort on the neighbouring Sparrhorn – until 1876 Tschingel accompanied Coolidge and his aunt to the Alps every year. She travelled in a specially built box, was fed by porters and passers-by alike, and soon acquired an international reputation. On the mountains, where her favoured drinks were red wine and cold tea, she was normally roped by a cord passed through her collar. Her main trouble was not lack of stamina, but bleeding paws. Early on, her master had four leather boots made, but these she quickly kicked off. Judging by the records, her paws appear to have hardened as she grew older. The black tip of her nose would sometimes attract sunburn so badly that it peeled, but the evidence suggests that she enjoyed mountaineering as much as her master. As a watchdog she remembered her early training, and would keep all-comers from any tent she was left to guard. On glaciers she had the ability, also noted in other dogs, of being able to detect hidden crevasses, possibly by extreme sensitivity to air coming up through the snow-covering. On the descent from the Diablerets the guide, seeing her skill, cried out: 'Let us follow the dog!'.

After her ascent of Monte Rosa in 1869, Tschingel was elected an 'Hon. A.C.' by members of the Alpine Club then at the Riffel. And after one of the fastest British climbers had gone up the Jungfrau and returned to the Aeggishorn hotel by eleven in the morning he received a telegram. Signed 'Tschingel,' it read: 'Bow wow, *I* could have done it much more quickly than that.'

At times Tschingel howled on the mountains, 'not, as I believe, for fear of herself, as she invariably got through the most difficult places with the most wonderful skill and agility – but because she knew we were in danger', Miss Brevoort wrote. The dog took time off to chase marmots, hares, foxes, and on one occasion spent two and a half hours in pursuit of chamois before rejoining her party a good deal higher up the mountain. When the humans camped, she would usually be sent first into the tent – and having discovered by trial and error which was the softest spot would be turned out by her master who at night would often try to make her his pillow 'as her body was much softer than a stone or a pair of boots'.

Tschingel's finest hour came in 1875 when on 24 July she made what was widely believed to have been the first unassisted canine ascent of Mont Blanc. At the Grands Mulets, where she had been stopped by deep snow six years previously, she appeared to have second thoughts. But once she had been persuaded to start all went well; as the party approached the summit she went on ahead, reached the summit, and returned to announce that the others had not much farther to go. On her return to Chamonix a special cannon was fired in her honour and 'she trotted into the village with her head erect and her tail wagging, immensely proud of herself', as Miss Brevoort wrote to her sister. 'The next day, lying luxuriously on a sofa in the hotel drawing-room she held a kind of state reception which was attended by several hundred persons, including all the guides.'

It was planned that Tschingel should crown her Alpine career the following year with an ascent of the Matterhorn. Miss Brevoort felt she was hardly up to it, an opinion that brought a pained reply from her nephew for whom Tschingel's sex was still unclear 'He must have grown much older since I saw him two weeks ago,' he wrote; 'if it suited *him* better I could do it in 2 days, or even 3, sleeping twice at the hut!!!' But Miss Brevoort would not be convinced. The opportunity never came again.

As Tschingel grew old, her coat turned white, she became almost blind, and her teeth dropped out. But on occasions she still wore her Sunday best collar with its silver medallions recording the peaks she had climbed and the passes she had crossed. Finally, in 1879, Coolidge decided that it would be kinder to have her put down; but that night she died in her sleep before the kitchen fire.

'I am at present in great affliction at the death of my dear old dog Tschingel, which took place on June 16,' he wrote to his friend C. E. Mathews, the historian of Mont Blanc. 'She was so much more a companion than a mere dog that I feel her loss very deeply.'

Forty years later Dr Monroe Thorington, the American climber and Alpine historian, visited Coolidge in his Grindelwald home. 'He had his man show me about,' Dr Thorington said. 'And then, just when I was leaving, he pointed to the door. There on a hook was Tschingel's collar with the little bangles shining in the sun. Not a word was said, but Coolidge managed something resembling a smile.'

Tschingel has had few successors. The Alpine avalanche services have developed and exploited the canine facility for smelling out humans so that more than one man has been dug out just in time. But these are no Tschingels, and her nearest descendants are the path-bound pets met below the snowline, the equivalent of fair-weather human mountaineers.

Yet a few years ago there was the example of Maccabeo, an Irish setter bitch, which suggests the reappearance of Tschingel's spirit a century on. The pet of a Gressoney hotel-keeper, Maccabeo was reported one day to be making for the Col de Lys, which leads from the Italian valley across the main watershed between the Lyskamm and Monte Rosa. What happened next is unknown, but a few days later Maccabeo turned up in Zermatt. She was duly returned across the frontier. But thereafter, every year until she finally disappeared at the age of eleven, she would roam off in the summer, whatever precautions were taken, and spend three months ambling in, up, and over the Monte Rosa group, enjoying the world above the snowline with a perversity which in the canine world no doubt raised an echo of *The Times*' rhetorical comment on mountaineering after the Matterhorn accident, 'Is it common sense? Is it allowable? Is it not wrong?'

Henriette d'Angeville, the 'thwarted maiden lady' who climbed Mont Blanc in 1838.

Queen Margherita of Italy, seen on the Lysjoch in August, 1893 after the inauguration of the Margherita hut.

CHAPTER TWELVE
The Female of the Species

The exploits of Tschingel and the eccentricities of her master, whose Alpine life linked the Golden Age with the 1920s, tended to give unfair prominence to Miss Brevoort, the central figure of the famous trio – 'the young American who climbs with his aunt and his dog'. She was, however, a fairly typical example of the independent-minded females who during the second half of the nineteenth century transformed mountaineering by women from a curiosity into a commonplace.

In today's Alpine huts and on today's Alpine peaks there is not so very much difference between male and female. It is not only that unisex is expressed in similarly utilitarian breeches and boots, anoraks and gloves. Physiologists have long ago shown that the female organism is as tough as the male at withstanding the rigours of wind, weather and similar hardship. Women's hands are in general smaller than men's, and are therefore able to make better use of small holds. The female of the species cannot normally carry as much weight as the male but in most other ways is quite as efficient a climbing machine.

All this makes it difficult to appreciate the impact of women in the Alps more than a century ago, or the furore that their presence was apt to create above the snowline. Yet their invasion of the mountains gradually did much to alter the context of the mountaineers' special world. If expedition food progressed beyond the leg of hardy mutton stuffed into the *sac*, domestication by women mountaineers had at least something to do with it. So with huts and their development from the primitive to the near-sybaritic. In addition it is difficult not to believe that the relationship between guide and employer was affected by the inclusion of women in mountaineering parties. Some were formidable in the true dictionary definition of 'fit to inspire apprehension'; with them even a Carrel or a Burgener would have found it difficult to get his own way in controversy.

The female invasion of this male field, which seriously got under way in the 1860s, was for its time a remarkable example of emancipation. 'The weaker sex' was still generally thought to be incapable of anything more strenuous than a quiet walk uphill. In an age when piano-legs were concealed to lessen the onset of dangerous thoughts, instructions on where to put hands, feet and the rest of the body, part and parcel of getting many amateurs to the top, could present obvious and embarrassing problems. As for a lady – a word which began to be replaced in this context by 'woman' only towards the end of the last century – marching unchaperoned on the mountain and even bivouacking or sleeping in a hut where only men might be present, this was a prospect which at first seemed too terrible to contemplate.

But many conservative mountaineers found an explanation for the extraordinary development when it did evolve. Thus Sir Edward Davidson, the great climber of the Silver Age, meeting Lord Fisher at the Riffelalp about the turn of the century, noted that two young women there were 'husbandeering,' not mountaineering. 'I suppose the places are so deadly dull that the young men fall an easy prey,' Fisher replied.

Even if such prejudice was overcome by a combination of vigour and brazenness, one practical problem remained: how on earth would it be possible for a woman, let alone a lady, to negotiate ice-walls and rock arêtes in the only clothes she could possibly be permitted to wear? The varying answers to this question run as constant themes through the story and it is unfortunate that so little information exists about the first significant ascent made by a woman. This was by Maria Paradis, a Chamonix girl aged eighteen who owned a stall from which she sold trinkets and fruit, and who in 1809 decided to climb Mont Blanc. Publicity was the main aim but it is difficult not to admire the young woman's initiative and courage. On the mountain the going was worse than expected and at one point she implored her guides: 'Throw me into a crevasse and go on yourselves'. However, they dragged her to the top, which she reached in rather poor condition, and brought her safely back to Chamonix where she lived to a considerable age, dispensing strawberries and cream from her stall together with accounts of the exploit.

Nothing is known about the dress in which this first woman's ascent of Mont Blanc was made, but the reverse is true of Henriette d'Angeville twenty-nine years later. This self-styled 'bride of Mont Blanc' was different from her predecessor in both social and Alpine sense, had a genuine love of mountains, and made her final, and twenty-first, climb – of the 10,250 foot Oldenhorn – in 1863 at the age of sixty-nine. She had visited Chamonix in 1828 and returned to the village a decade later, determined, it was stated, to equal the publicity given to George Sand, who had arrived dressed as a man, accompanied by a young man dressed as a girl. Henriette d'Angeville's outfit consisted of peg-top check trousers under a voluminous belted cloak, a long black boa and a feather beret. 'She goes as well as we do, and fears nothing', commented one of her guides as they set out for the mountain on 3 September. She did go well: reached the top in high spirits: released a carrier-pigeon bearing the news of her success and was told by her guides as they lifted her on their shoulders: 'Now, mademoiselle, you shall go higher than Mont Blanc.'

By the date of Henriette d'Angeville's last climb, more than twenty years later, the climate of mountaineering had been altered by the exploits first of the Swiss and then of the British who founded the Alpine Club. Although there had still been relatively little genuine mountaineering by women, an increasing number had travelled through the Alps in the 1840s and 1850s not

An 1860 mountaineering party of husbands and wives.

as eccentrics but as wives, or sisters, who played second fiddle to husbands or brothers. In the 1840s George Barnard the artist and Michael Faraday the scientist took their wives on a foursome holiday through the Alps. A few years later Alfred Wills, on his honeymoon, persuaded Mrs Wills to camp out on the Mer de Glace. There were the Gilberts and Churchills, while Mrs Freshfield, mother of a later president of the Alpine Club, made excursions above the snowline in the 1850s and was suitably photographed in voluminous skirts and holding a giant alpenstock.

These women made the way easier for their successors; they broke the ice, if not of the mountains at least of public opinion. Yet their comparatively simple strolls did not demand that they should tackle the dress problem seriously; this was left to the next decade. Discardable skirts worn over breeches; a cord-and-ring device on the skirt by which it might 'be drawn up at a moment's notice to the required height'; trousers; and eventually bloomers – all these were experimented with, supplemented by broad-brimmed hats which, as one climber put it, 'relieved me from the encumbrance of a parasol'. But at least one conventional garment was useful. 'That awful snow-slope which had taken more than two hours to get up, we were down in about five minutes,' wrote Eleanor Hornby of her ascent of the Finsteraarhorn. 'I made a sledge of my petticoats and they dragged me down; I hardly walked a step till we were down at the glacier.'

The tone was set by the cord-and-ring skirt device, its main devotee being

Prince Arthur, Duke of Connaught (centre, holding Alpenstock) at the Grands Mulets, Mont Blanc, in 1864, at the age of 14.

Mrs Cole, who described her journeys in *A Lady's Tour round Monte Rosa*.

Every lady engaged on an Alpine journey should have a dress of some light woollen material, such as carmelite or alpaca which, in the case of bad weather, does not look utterly forlorn when it has once been wetted and dried [she wrote]. Small rings should be sewn inside the seams of the dresses and a cord passed through them, the ends of which should be knotted together in such a way that the whole dress may be drawn up at a moment's notice to the required height. A riding skirt, without a body, which can be slipped on and off in a moment, is also invaluable.

A variation on the slipping-on-and-off practice was devised by another climber who wore her brother's riding breeches under a crinoline; once out of sight of the hotel, off came the crinoline which was then carried by a guide until the party returned to civilisation.

In 1859 there appeared the redoubtable Lucy Walker, daughter of Francis and sister of Horace Walker, who were to make the first ascent of the Brenva ice-ridge. When she decided to climb the Altels her father told her that Melchior Anderegg would be the best guide to employ, and outside the inn she asked a young man, apparently a porter, where she could find him. 'I am Anderegg', he replied: the start of a partnership during which they made no less than ninety-eight expeditions in more than twenty years.

In many respects Miss Walker was the antithesis of the Victorian woman mountaineer as thought of at the time. She suffered from slight mountain sickness throughout but fought it off with doses of sponge-cake and champagne or asti. She had none of the 'horsey' preoccupations of the rugged female and always wore a white print dress whose shape had to be 'renewed' after each expedition. This dress limited her activities, but the limitation did not worry her, and she was always pleased to explain why she had not climbed one particular summit. She would describe how a rival, having reached the top, rebuked a member of the Alpine Club who had said no woman could manage it. 'No,' he replied. 'I said, "No lady".'

Throughout the 1860s others followed Miss Walker's lead in tackling serious peaks. Miss Straton, who eventually married her guide, Jean Charlet; Emmeline Lewis-Lloyd, who climbed with Miss Straton for many years; the Bird sisters; and the Pigeon sisters who in 1869 made the first crossing of the Sesiajoch into Italy and took charge of the party when their guide lost the way. 'We were the very first, I think, to go unattended by a male protector, and we got on very well,' one of them later wrote: 'but then two together must be pleasanter than one alone, when you must have guides.'

Eventually there arrived the American Miss Brevoort, as confident as a ship under full sail, determined to sweep all before her in what she had discovered to be the delightful occupation of mountain climbing. It was inevitable that some rivalry should develop between Miss Brevoort and Miss Walker, and this reached its climax in the struggle to make the first lady's ascent of the Matterhorn. In 1867 Félicité Carrel, daughter of a guide, had reached the point on the Italian ridge 350 feet below the summit later named after her as the Col Félicité. However, her success would no doubt have been considered in the Maria Paradis class, leaving 'first ascent by a lady' still to be claimed. One attempt on this was made in 1868 by Miss Lewis-Lloyd and Miss Straton, who were forced to retreat by stone falls. The following year Miss Brevoort crossed the Théodule from Zermatt with her nephew, left Tschingel at Breuil, and spent the next night high up on the Italian ridge. Then storms forced the party to retreat.

Bad weather kept her from the peak the following year but in 1871 all appeared ready. In mid-July she and her nephew climbed the Eiger, confided to an English acquaintance, E. H. Whitwell, that they would soon be attempting the Matterhorn, and then turned in a leisurely way towards Zermatt where they arrived on 23 July. They went to their rooms in the Monte Rosa and prepared for dinner. Their guide, Christian Almer, carried on below with the business of settling details for the attempt to be made the following day.

Shortly afterwards there came his anguished cry from the corridor: 'A young lady has climbed the Matterhorn!'

Miss Brevoort had no doubt as to who it must be. What was revealed only later were the details. Whitwell, patriotically feeling that an English woman rather than an American should be first on the top, had hurried to Zermatt, fortuitously found Miss Walker, and warned her of what was afoot. Her brother had broken an arm but a young friend, Frederick Gardiner, just arrived in Zermatt, was able to take his place. Without delay, Lucy Walker set out with her sixty-three-year-old father, Gardiner and Melchior Anderegg. She got to the top.

But Miss Brevoort was to win a consolation prize. On 4 September she left Zermatt with her nephew and the Almers. They spent the night at the Hörnli, climbed the mountain on the fifth and descended to the Cravatte, where they slept before descending to Breuil: the fourth traverse of the peak – but the first by a lady. The first ascent by a woman, and the first traverse, of what only six years before had been the most formidable of the great unclimbed mountains of the central Alps, represented a milestone. Before, it had been admitted, even if with some reluctance, that there was a place for women on some mountains. Now, just as reluctantly, the 'some' had to be removed.

In the wake of Lucy Walker and Miss Brevoort there came such figures as Mrs Jackson, who made 150 expeditions during the 'seventies and 'eighties, and Eleanor Hornby, whose privately printed notes give an indication of the problems the ladies were by this time tackling.

There was no footing at all in the chimney [she wrote of an ascent of the Nuvolao in the Dolomites] and I had to worm myself up till I could get on my knees on a flat stone, and I kept getting my head under this stone, and could not get beyond it. I lost my hat and the net off my hair, but at last accomplished it. I had previously lost a red shawl, and the skirt of my dress was left intentionally below, so that the Nuvolao was strewn with my property.

Despite her climbs in the Dolomites, Miss Hornby lacked the attack and bite of at least one of her contemporaries, the astonishing Kathleen Richardson, an Englishwoman who spent most of her life in France and whose record would in modern terms qualify her as a tigress. Slender, short, green-eyed;

Miss Emmeline Lewis-Lloyd (second from left) and the guide Jean Charlet (second from right) who later married her mountaineering companion, Miss Straton.

Miss Meta Brevoort (1825–1876), the American who introduced her nephew, the Rev. W.A.B. Coolidge, to the Alps in 1864 and who then climbed with him regularly until her death.

looking, it has been claimed, as frail as a Dresden shepherdess, she was climbing in the Engadine in the 1870s at the age of seventeen, and while in her twenties became the 'legendary Miss Richardson' of whom her guides said: 'She does not eat and she walks like the Devil.' In her eleven seasons she made 116 *grandes courses*, including all the well-known and many of the harder peaks, as well as sixty minor ascents. Six of her major climbs were firsts and another fourteen were firsts by a woman. In five days she climbed the Aiguille Verte, and the Aiguille de Talèfre as well as traversing the Petit and the Grand Dru. On another occasion she climbed the Matterhorn, Monte Rosa, the Weisshorn and the Rothorn in eight days. She climbed all the five peaks of the Grands Charmoz in a single expedition, set up records for speed and endurance that discomfited many male climbers, and succeeded, where Miss Brevoort failed, in making the first lady's ascent of the Meije.

It was after this climb that she met the French Alpiniste Mary Paillon. Mlle Paillon's mother had been up Mont Blanc, bivouacked out at 10,000 feet on the Matterhorn at the age of sixty, had traversed the chain of the Belledone at seventy-five in an expedition which involved nineteen hours going in a temperature of minus eighteen degrees, and was still climbing five years later. Her daughter and Miss Richardson climbed together for many seasons and their mutual affection was shown when they were about to reach the top of the central Aiguille d'Arve in the Dauphiné. Miss Richardson waited for her companion to reach her, then pushed her ahead with the words: 'You go first. I have the Meije; you take the Aiguille d'Arve.'

Miss Richardson represented the new class of woman climber who was competent to tackle anything that a man could tackle, and frequently did so. Miss Bristow traversed the Grépon with Mummery, and inspired the phrase

194

'an easy day for a lady'. Gertrude Bell, that extraordinary character who created a class of her own wherever she went, climbed the Meije, the Pelvoux, the Écrins and the Matterhorn, among other peaks, in a single season.

This period during which women for the first time began to be regarded in mountaineering circles as mountaineers first and women second, saw the start of the modern era with the formation, almost exactly half a century after the Alpine Club, of the Ladies' Alpine Club. Its moving spirit was a woman who appears on the mountain scene from 1880 onwards in various guises: first in her maiden name of Miss Hawkins-Whitshead; then as Mrs Burnaby, wife of Colonel Burnaby, killed in Africa after his *Ride to Khiva*; then as Mrs Main; and finally, after the death of Mr Main, as Mrs Aubrey Le Blond.

Mrs Le Blond – the name in which most of her books were written, and by which she is least confusingly remembered – could give a deceptive appearance of fragility and for many years her lady's maid accompanied her to the highest huts. One of her main discoveries during an ascent of Mont Blanc was that she had never before put on her own boots. 'For several years longer', she admitted, 'it did not occur to me that I could do without a maid, and it was not until one of the species had eloped with a courier that I gained my independence of all assistance of the sort that they did, or more often did not, render.' She wrote about her climbing experiences at length, and with something of a gush, but had a strong and genuine love of the mountains. If some of the greybeards were a little allergic to her chatter, at least one member of the Alpine Club, T. G. Bonney, praised her in his presidential address as one 'whom our stern Salic law prevents us from numbering among our members'.

Mrs Le Blond belonged to the Lyceum Club, a London club for ladies, a number of whom were mountaineers. This body banded itself into a section within the club and this in turn became in 1908 the Ladies' Alpine Club. The French and Swiss Alpine Clubs had admitted women members for many years while the American Alpine Club had done so since the first years of the century. But the Ladies' Alpine Club was the first mountaineering organisation for women alone. The second was the Ladies' Scottish Climbing Club, formed in the same year. A decade later came the Pinnacle Club, the first climbing club for women which demanded a rock-climbing rather than a mountaineering qualification.

As in so many spheres the First World War was one great watershed and the Second World War another. After 1918 the exploits of women mountaineers not only became more numerous but began to be absorbed almost without comment into the general story of Alpine exploration and activity. As far back as the 1880s a few women had climbed without guides, although always with male companions and usually with their husbands – the most famous example possibly being Mrs Norman Neruda. Between the wars their numbers increased and the first ropes of guideless women mountaineers appeared on the scene. After 1945 climbs by women became so normal that little less than an ascent of the Eigerwand would bring them into the news. When in the summer of 1960 a mass ascent was made of Monte Rosa it was noticed only in passing that more than a hundred women made the climb.

Mrs Aubrey Le Blond, the British woman mountaineer, with her guide, Joseph Imboden.

CHAPTER THIRTEEN
The Masters

Right F.J.Hugi, the Soleure geologist, and his party during their attempt in 1828 to reach the Jungfrau from the north.

Francois Favret, one of the Chamonix guides who accompanied Albert Smith to the summit of Mont Blanc in 1854.

It is difficult to over-estimate the physical changes which have taken place in the Alps during the last hundred years – the urbanisation of the lower valleys made more accessible from the large towns, the transformation of upper valleys by hydro-electric schemes, and more recently the criss-crossing of the higher slopes by cable-ways, for tourists in summer and skiers in winter. Yet these developments have been more than equalled by changes in the Alpine guide.

More than a century ago Peter Bohren, turning to an Englishman who queried the order of descent after a climb on the Wetterhorn, quickly silenced him: 'Herr, you are master in the valley; I am master here.' But in those days they were strange masters, and all except the small handful at the top of the profession often took lessons from their pupils. In an age when the Alps were being explored the guide supplied the local knowledge and the brawn; even the mediocre man who had lived in an area all his life – as his family had probably done for generations – knew far more about its idiosyncracies than the most enthusiastic and regular visitor. Even the second-class guide was more competent to cut steps for long periods, hold his balance naturally in steep places and travel for hour after hour over rough country than most of the muscular Christians who employed him. In level walking the pick of the early mountaineers who had made pedestrianism their hobby could equal the men they employed; on the mountains, which they visited for a few months each year, they were only very rarely the match for those accustomed to the up-and-down of near-vertical places since toddling days.

But the guide's qualifications usually stopped here. Unless he was one of those exceptional men who had travelled extensively with a regular employer, he would have little knowledge of mountains outside his own locality, or of the peculiar conditions of wind and weather which might be expected away from it and on which the safety of a party might rest. He was unlikely to know very much about maps or map-reading – perhaps understandably since in the early days map-makers were apt to let a strong imagination make up for lack of knowledge – and he was usually ignorant of all except the most famous accounts of ascents made even in his home territory. He would, moreover, be distinctly susceptible to mythology and legend accumulated over the cen-

Jean-Michel Cachet, a
Chamonix guide who took
part in the second ascent
of Mont Blanc on 5 July
1787.

'Carrying a lady's shawl
across the Mer de Glace'
one of the tasks which even
leading guides might have
to perform before the
system was changed in
Chamonix.

turies. Time after time in the annals of Alpine exploration, there crops up some equivalent to Whymper's Matterhorn encircled, for the local men, by that 'cordon beyond which one did not go'. Thus on the mountain 'the master' might sometimes be unsure of himself and the pupil-amateur might instinctively tend to take charge, with all the perils of divided control which that could bring.

This has very little in common with the guides of today. Nowadays they will probably speak three or four languages, will be in at least what advertising departments call the B category and may well be in the A class. It was a sign of the times when in June 1964 Italian guides took half-page advertisements in *La Stampa* and the *Corriere della Sera*, urging that climbers should use their services for ascents of the Matterhorn. In most valleys the guide will be among the élite and in many he will be a well-known personality, sought-out by TV interviewers and with a sizable clip of cuttings to his name in the newspaper files. Socially he will have to be kept up with, and occasionally he may be a best-selling author.

Nor is this all. Just as today's expert farmer has to be, if not his own engineer and mechanic, at least a man understanding engineers and mechanics, so the modern Alpine guide needs a wide range of contacts with modern technology, from the short-wave radio which keeps him in touch with huts, to the helicopter which both supplies them and provides rescue services, and the latest developments in weather-forecasting.

These contrasts between the guides of the heroic age and those of today have come about as the social climate of Europe has changed and as the mountains have been transformed from the exclusive playground for gentlemen into a money-making tourist attraction. There is another reason for the contrast: the evolution of guiding from a spare-time occupation for the few summer months into a profession to be followed for most of the year, with little more than a temporary break in the late autumn and early spring as the weather rules out much serious mountaineering. Furthermore to winter guiding there has been added the *bonne bouche* of winter ski-instruction, which to some extent create a bridge between the classes.

The social demarcation line between professional and amateur is not the only one which has tended to disappear since the days when many of the pioneers whistled up their guides much as they might take on a new gardener. More than one guide has in recent decades relinquished his vocation for a while and climbed *en amateur*. More than one enthusiastic amateur, faced with the prospect of spending only a few weeks a year in the mountains, has discovered that formation of a climbing school, judicious writing, and the even more judicious acceptance of sponsorship for expeditions beyond the Alps, have offered the chance of making a living from mountaineering.

The gulf between 1870 and the 1970s is deep; but there are at least two similarities between then and now. In the nineteenth century, as well as today, guides at the top of their profession were not only better but very much better indeed than the run-of-the-mill men. This is so despite the fact that the overall difference tended to decrease as guides' corporations and their

The walls of Mont Aiguille, first climbed in 1492 – and not climbed again until 1834.

regulations spread during the nineteenth century; it has decreased even more today, when guiding is in general as strictly controlled as any other profession, and no one failing to reach a high standard is able to practise. Nevertheless not every advocate is a Carson or a Birkett; not every politician a Churchill or a Lloyd George; and not every guide is a Christian Almer, a Joseph Knubel or a Gaston Rebuffat. Now, as then, a handful of exceptional men stand head and shoulders above the rest.

One other similarity unites the guides of yesterday and today. The profession is demanding and dangerous. Its rewards are now high, in both cash and esteem, but the man who is able to satisfy the stringent demands required for his guide's certificate is likely to rise to the surface anywhere. Thus it is fair to assume that mountains have a particular appeal, that guiding has a fascination beyond its financial rewards, and that Auguste Balmat, making his twelfth ascent of Mont Blanc at the age of fifty-three, Christian Almer celebrating his golden wedding on the Wetterhorn, had something in common with the commando-like figures to be met today in the guides' centres at Chamonix, Grindelwald or Zermatt. Scrape away the mythology, consider the guide a human being earning his living rather than a legendary figure twice life-size, and he still stands in relation to the Alps as devotee rather than worker, in some respects nearer to Ruskin than to most Alpine visitors.

Most guides are individualists. The reason is no 'wind on the heath, brother' affectation, but the plain fact that a man on a mountain is out on his own – paradoxically enough, almost more on his own when he is responsible for someone else. Mountain problems cannot often be answered by rule of thumb and the mountain guide, more than most men, is dependent on his own initiative and enterprise for staying alive. Yet if drivers of cars and carriers of arms must be licensed and controlled in one way or another, so must men basically responsible for mountain survival. So for more than a century and a half guides have worked within the framework of corporations, societies and companies, the predecessors of the Guides Bureaux that are a familiar sight in most Alpine centres.

The first corporation was started in Chamonix in 1823, when after the Napoleonic Wars more travellers wanted to climb Mont Blanc and even more wanted to make excursions on the surrounding peaks and glaciers.

The new organisation did many useful things, laying down rough standards which novice guides had to reach, fixing tariffs for specific expeditions and stating the number of guides which travellers had to take on each. When the corporation was formed with forty men on its roster the rules were complicated and numerous enough; before the end of the century they had expanded to seventy-one separate articles. The corporation thus quickly grew into a bureaucracy which served second-rate men well enough but was disliked by the first-class. Mountain excursions in the Chamonix area a century and a half ago ranged – as they still do today – from the charmingly simple to the desperately dangerous. A guide would be needed 'to carry a lady's shawl across the Mer de Glace', to cut steps for long periods up the most dangerous ice-wall in the area and to make expeditions between these two extremes.

The Rigi at sunrise, painted on glass by the Bernese artist Franz Niklaus König. The picture, illuminated from behind, was exhibited in Switzerland, Germany and France in the early 1820's. (Property of the Kunstmuseum, Bern, Switzerland.)

Yet every traveller had to take the man who had reached the top of the rota. Thus the first-class guide anxious to work with a first-class party in making new routes might find himself landed with shawl-carrying; the able mountaineer might find his man competent for little else. There were few better ways of putting a premium on mediocrity.

This was bad enough in the first half of the nineteenth century but became intolerable from the 1850s onwards and many of the best guides connived with their employers at finding loopholes in the regulations. One was Auguste Balmat who met Alfred Wills in 1854 at Sallanches, outside the Chamonix boundary, and then reached Chamonix with him by way of the Col de Voza; for if a guide were hired outside the jurisdiction of Chamonix and then entered it by way of a pass, he could continue working for the same employer, whatever his position on the rota. Balmat, many cuts above the average, was adept at evading the regulations. On being reprimanded for taking Wills and Mrs

Guides outside Grindelwald church in the 1880s.

Wills on the Mer de Glace without a second guide, he replied that the regulations spoke only of a guide for *chaque monsieur*. No mention was made of ladies.

While the corporation rules provided safeguards for ordinary travellers they thus hampered real mountaineering. Even worse, as the sport became more popular, the system tended to spread and Hudson and Kennedy arriving in Courmayeur in 1855 found that a new corporation on Chamonix lines had just been set up. Local chamois-hunters outside the new organisation were bullied into withholding help, and it was only with difficulty that the Englishmen were even able to hire porters. But this incident had one unexpected result. Disgusted with what they considered an iniquitous system, Hudson and Kennedy climbed Mont Blanc without guides. To show the strength of his feelings, Kennedy left in Chamonix a substantial contribution to a relief fund opened following a disastrous fire. But the cheque was to be cashed only

Three generations of
Courmayeur guides – and
of sculpture: Giuseppe
Petigax, Emile Rey and
Mario Puchoz.

A corner of the Alpine
Museum, Courmayeur,
showing portraits of
famous guides.

206

when an English traveller was allowed to choose his own guides and their number.

The coming of the real mountaineer, interested in more than making the routine ascent of Mont Blanc, eventually brought about a relaxation of these rules, but guides' corporations appeared elsewhere in the Alps: in the Oberland in 1856, subsequently in most other centres; usually modelled to greater or lesser degree on the Chamonix prototype.

The men who entered the profession as it developed with the spread of mountaineering, tended to come from specific families. Thus on the Chamonix roll of 1898 there were 38 Simonds, 28 Couttets, 19 Ducroz, 18 Balmats, 16 Payots and 16 Ravanels among the 284 names, while a catalogue of 177 Zermatt men issued a few years later included 14 Bieners, 13 Burgeners and 19 Perrens. Few of these men became rich. François Couttet might develop into a hotelier but he was the exception. Michel Croz died in debt and it was financial worry, not the mountains, that killed Auguste Balmat at the age of fifty-four.

Today there are still those for whom the guide as film star (Luis Trenker in the 1930s, for instance) or the guide as successful author (any number of contemporary examples) is something of an anachronism. The reality is that the peasant world from which the guide traditionally comes is in the Alps being assimilated out of existence by the expanding tourist industry. Thus he no longer has to step from one world to another before he enters professional practice. He trains almost officially, much as the student about to enter any other profession would train. He receives his licence to operate in a way not so very different from the lawyer or the doctor. If he wishes to write, or to exercise his other talents, he does so in a milieu where such activities cause little surprise.

The Ruskin Stone outside
Chamonix.

CHAPTER FOURTEEN

Phantom-Fair

Both painters and writers have come to the Alps, looked at them with perceptive eyes, and interpreted them in a way enabling other men to understand the mountains better. But there have been important differences between the two kinds of artist, and for more than one reason. Perhaps most important is the fact that by force of circumstance more painters have looked at the mountains from outside, as strangers; more writers have rubbed their noses on the rock and learned by the hard experience of triumph and tribulation.

Some of the outsiders certainly knew what mountains were about and William Pars, Francis Towne and the Cozens are only the most obvious examples. But from Titian, who introduced his native Dolomites into so many scenes, through George Barnard and Elijah Walton of Victorian times to the Kokoschka who stayed at the Riffelalp until he felt the Matterhorn in his bones, it is the rarer painter who has portrayed the Alps effectively: the man who from birth has deliberately sought out a special relationship with the mountains. Barnard and Walton knew their way above the snowline even though their election to the Alpine Club was on artistic qualifications. Gabriel Loppé painted if not as mountaineer at least as a man who had strong physical awareness of the mountains he painted. Later still E. T. Coleman, an original member of the club who spent three seasons on or about Mont Blanc preparing his *Scenes from the Snowfields*, deliberately set out to be an Alpine painter. As for E. T. Compton, his artistic and his climbing careers are as Mumm put it, 'so closely combined that it is impossible to treat them separately'. To understand the Alps one must reflect on how such artists have seen them, and on the differences between the Swiss, who were bred to the landscape, and the British who sought it out in scientific or holiday mood.

A good deal of chocolate-box Jungfrau material must be skipped over as quickly as possible. Knowing what one likes is no less a criterion in mountain painting than in others and one can only guess at the Faulhorn described in the *Alpine Journal* as 'the most preposterous picture of its kind that ever disgraced the walls of an exhibition'. At the other end of the spectrum, how many mountaineers honestly sing the praises of Kokoschka's *Matterhorn*?

Literature has at first glance an easier task, since it is simpler to convey the excitement of action than the beauty of solitude, simpler to write effectively about mountaineering than to paint mountains effectively. To start with, nothing more is needed than a notebook to jog the memory; and, as all the world knows, 'anyone can write'. This at least is too often the accepted theory, and the fine inspiration that can be evoked by the Alps shows through in its literature as a thin white thread often in danger of concealment among the grey mass of second-rate material bundled round it. Even more than in pictorial art, the records are overloaded by the amateur, and for every Alpine equivalent of *The Stag at Bay* there is the regurgitation of mountain memories which were fun at the time but are trite in retrospect. Not every contemplative artist is a Ruskin; not every mountaineer a Whymper, able to work away at his manuscript until there rises from it the authentic thunder of the falling rocks. There are mountain poets galore but few such as Arnold whose 'Obermann Once More' contains the finest lines ever written about the Alps. There are few part-time writers who can, like the late Lord Schuster, create in a few casual sentences a mountain landscape as pin-sharp and visible as any photograph. The pure gold exists, tucked away between the pages of the *Alpine Journal*, concealed in pamphlets and lectures and papers, and occasionally found between the hard covers of a book. But a good deal of dross has to be discarded before the gold is revealed.

Until the Romantic Revolution there was no need for description, let alone interpretation. In literature the occasional appearance of the Alps brought forth only the passing gasp of horror. Gesner and Simler were exceptions; most Englishmen agreed with Shakespeare who has Caesar telling Anthony that

> On the Alps
> It is reported thou didst eat strange flesh
> Which some did die to look upon.

A century and a half later Walpole and Gray, making the Grand Tour, felt much the same: 'The Road! winding round a prodigious mountain, and surrounded with others, all shagged with hanging woods, obscured with pines or lost in clouds!' exclaimed Walpole of the track to the Grande Chartreuse. As for Gray, 'the Mont Cenis, I confess', he wrote, 'carries the permission mountains have of being frightful rather too far, and its honours were accompanied with too much danger to give one time to reflect upon their beauties'.

All this changed, if not overnight at least quickly. Wordsworth, Shelley, Byron and Keats were among those who first sang the glories of the Alpine world. They were soon supported, although obliquely, by scientists who could not prevent a touch of Alpine enthusiasm from slipping into accounts of their expeditions. By the mid-nineteenth century the reading public were being made aware of the world above the snowline. They knew that it was possible to look at the Alps not only from below but from their innermost and highest recesses. Here was a unexplored world, and with the birth and growth of mountaineering it was possible for it to be described by those who knew its beauties as well as its perils, its possibilities for mental uplift as well as for physical exercise. It would be ingenuous to claim that the best was made of a great opportunity. This is hardly surprising. The final judgement of Anthony

Hope's *Prisoner of Zenda* was that 'fate doesn't always make the best men kings', and the last judgement on many Alpine pioneers is that fate rarely made the best of them writers.

Ironically the inability of many giants of the Golden Age to communicate their experiences was highlighted by the arch-aesthete of the times. For Ruskin saw farther and more percipiently than many of those who arose morning after morning to strike a new summit from the list of the unclimbed. It is true that he was limited by his view that 'the real beauty of the Alps is to be seen, and seen only, where all may see it, the child, the cripple, and the man of grey hairs'; he genuinely believed that 'all the best views of hills are at the bottom of them', a natural enough conclusion since he had never fully entered the Alpine world. Nevertheless he was able to glimpse from afar what many mountaineers were unable to see at close quarters. His fourth volume of *Modern Painters*, with its sub-title 'Of Mountain Beauty', published in 1856, revealed him to be a close observer of Alpine form and a sensitive reactor to the moods of mountains. The book was enough to qualify him for membership of the Alpine Club, an item in his long list of books, essays and papers which throughout the second half of the last century gradually encouraged the English-speaking world to see the Alps in a new light.

Ruskin did as much as he could, not only with his paintings but by his writings. But he was irked by the fact that so many of the men who forced their way into that upper world, which he knew only at secondhand, lacked his vision and failed to preach the new Alpine gospel. Whatever his defects, he believed that the Alps were a good thing and deplored the fact that men better than himself above the snowline were not thundering the news from the roof-tops. Among the scientists he had a soft spot for Forbes, whose geological speculations were from the first laced with Alpine wonder and who enjoyed hot-footing it for the nearest summit from which he could see 'the field of his summer's campaign spread out before him, its wonders, its beauties, and its difficulties, to be explained, to be admitted, and to be overcome'. But most men of science, he believed, would willingly see any of the Alps ground down into gravel, if only they could be the first to exhibit a pebble of it at the Royal Institution.

But surely the mountaineers, the men who deliberately set out for pleasure to explore the new snow and ice world, could see with vision and describe with understanding? This, Ruskin was apt to lament, was not so.

Believe me, gentlemen [he once told an Oxford audience] your power of seeing mountains cannot be developed either by your vanity, your curiosity, or your love of muscular exercise. It depends on the cultivation of the instrument of sight itself, and of the sense that causes it ....

Ruskin was not alone. Trollope seems to have held much the same view, judging by the reference which his Mr Grey of *Can You Forgive Her?* makes to members of the Alpine Club. 'They rob the mountains of their poetry, which is or should be their greatest charm,' says Grey. 'Mont Blanc can have no mystery for a man who has been up it half a dozen times. It is like getting behind the scenes at the ballet or making a conjuror explain his tricks.' This opinion was held by more than one literary man of the period, and the historian John Richard Green was quick to claim that the attitude revealed itself sharply in the available literature. 'What is it [he asked] which makes men in Alpine travel books write as men never write elsewhere?' In his *Sunset on Mont Blanc* Leslie Stephen was to convince the reader that Trollope was writing nonsense. Green's stricture might with a few amendments have applied to much run-of-the-mill historical writing. Yet Trollope and Green and Ruskin were all in fact more than justified by *most* accounts which ordinary readers were receiving from above the snowline.

Peaks, Passes and Glaciers and its continuation in the early numbers of the *Alpine Journal* can be read with pleasure today as period pieces or as topographical records of exploration; very few can be enjoyed as literature. They describe, usually in pedestrian detail, but they do not interpret; their authors record but, in Ruskin's meaning of the word, they do not see. And like the parish magazine or the school journal, they have a maddening collection of 'in' jokes, so that fleas, hard mutton, and vinegarish wine crop up, cliché-like, at the slightest excuse. The Mont Blanc pamphlets were followed by what has justly been called the pemmican of Alpine literature.

There are a few passages in Alfred Wills's *Wanderings among the High Alps* which would have satisfied even Ruskin, and his understanding of the matter was shown when proposing Geoffrey Winthrop Young for the Alpine Club, almost half a century after the famous ascent of the Wetterhorn in 1854: 'The Alps may profoundly influence your philosophy of life when you are old enough to have one.' J. F. Hardy, standing where the three ice-streams meet to form the Aletsch Glacier and noting: 'It is the Place de la Concorde of Nature; wherever you look there is a grand road and a lofty dome', showed a touch of imagination. There are other examples which with care can be picked from the pages of *Peaks, Passes and Glaciers*, but in general they excite, when they do excite, by their story of great deeds doughtily done. It is not until 1871 that Alpine literature, within the dictionary definition of literature as 'writings esteemed for beauty of form or emotional effect', emerges live from the chrysalis. Only then do there appear three books which support Young's thesis that 'a solid mountain block does affect us in some way spiritually'.

In 1871 there came Whymper's *Scrambles amongst the Alps*, Tyndall's *Hours of Exercise in the Alps*, and Leslie Stephen's *The Playground of Europe*. The three books were different in almost every possibly way. Whymper told a tale of heroic proportions, describing an Alpine world already fast disappearing; a tale, moreover, on which he had worked for five years, with a resolute determination of demon quality. Tyndall's papers and essays in which he almost casually recalled his mountaineering exploits between 1860 and 1869 were another affair; marred in places by his obsession for scientific balance but written with the ease of a man to whom writing was part of the day's work. Finally there was Stephen, the eloquent writer who was a fine mountaineer. His sport had led him into secret places which few men knew. He looked around, really 'seeing' and then effortlessly explaining what he saw.

Frontispiece of the first volume of *Peaks, Passes and Glaciers*, the predecessor of *The Alpine Journal*.

Sir Alfred Wills, whose ascent of the Wetterhorn in 1854 opened the Golden Age of Alpine exploration.

Despite their differences, the epic story of conquest, the scientific-discursive narrative, and the interpretive essay of 1871 had one quality in common: it was impossible to read any of them without seeing the Alps in a new light. Moreover it was difficult to read any of them without beginning to wonder more deeply about the springs of emotion that drove men not only to climb mountains but to look at them and to study them. Whymper had his great drama to relate, Tyndall and Stephen both had their firsts and could make the blood run faster with their stories of dangers faced and overcome; yet, despite this, mountain conquest was not the most important thing they had to describe. Their experience had in some way transformed them, and though Whymper might attribute the result to hard exercise in clean air, Tyndall stake a claim for fresh knowledge found above the snowline and Stephen be driven to ask metaphysically 'where does Mont Blanc end, and where do I begin?', they were all changed men.

Thus the Alps meant more to these three and to their small band of successors, than to those who wrote of their climbs, described pleasant scenes, and used the mountains as stock-in-trade for poems or fiction. Even poets did not always see with the same perceptive eye and if Tennyson had only used the Trümmelbach Falls for his 'wreaths of dangling watersmoke', the Grindelwald glaciers for 'the firths of ice' and the cottage smoke in Meiringen seen from the Brünig for 'the azure pillars of the hearth'; if he had only transformed the Silberhorn and the Kleine Silberhorn in 'The Princess' into 'walk with Death and Morning on the Silver Horns' – then it would be possible to claim that the truth of the matter had escaped him. But seeing Monte Rosa 'phantom-fair' from the grandstand roof of Milan cathedral, he showed himself to be among those for whom the Alps were a transforming stimulant.

During the century which has elapsed since the Victorian public had the Alps sprung upon them by Whymper, Stephen and Tyndall, the shelves have been filled a score of times. 'Alpine literature' is almost a university subject in its own right with divisions, subdivisions and demi-semi-sub-divisions dealing with topography, history, fauna and flora, and mountaineering technique among its countless aspects. Alpine fiction alone fills many shelves, from Anne Hector's *A Second Life* in 1885 when a guide helped the heroine to disappear – 'Lost in a crevasse' – to escape a wicked husband, down to the contemporary novels which tend to be excoriated in the *Alpine Journal*. The avalanche has always been available as *deus ex machina*, the humble guide a ready foil for the city slicker, while more than half a century ago the very act of ascent could be an act of cliff-hanging suspense: in Gertrude Warden's *The Crime in the Alps* an aneroid barometer was ingeniously linked to explode a bomb at a certain height.

The mountaineer deciding whether to tackle a 'severe' or only a 'very difficult' route, the botanist delightedly checking that his find of the lesser something-or-other is five hundred feet higher than the previous record for the flower, the historian correlating on the ground those tangled stories of early ascents, all use some form of 'Alpine literature' as tools of enjoyment. Yet it is none of these which concern us here. It is rather the successors to Whymper and Stephen and Tyndall who, consciously or unknowingly, have shown how the Alps can be used as great literature or great painting or great music is used: to add a fresh tingle to life, to bring into focus, to sharpen up the image, as well as to create an emotion that goes beyond the aesthetic enjoyment of fine scenery.

There are very few such successors. Few mountain writers fail to pull out the occasional telling phrase; most of them, however wildly they strike, do not always fail to hit the nail on the head. But to do something more, to reveal, on page after page, the quality in the Alps that other men miss, requires perception of mind and concentration of outlook that is always genius and sometimes monomania. Reading the relatively few who have succeeded will enable even the most casual visitor to understand the Alps better and to catch a glimpse of what has driven mountaineers into climbing them.

There are first the one-book men. Whymper himself can be numbered among them; although he described his South American explorations in *Travels amongst the Great Andes of the Equator*, and wrote much other miscellanea, none of this approaches the quality of *Scrambles*. So too with Guido Rey. While his *Peaks and Precipices* is a fine book by any standards, the essence of his mountain beliefs is concentrated in one book that genuinely merits the word 'extraordinary': *The Matterhorn*, which communicates to the reader one man's passion for an individual mountain which is extraordinarily revealing about the power of the Alps over a human being. In much the same way there is Julius Kugy's long discursive autobiography which even in translation retains the subtleties of how, in Bourdillon's words, mountains 'move us in some way which nothing else can'.

It is not always – although it is usually – such active mountaineers who succeed in conveying to the layman the meaning mountains have for them. The professional writers have a head lead in the business and it is not surprising that some of Robert Louis Stevenson's essays from Davos give such a perceptive idea of the Alps in winter. So too with John Addington Symonds recovering in the Engadine, an invalid forever on the edge of bursting into mountain enthusiasm, a master-craftsman who time after time reveals the fascination of Alpine scenery almost in passing.

Symond's life overlaps with that of his almost complete antithesis – A. F. Mummery, weak-backed and frail-looking yet possibly the finest rock climber of his age. Mummery is an extraordinary example of the amateur writer who makes every textbook mistake yet succeeds in a way professionals must envy. Horribly hearty, larding his text with 'in' jokes, as apt as the worst *Journal* writer to expand on the fleas, guides and cold goat, Mummery nevertheless conveys to the modern climber, walker or even motorist, the exhilaration of the second stage of climbing in the Alps, the excitement and challenge of the period when great rock pinnacles could at last be tackled by bold planning and athletic daring. No one can claim that Mummery set out to 'explain' the attraction of the Alps in the manner of such masters as Conway or Geoffrey Winthrop Young. Nevertheless the message comes through.

Conway and Young, together with Claud Schuster, link the world of the Victorians if not with the present day at least with the day before yesterday. All three reached similar pinnacles of Alpine interpretation, all explain, to the reader with a preference for the plains, the fascination of the heights. Conway, art critic and collector, gives an impression of almost double vision, of a man seeing the Alps half as aesthete, half as mountaineer. He is at his best in *The Alps*, although *Mountain Memories and The Alps from End to End* both add something to a layman's understanding of Alpine travel – as do his numerous papers scattered through the *Alpine Journal*.

Less prolific, more reserved in expression and more spare of words, Claud Schuster, first barrister, then civil servant, gave in *Peaks and Pleasant Pastures* the epitome of Alpine appreciation. More than half a century old, the book should convince the most sceptical that mountaineering – at least mountaineering old-style – is the most civilised sport in the world. 'Fluent on paper' as his biographer in the *Dictionary of National Biography* puts it, Schuster paints the physical struggles of mountaineering against the intellectual rewards in a way that few men have done before or since.

One of the few was Geoffrey Winthrop Young, mountaineer and poet in almost equal measure and a legendary figure long before his death in 1958. Between 1897 and the First World War, when he lost a leg while serving with an ambulance unit on the Italian Front, Young made a great number of extremely difficult first ascents in the Alps – the Younggrat on the Breithorn, the south face of the Täschhorn, the Brouillard ridge of Mont Blanc from the Col Émile Rey and the south face of the Écrins in the Dauphiné to number only a few. These were remarkable climbs judged by any standards. So were his achievements after the war, when on one leg and 'the peg', he climbed the Matterhorn, the Requin, the Grépon, Monte Rosa, the Zinal-Rothorn and

the Weisshorn to within five hundred feet of its summit. This was part private battle with disablement, part encouragement to the thousands of post-war wounded.

But it is not only for his climbing achievements that Young is mainly remembered today. Just as important was his authorship of *On High Hills*, of *Mountains with a Difference* and of three small volumes of poems. In the first he describes his pre-war climbs in a way which brings them alive to those who have never seen the mountains; in the poems he translates into terms that the ordinary man can understand the mental and physical delight that comes from grappling with stern problems. Young indulged, perhaps too often, in convolutions of style and a delight in rare words. He had a weakness for 'Alpine uplift', those 'mystical emotions and elevated thoughts (which) may please the writer but ... are not demanded or expected by the reader'. Despite this, if there is any one book which explains the fascination of mountaineering more persuasively than *Peaks and Pleasant Pastures* it is *On High Hills* – just as there is still no better guide to the basic principles of mountaineering than the fifty-year-old *Mountain Craft*.

From a few other men who have both climbed and written it is possible to gain some impression of what the Alps can mean. Michael Roberts' poetry, George Leigh-Mallory's defence of mountaineering which he called *The Mountaineer as Artist*, and Arnold Lunn's polemics on the Alps and Alpinism all present this in various ways. All were written by men who felt it necessary to explain to others what they had found in the Alps, and who succeeded in the task. There are, of course, more recent authors, and some convey in remarkable manner the exaltations and terrors of the most difficult and challenging climbs. But in an age of specialisation they are apt to lose the mountain splendour among the mountain difficulties, to miss the wider appeals of the range while concentrating on the rigours of solving the 'last great problem'. There is not necessarily anything wrong in this, but it means that the visitor anxious to see the Alps steadily and whole is likely to find the best pointers in past literature rather than present.

Geoffrey Winthrop Young with his guide, Joseph Knubel.

Page 219 The seracs of the Upper Grindelwald Glacier.

Page 220 The most famous shape in the Alps: the Matterhorn from Zermatt.

PART THREE
Peak Points
and Last Strongholds

The number of mountains in the Alps depends mainly on definition, while the number of *Viertausender*, the summits which reach the magic 4,000 metres, depends on the survey figure used. Of these thousands of peaks rising between the Mediterranean and the Bohemian rectangle, some have by their commanding height or position helped to guide the story of the Alps and to create the human background of the range as it exists today. Others have exercised the same influence by their beauty or been given a particular niche in history by chance circumstance. Thus Rochemelon, the most southerly of the Graians, would be unremarkable, despite its fine view, had not Bonfacius Rotarius, having escaped from infidel hands in the Far East, climbed it in 1358 and hewed a chapel from the summit rocks, thus marking what was probably the first ascent of an Alpine snow-peak. Pilatus, even without its railway and its grand-stand view, would be worth ascending for a sight of the little marshy lake near the summit from which the ghost of Pontius Pilate failed to arise and meet the taunts of Pastor John Muller in 1585 – a failure which put an end to the legend. The Velan is worth seeing if only for the last eight lines of Arnold's 'Obermann Once More'; the Jungfrau for its open-bosomed display of snow and ice, almost too blatant to be believed. A flutter of interest must pass through even the most unimaginative mind on regarding the Gross Glockner or the Ortler and recalling that the Glockner was first climbed by the local bishop in 1800 and the Ortler four years later on the orders of Archduke John, brother of the last Holy Roman Emperor. Franz Altgraf von Salm-Reifferscheid-Krantheim, bishop of Gurk, suitably black-suited and hatted, approaching the Glockner on a white horse in Scheffer von Leonhardshoff's painting, was merely one in a long line of climbing clerics which has included Placidus à Spescha; the prior of the St Bernard Hospice who made the first ascent of the Velan in 1779; *curé* Clément of Champéry, who climbed the Dent du Midi five years later, and many others down to the days of Achille Ratti, Pope Pius XI, whose one book was *Climbs on Alpine Peaks*.

Over the years the great barrier between the northern plains and southern Europe, crossed for centuries only with reluctance and caution, has thus been transformed into a chain of snow- and rock-peaks rich with the memories of human hope and endeavour. Here are the stories of a few of them.

Le Mont Inaccessible; from
Simler et les origines de l'
Alpinisme jusqu'en 1600.

CHAPTER FIFTEEN

Mont Aiguille

The traveller reaching the crest of the Col d'Allimas from Gresse, a small village thirty miles south of Grenoble, is faced without warning, and almost with shock, by what the Michelin Guide to the French Alps calls '*une saisissante apparition*'. The words are strong, but no stronger than they should be. What appears as a sudden revelation is Mont Aiguille, one of the 'Seven Wonders of Dauphiné', and from here, as from so many angles, fully justifying John Ball's description of 'one of the most wonderful and extraordinary of the minor summits of the Alps'.

In front the road twists down among meadows golden with flowers in spring before rising to the farming hamlet of La Bâtie. Beyond, some three miles away, a skyline spectacle of improbable shape and impressive grandeur, the mountain looms up, its vertical precipices forming the northern side of a massive rock-ship riding prow-high from a sea of fields. With a summit plateau half a mile long, a quarter of a mile wide, the mountain is cut off from the Vercors plateau to the west by a col some 1,500 feet lower, a col which emphasises the isolation of the peak and converts what would otherwise be a cliff-girt peninsula into one of the most extraordinary mountains in Europe.

From all sides Mont Aiguille looks magnificent and from all sides it looks different. As with Suilven, the lonely peak which rears up from Sutherland's level floor of Lewisian gneiss in north-west Scotland, it is difficult to believe that the mountain seen from north or south is the animal seen from east or west. From the east, in particular, Mont Aiguille stands up like a paper-knife on edge. From the south it rises as a natural fortress, its vertical sides apparently impregnable. From the Col d'Allimas on the north the impression of anchored ship is irresistible. And from the west, where the top of the Grand Veymont, nearly a thousand feet higher, commands an almost eagle's-nest vista, Mont Aiguille's summit plateau appears like a 'Lost World' on which one might find the survivals of an earlier age.

Yet if its form is astonishing and its presence awesome, its history is no less. Mont Inaccessible was for long its name, and inaccessible to all but rock experts it still looks. Yet this extraordinary peak was the scene of the exploit which opened Alpine rock-climbing history. For it was scaled for the first time in 1492, its conquerors setting out from Grenoble a few weeks before Columbus set out for America. And the letter describing the scene on the summit has rightly been called 'the Magna Carta of Alpinism'.

The remarkable climb was made by royal command after Charles VIII had spent the night of 6 November at the nearby village of St Maurice en Trièves. Charles was presumably piqued by the idea that any part of his kingdom should be inaccessible and on returning from Italy decided to put matters right. Little is known even of Antoine de Ville, lord of Dompjulien and of Beaupré – two places in Lorraine – on whose shoulders the royal orders now descended. Significantly, however, Dompjulien is described as the king's '*capitaine des schelliers*' – the officer in charge of the laddermen who assaulted walled towns, and probably responsible also for much other siege apparatus.

He and his party arrived at the foot of the mountain in late June, and it seems that some time was spent conferring with local people and preparing the ladders and '*subtils engins*' with which the ascent was to be made. One measurement of the summit plateau is given as '*une traict d'arbaleste*', and it is not inconceivable that some method of throwing up ropes with or without grappling-irons, was adapted from contemporary methods of siege warfare.

Reporting for climbing duty was Dompjulien himself; his almoner François de Bosco; Sebastien de Carect, a royal chaplain who had probably been sent to vouch for what happened; and a handful of others who appear to have numbered between half a dozen and half a score. The climb was made on Tuesday, 26 June, and the only indication of what it involved is given by de Bosco's statement that 'one had to ascend half a league by ladders and then a league by a route horrible to behold and even more terrible to come down than to go up'. However, there seems little doubt that the route was substantially the same as that followed centuries later, at the south-western corner of the precipices, where a series of chimneys leads upwards into the heart of the mountain.

Arrived on top, the party found a green meadow 'a quarter of a league in width and an arbalest-shot in length', covered with flowers and sloping up towards the east. In addition Dompjulien and de Bosco reported wild sparrows of three different colours, red, black and grey; ravens with red feet; other extraordinary and unknown birds and '*une forte belle garenne de chamois*' – an extremely beautiful herd of chamois, including young apparently born that year. Dompjulien added that there was no way by which the animals could leave the summit, a remark which raises the question of how they got to the plateau in the first place. However, having so nobly succeeded in his enterprise, he was doubtless anxious to deliver the best possible account to the royal ears.

In de Bosco's words, the party 'having said Mass on the said mountain, ate, drank, and reposed thereon'. They built a hut, presumably of stone blocks prised from the plateau, the vestiges of which were still visible three and a half centuries later. Then they set up three crosses, one on each of the three highest points.

These preliminaries over, the royal chaplain baptised the mountain in the name of the Holy Trinity, dropping its earlier title of Mont Inaccessible, which was no longer true, for Equille For. Now the party might have been expected to descend. The climb had been difficult enough and it is improbable that they would have burdened themselves with much in the way of provisions. However, instead of returning, Dompjulien and his companions set up camp. They were to remain on the summit for six days and it seems likely that some of the local men were sent down to bring up supplies. Certainly a descent was made by at least one of the party before very long.

For on 28 June Dompjulien prepared a letter. Dated from the summit and addressed to the president of the assembly in Grenoble, it reported that the writer had arrived at the top. The letter was taken to the foot of the mountain, whence a messenger carried it to Grenoble. Here the parliament turned to Yves Levy, the *huissier* or sheriff's officer, who was immediately despatched to see for himself whether the mountain had really been scaled. He was expected to join the summit party; but, as he explained on his return to Grenoble on 5 July, he did not wish to expose himself to the chance of getting killed. Instead he reported that he had seen the summit party and handed over the sworn witness of four men who on 1 July had braved the dangers, climbed the ladders and, apparently on the same day, descended to sign a statement and hand it to the waiting sheriff's officer. These men were four local notables, and they had carried up in sacks three pairs of coneys, one black, one white and one grey, leaving them on the summit in the hope that they would breed there.

The following day Dompjulien and his party descended. Despite the stir that the expedition must have caused, despite the fact that local 'gentry' had been on the top, that the whole operation had gone off without hitch, Mont Aiguille was now left in peace; not for a decade, not for a century, but for nearly three hundred and fifty years. Dynasties rose and fell, armies passed through or round this western fringe of the Dauphiné. Grenoble, less than forty miles to the north, grew into one of the great fortified cities of southern France. Yet not until 1834 was another ascent made of Mont Aiguille.

On 16 June of that year the *curé* of Chichiliane, a hamlet south of the peak, reached the summit with Eugène de Rochas, a lawyer from the town of Gap, forty miles away, and a number of local men. Little is known of the reason for their enterprise or of the difficulties they experienced, although a brief report says that they used ropes, ladders and mason's hammers – the latter presumably to cut foot- and hand-holds where God had failed to provide them. This party was followed in 1849 by two men from La Bâtie, the hamlet under the northern lee of the mountain, and a companion from Gresse, all of whom left their names on a small iron cross which they planted on the summit.

Attempts to climb the mountain were made in the early 1870s but not until 1877 did man again set foot on the summit of Mont Aiguille. This time the ascent was of a different kind: the first 'tourist' climb, made in September by Edouard Rochat, a member of the Paris section of the French Alpine Club, who set out from Clelles with a local guide. Whether the man had taken part in the ascent of 1849 is uncertain but he knew at least the lower part of the

route. First to be negotiated was a narrow rising ledge, not difficult on the whole but very exposed, with the sheer face of the mountain on one side and an equally sheer drop on the other. There was one particularly nasty spot where the ledge virtually disappeared and minor acrobatics were called for; this was followed by a stretch only to be negotiated on the stomach, followed by a wriggle between two rocks so close together that 'anyone in the slightest bit fat would be forced to hang over the edge as he made the passage'. After a hundred yards of this, the route led into the heart of the mountain, and to the foot of a huge perpendicular chimney. On either side there rose sheer walls; in front the bed of the chimney; behind, framed by the rock-walls, lay a vertical view of the distant country. The situation was impressive, although lacking the dramatic exposure of the traverse which had just been completed.

The party now advanced without great difficulty. Only two places caused trouble. Where the gulley-bed became first perpendicular, then overhanging, progress could be made only by back-and-knee work in which the body was strenuously levered upwards. Eventually the two men came out on the summit plateau, an hour and thirty-five minutes after starting the climb. Looking about them they saw the gently rising slope, a few juniper bushes and a few stunted pines. They hacked down some of the junipers, made for the highest point, and there started the bonfire they had promised to light. They spent nearly three hours on the summit, waiting for the weather to clear. Then they descended, taking slightly longer than on the upward climb since there was a constant danger of sending down stones.

The first tourist ascent was made at a significant moment. As Edouard Rochat noted in the description he wrote for the *Annuaire* of the French Alpine Club, a railway was to link Grenoble to Gap the following year, passing within sight of Mont Aiguille. There would even be a station at Clelles. If these remarks were not enough to foreshadow things to come, M. Rochat went on to point out that three and a quarter hours walking from the station would bring a climber to the base of the rocks. In fact a carriage could be taken part of the way, and two hours or less were required for the climb. All this made the mountain accessible not only from Grenoble but from much farther afield. Had M. Rochat lived a century later he might have speculated on whether it might just be possible to climb Mont Aiguille in a long day, Paris back to Paris by using the autoroute du Sud.

The following year, 1878, the Section d'Isère of the French Alpine Club took notice of the peak and in October more than three hundred feet of iron rope were fixed across the more difficult parts of the ascent and pitons hammered in at places so that a doubled rope could be used in the descent. Today Mont Aiguille combines modern accessibility and ancient mystery. It has made much of the Alpine progress from inaccessible to 'an easy day for a lady'. Yet still, as M. Rochat wrote nearly a century ago, 'established Alpinistes have no wish to leave the high mountains to make an ascent of a mere 2,097 metres especially since, the reputation of Mont Aiguille being what it is, they may fear that their attempt will be a failure'. At the top of a ladder, in some medieval paradise, Dompjulien must be laughing his head off.

One of Elijah Walton's water-colours from *The Bernese Oberland*.

227

CHAPTER SIXTEEN
The Rigi

The motorist who drives from Zurich to Zug can take the motorway, the older and more beautiful route No. 4 that follows the Sihl Valley or the yellow and more wiggling road that crosses the line of switchback summits between the Albisberg and the Uetliberg, the last despairing attempt of the Alps to put a foot in the suburbs of Zurich.

Soon after he has crossed the Albis Pass and curved down via the yellow wiggles into the undistinguished agricultural country beyond, he will see rising from the horizon to the south a large and not altogether prepossessing lump. It is not high as heights go in this part of the world. It is not particularly shapely in form, and in detail from some angles it resembles the gigantic spoil-heaps which marred mining country before the conservationists began to take the landscape in hand. At first glance there seems something faintly presumptuous that this should be considered a mountain at àll, and faintly ridiculous that it should be considered a part of the Alps. Yet this is the broad northern bulk of the Rigi, the culmination of the ridge rising between the Lake of Lucerne and the Zugersee that for more than a century has provided countless thousands of visitors with the grandstand for a topographical world Cup Final that has few competitors in Europe.

Since Victorian times the Rigi has offered the ultimate in mountain sightseeing. If this sounds ominous, worse is to follow. The Rigi has not one mountain railway but three – or, to be more accurate, two mountain railways to the summit and a cable-car system that joins one of them half way up. It has, moreover, not only a hundred-bed summit hotel but more than a dozen other hotels and pensions scattered about its slopes and ridges. More than seven hundred men, women and children can sleep overnight in them to await the spectacle of the sunrise, an almost Druidic ceremony repeated every morning of the year. Thus at first glance it would be easy to consider the tourist paraphernalia of the Rigi not as a tribute from man to Nature but as an example of how man can spit in the face of the environment. However, it is difficult to maintain the critical attitude. One is reminded of *White Horse Inn*, that chocolate-box confection of a musical that teeters on the brink of parody. In that, after the titillation of the prologue, the stage curtains are drawn back – or 'the morning mists arise' – and with a belch of music and entrance of the

228

dancing girls the whole thing bursts into a life that only the most curmudge-only can fail to enjoy.

So with the Rigi. Here the transformation comes about mid-morning, especially for the traveller who has gained height by his own feet and is pleased with the fact. The cow-bells are clanging as though Swiss public relations are working overtime. The view is opening out. The overnight guests are being disposed of, the sun-blinds wound down, the shutters of kiosks unlatched, cardboard cases of beer opened for the day. The first old dears with their badged sticks are already on the hoof. From the lakeside bases surrounding the mountain, the hundreds determined to get a glimpse of what Victor Hugo called 'that unbelievable horizon' are already on their way. Unless the weather turns nasty, the cameras will be clicking all day, an offering to the colour-film makers and a tribute to the irrepressible optimism of the human race. The spirit is as infectious as that of a Cup Final crowd or a Nürnburg rally, and one capitulates before the main attack has even begun.

The Rigi-Kulm, highest point on the mountain, rises to only 5,896 feet, the northern prow-like promontory of a ridge bounded by the Lake of Lucerne on the south-west, the Zugersee on the north-east, the Lowerzer See on the south-east, and on the south the low-lying country which in pre-historic times was part of a greatly enlarged Lake Lucerne from which the Rigi rose as an island. On the north, steep slopes are divided by the terrace of the Seebodenalp and across the whole of this escarpment can be seen the broad bands of *Riginen* which give the mountain its name. On east and west, as the main ridge slopes back with decreasing height, the ground is less steep, more meadow-like, with a picture-book mingling of pasture and woodland.

High on the western slopes, at Rigi-Kaltbad, to which the cable-way swings up passengers from Weggis, there emerges the cool spring that early in the eighteenth century set off the familiar progress. First pilgrims travelled to sample alleged healing powers; then came the little church of 'Our Lady of the Snows.' Today there is the health resort, served by cable-way and by rack-railway from Vitznau, and boasting more than half a dozen hotels.

This railway, certainly the first of its kind in Switzerland, allegedly the first in Europe, and apparently the second in the world – the Americans won a first with the line up Mount Washington – was built up the easy ground from Vitznau a century ago. Before this visitors were served by the guides, the porters, and the horses which made use of three main mule-tracks. In addition there were the *chaises à porter* for ladies who did not wish to ride or walk, for invalids and for the elderly. Labour was always available, and Murray's guide for 1838 adds that: 'In the height of summer, when the concourse of visitors is immense, it is a good plan to send a lad up the mountain before you to secure beds at the Rigi-Kulm inn.'

This building was something like a barracks, and housed forty beds in rooms not unlike cabins. During the summer large numbers would be turned away every evening, and at times it was difficult to get beds, food or attention. Just what conditions were like is made brutally clear by Mr Murray in the way for which he was famous:

The house presents a scene of the utmost confusion, servant maids hurrying in one direction, couriers and guides in another, while gentlemen with poles and knapsacks block up the passages [he wrote]. Most of the languages of Europe, muttered usually in terms of abuse and complaint, and the all-pervading fumes of tobacco, enter largely as ingredients into this Babel of sounds and smells, and add to the discomfort of the fatigued traveller. In the evening the guests are collected at a *table d'hôte* supper; after which most persons are glad to repair to rest. It takes some time, however, before the hubbub of voices and the trampling of feet subside; and, not infrequently, a few roystering German students prolong their potations and noise far into the night.

Niklaus Riggenbach, the Basle engineer who humbly called himself only a mechanic, was the man who began to alter all this, and from Vitznau carriages – painted red to distinguish them from the blue ones that come up the other side of the mountain from Arth-Goldau – still use today the line laid out under his supervision in 1870. Soon after Riggenbach himself had driven 'the City of Lucerne' on its inaugural run, the system was carrying 100,000 passengers a year; today the figure tops the half-million. The track rises gradually up the easy slopes to Rigi-Kaltbad, then continues more steeply up the crest of the ridge which rises above the easternmost arm of the Lake of Lucerne to Staffel. Here the line from Arth-Goldau comes in, and for the remaining few hundred yards the two lines run parallel, the trains like horses driven in tandem, the blue and the red drawing a double load of sightseers to the top.

All travellers debouch a few yards below the summit. Here is station and Swiss flag, ancient carriages hauled up railwaywise nearly 6,000 feet for no apparent reason other than to give more colour to an already colourful scene; the great Hotel Rigi-Kulm, with a hundred beds, huge restaurant hall, conference room, bowling green and tourist-house; and, a little higher and a little aloof, the summit itself, a flat space on which, in earlier times, there stood the inevitable cross and an eighteen-foot wooden erection climbed by ladder – 'puny additional elevation to that of the mountain, though some ascend it to see the view to the advantage', noted Murray.

Here, for at least a century and a half, have come the incorrigible mountain romantics, as well as many others. Goethe, Longfellow, Wordsworth and the elder Dumas, Fennimore Cooper and Mark Twain were among the writers. Here wickedly observant, came Alphonse Daudet, creator of the immortal Tartarin, that cautious adventurer from southern France who climbed the mountain bowed down with Alpine paraphernalia and conjuring up the greatest perils until suddenly an 'immense hotel with its three hundred windows became visible to him a little farther on between the great lamps, which burned brightly in the fog'.

The Empress Marie-Louise was carried to the summit of the Rigi in 1814. Prince Albert, bringing back to the young Queen Victoria a book of views chronicling a Swiss tour, brought a pressed Alpenrose from the Rigi. The Rumanian Princess Kolzoff-Masalsky climbed the mountain in 1855 before making what she believed was the first ascent of the Mönch. Queen Victoria herself came in 1868, ascending the mountain in the company of the faithful John Brown. Four years later Martin Conway, just sixteen, failed to reach the top with a companion. 'We were too proud to go up by train and too slow to reach the top in time if we were to catch the last boat for Brunnen and join the parents that evening at Axenstein,' he wrote. 'The Staffel was our highest point. We ignominiously descended by rail.'

Wagner came here, writing the *Siegfried Idyll* across the Lake at Tribschen and claiming to have used the three notes of the local *rang de vaches* as a key musical phrase in *Tristan and Isolde*. Rachmaninov lived at Hertenstein just below the Rigi. Victor Hugo wrote of the summit view, commenting: 'In the face of this indescribable spectacle, one understands why the half-wits swarm throughout Switzerland and Savoy. The Alps create many idiots. It is not given to every human being to appreciate such marvels or, without being blinded and dazzled, to promenade from sun-up to sunset above a panorama stretching for fifty leagues.'

All came for the view; or, more specifically, for the view at sunrise, after which, as one Victorian writer put it, 'it seems as if nothing in nature can ever again be so beautiful'. This was George Cheever who epitomised the age of fruity topographical description which demanded at least one passing reference to the Almighty. 'It was as if an angel had flown round the horizon of mountain ranges, and lighted up each of their white pyramidal points in succession, like a row of gigantic lamps burning with rosy fires,' Cheever declared, before comparing the dawn pageant to a 'supernatural revelation, where mighty spirits were the actors between earth and heaven'.

That writer after writer should so stretch themselves, having been wakened by the bellow of the *Alpenhorn*, blown as a pre-dawn warning, says much for the Rigi view. It is, in fact, the almost perfect example of the great panorama. The catalogue of peaks and fourteen lakes on a 124-mile stretch of the main Alpine chain that can be rolled off on a good morning is only a part of that perfection. The immensely satisfying way in which this collection is arranged gives it a quality more than counter-balancing the awfulness of a peak point at tourist time.

As the photographer in search of a view soon discovers, the finest horizon needs a foreground as certainly as a pearl necklace demands the firm white flesh of a nice neck. Here the Rigi provides not only foreground but midground as well at almost all points of the compass. The ridge of the mountain itself, stretching away south past the Dossen to the Rigi Hochfluh above Brunnen, is broken into effectively scenic Alpine meadows, littered with cows and chalets, and at just the right depth below the summit to set off the more distant view. To the east, across the Lowerzer See, rise the extraordinary peaks of the lesser and greater Mythen. To the north, and for once meriting the tired description of 'almost at one's feet', Küssnacht stands on the neck of land between the Zugersee and the Lake of Lucerne.

All this detail sets off the horizon. This is just as well. The distant view from the Rigi – which, as early writers pointed out, can be seen merely by turning full circle, with never a tramp to secondary vantage-point – has a

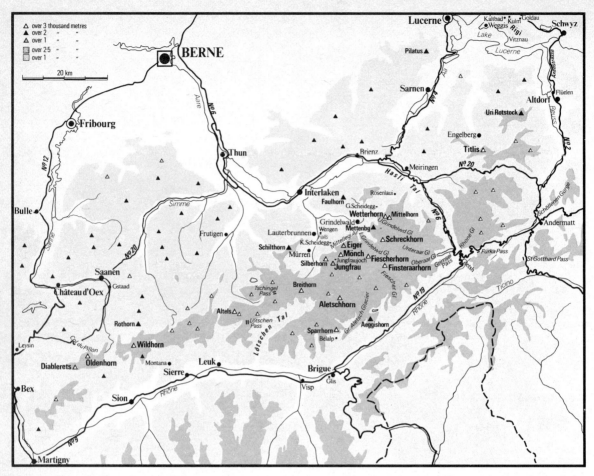

The Bernese Oberland

special quality given by the peak's situation on the southern edge of the Swiss midlands, half way between Alps and Jura, and offers the best of both scenic worlds. Yet it would be unfair to suggest that the distant peaks loom as overwhelmingly large in the landscape as suggested by the publicity brochures. The giants of the Oberland, which rise up in artists' impressions as though they were being studied through a ten-thousand-inch telephoto lens, must be picked out among the clutter on the horizon with a good deal of care. They are bigger than pin-points; but not much. Due east the Säntis, over which the sun rises in midsummer, is pimple rather than peak. The summit of the Titlis to the south may 'shimmer with its virgin snows' *à la* prospectus, but it still needs care in identification.

The Rigi view, just because of what it offers – a horizon five hundred miles in circumference is the figure usually quoted – thus makes the demands of its class: study and attention, and if possible a personal knowledge of the massive detail which suggests that the view includes the whole heartland of Europe. On the north, beyond Zurich and a sliver of lake, lies southern Germany, the shadow of Baden and Württemberg to the east and to the west the dark lines of the Black Forest. Further west still, beyond the Sempacher See with its memories of the most famous battle in Swiss history, rises the dim

232

shape of the Jura; good vision plus adequate faith can even discover the outline of the Weissenstein above Soleure.

South-east to south-west rise the Alps; the snowy ridge of the Glärnisch, the broad bulk of the Tödi, the more rocky Uri-Rotstock and the Titlis – all leading the eye towards the more distant Oberland where the Finsteraarhorn, the Schreckhorn, the Wetterhorn peaks and the trinity of Mönch, Eiger and Jungfrau can be ticked off with the aid of field-glasses. All this and the foreground too.

A century ago the Rigi was in the vanguard of sub-Alpine development, its popularity a forerunner of the fame which spread up so many valleys during the next few decades. Today it has an almost urbanised environment, an air of being a municipalised mountain top from which to look at the view, a not too incongruous outlier of Lucerne. For the Alps it may be the shape of things to come.

CHAPTER SEVENTEEN

The Wetterhorn

The downhill walk from the Kleine Scheidegg above Wengen to the tourist centre of Grindelwald is one of the most popular five-mile strolls in the Alps. From Grindelwald one can return to Interlaken, or be taken in ease back over the Scheidegg to a destination on the other side of the bump. The track can be lost only by an almost perverse combination of effort and imagination. Stations between starting and finishing point, merged discreetly into the landscape, like most of the railway line itself, are an added inducement to those for whom even a few miles of descent are apt to be too much.

However, this alone does not account for the number of enthusiasts who pick their way downhill in late spring when the ski-slopes have disappeared into melting drifts from which flowers burst at the hint of an opening camera-case. It does not account for the throng in summer, when walkers congregate round the hamlets of Metten or Alpiglen like strollers at a café during the evening promenade. The downhill path to Grindelwald is the easiest of easy trots, but two things make it incomparable. One is the towering Eigerwand on the right hand. The other is the view ahead, a close-up shot of one tiny portion of the huge panorama of the Oberland seen from Berne.

The centre-piece of this view is the Wetterhorn – or, to be quite accurate, the second highest of the three Wetterhörner. The slopes near Alpiglen are, at 5,850 feet, only slightly less than half the Wetterhorn's 12,149 feet. Thus the mountain is seen from roughly mid-height, virtually from top to bottom. The upper Grindelwald glacier artistically pushes out its white snout between the mountain and the nearer Mettenberg, and the architectural steep lower slopes provide the ideal pediment for the receding upper stretches. These give back in proportions correct enough to underline Whistler's complaint about Nature creeping up on him. Seen from the path down to Grindelwald, the Wetterhorn is the almost perfect mountain.

It is also a mountain whose early history is even now so riddled with uncertainties as to present more questions than answers. Perhaps this is hardly surprising. For the highest peak of the Wetterhörner, the Mittelhorn, modestly hides away from most viewpoints, while the peak that hangs over Grindelwald was known for years – particularly in the Haslithal, the valley beyond Grindelwald – as the Hasle Jungfrau. The early ascents have, furthermore,

The Wetterhorn from the Kleine Scheidegg – Grindelwald path. The snout of the upper Grindelwald Glacier can be seen between the Wetterhorn and the neighbouring Mettenberg.

tended to subdivide into those made from Grindelwald, a major tourist centre since men first came to look at the two Grindelwald Glaciers in the eighteenth century, and those made from Rosenlaui, a much smaller place which lies over the hump towards the Haslithal.

From the jungle of dates and contradictions two things are clear. The first is that early attempts to climb the three peaks of the Wetterhörner – whose respective heights do not seem to have been agreed upon until some time afterwards – were bunched in two groups, one in 1844 and 1845, and one a decade later. The second fact is ironic: although most early attempts on the group were made by the Swiss, guides and amateurs alike, Sir Alfred Wills's ascent of the Hasle Jungfrau or Wetterhorn in 1854 is almost universally accepted as the start of the Golden Age in which the British played such a prominent part.

The first campaign opened in the summer of 1844 and was carried out by the 'disciples' of Agassiz who had recently established their Hôtel des Neuchâtelois on the Unteraar Glacier which runs, as it were, at the 'back' of the Wetterhörner as seen from Grindelwald. On 28 August, Édouard Desor and Daniel Dollfus-Ausset climbed with two companions and six guides the southernmost and lowest of the three Wetterhörner, the 12,110 feet Rosenhorn, named by Desor since it appeared to dominate the Rosenlaui glacier. Three days later two of the guides, Johann Jaun and Melchior Bannholzer from the village of Meiringen, climbed the Hasle Jungfrau from Rosenlaui and then went on to the Hôtel des Neuchâtelois. This was of course the first ascent of what is now generally called the Wetterhorn, and since it is only some fifty feet lower than the second peak in the group, the 12,166 feet Mittelhorn, it seems likely that the men believed they were climbing what had eluded them a few days earlier, and had now reached the highest of the three summits.

Uncertainty begins the following year with a disputed ascent of the Hasle Jungfrau by Dr Roth, an Interlaken physician, and a local forester. Little interest was shown at the time in a small note appearing in a Swiss paper, signed by Roth and his forester, stating that they had made the ascent of the 'highest peak of the Wetterhörner' with three Grindelwald guides. Now the Hasle Jungfrau was not 'the highest peak', although internal evidence suggests that Roth thought it was; and the fact that he and his companion were accompanied by three Grindelwald men is not proof positive that they climbed from Grindelwald. Two days after Roth's climb – about which there was controversy when the 1844 report was noted a century later – there came the genuine first ascent of the highest of the Wetterhörner. It was made by a Scotsman, S. T. Speer, whose guides provided him with this particular niche in history. For he was intent on climbing the peak which dominates Grindelwald, no doubt hoping to make the first tourist ascent. But Johann Jaun was regularly employed by Agassiz, wished to reserve for his Swiss employer the first tourist ascent of the Hasle Jungfrau, and therefore led his English employer up the Mittelhorn, subsequently shown to be the highest of the three peaks.

When Speer first saw the upper snows of the mountain he considered the

Sir Alfred Wills and his guide Auguste Balmat.

ascent impossible, but was told that this was not so. 'I therefore held my peace,' he wrote, 'thinking myself in right good company.' The final slope was steep, difficult and dangerous. The leading guides cut large steps or 'holes' as Speer described them. As the highest available of these was grasped, each member of the party gingerly hauled himself up and lay in contact with the snow while the others then moved up, a caterpillar-like progress that was cold and certainly increased the dangers of a slip. They had been climbing for three hours on the upper portion of the mountain when, says Speer,

the guides confidently affirmed that in another hour (if no accident occurred) we should attain the summit; the banner was accordingly prepared, and after a few minutes' repose, taken by cautiously turning round and placing our backs against the snow, we stretched upwards once more, the guides singing national songs, and the utmost gaiety pervading the whole party at the prospect of so success-ful a result. The brilliant white summit of the peak appeared just above us, and when within thirty or forty feet of its apex, the *guide chef*, considerately thinking that his employer would naturally wish to be the first to tread this unconquered summit, reversed the ropes, and placing me first in the line, directed me to take the hatchet and cautiously cut the few remaining steps necessary. These injunctions I obeyed to the best of my abilities, and at one o'clock precisely the red banner fluttered on the summit of the central peak of the Wetterhorn.

Three weeks later Jaun led Agassiz to the same central plateau from which the three peaks rise and then turned up the final slopes of the Hasle Jungfrau. The ascent was the last of these made in the 1840s The story reopened a decade later with the arrival in Grindelwald of J. Eardley Blackwell who, 'being an idle man ... loved the excitement, and always felt a desire to accomplish what others had done before him'. During June 1854 Blackwell made two attempts on the Hasle Jungfrau. The first was made from Grindel-wald and was unsuccessful; the second, made from Rosenlaui, was successful; and an iron flag, found later in the year only some ten feet below the summit, was probably carried up by Blackwell and his guides. But Blackwell's climbs became of interest only later, after the events of September 1854, which provide a convenient starting post for the story of 'sporting' mountaineering.

These events began with the arrival in the Oberland of Alfred Wills, then a twenty-six-year-old barrister. His mountaineering coincided with his honey-moon, and Wills had already introduced his wife to glacier-camping on the Mer de Glace. They arived in Interlaken with Auguste Balmat. Will's first aim was to climb the Jungfrau but this was ruled out on the ground of time, since it could only be approached from the south. The Finsteraarhorn and the Schreckhorn were also considered impossible, since an attempt on either would make it necessary to sleep on the glacier, and the season was by now considered too far advanced for this. Wills then suggested the Wetterhorn – meaning the Hasle Jungfrau. The local guide Ulrich Lauener said that this was practicable, and added that the mountain had not been climbed before. It is clear that he meant 'not climbed before from Grindelwald', and there is considerable evidence suggesting that this was genuinely believed to be the case, not only in Grindelwald itself but throughout the whole area.

The following day Wills arrived in the village to find a bustle of preparation so great that he feared his wife might take alarm. He also found that Lauener now insisted on bringing a second Oberland man, Peter Bohren, in addition to Balmat and to Auguste Simond, a Chamonix friend who had already been engaged. There would also be the inevitable porter, bringing the party's total to six, and provisions had to be carried for them all. There was 'a great basket with ropes' – probably one of the wickerwork panniers carried on the back – and there were crampons, as well as what Wills vaguely describes as 'other necessaries for an excursion of this sort'. The preparations staggered him. So in a different way did the landlord of the inn who, as they prepared to leave, came forward, shook Balmat by the hand, and said: 'Try to return alive, all of you; but ...'

They left at 1.30, walking south across the meadows by the river. Before them, half-right, there rose the walls of the Wetterhorn across which, hundreds of feet up, could be traced out the line of the Enge, a narrow path that ascends and then contours the rocky buttresses above the Upper Grindelwald Glacier. They passed Peter Bohren's home, reached the Enge, and had not gone far along it before they were caught up by Lauener, who had remained behind to collect the 'flagge' which it was customary to place on summits as a mark of victory. Wills now understood why the flag had been collected at the blacksmith's. Strapped on Lauener's back was a sheet of iron three feet long and two feet wide, attached to a bar of the same metal, ten or twelve feet long, and as thick as a man's thumb.

They reached the Gleckstein cave before dusk. One huge boulder had fallen on two others, and the trilothon itself butted up against rocks. Earth and moss filled the cracks and left only a narrow entrance. Before it was dark, while the rest of the men prepared the meal, Wills and Balmat made beds on the thick floor-covering of short mountain hay, having hunted fleas from the blankets.

This was quite normal. From Whymper's guide who commented that all men were the same – 'we have them' – fleas occupy a position in the literature equalled only by tough mutton, rocky beds and summit champagne. Wills, himself a connoisseur, on first visiting the Hôtel du Monte Rosa at Saas, considered that the specimens there were insupportable. 'Their size, and the fierceness of their appetite', he added, 'exceeded anything of the kind I ever knew; and when a cold or wet day drove one near the fire, their attacks became unendurable; and there was nothing for it, but to retire, and have a grand hunt, and we always found.'

They left at 4.30 the following morning, having sent the porter back to Grindelwald. First they crossed a limb of the Upper Grindelwald Glacier; then they took to the rocks and, with what Wills called 'the worst piece of scrambling I ever did', made their way up towards the snowy plateau from which the peak rises.

And here, high on the mountain, they realised they were not alone. Below, moving on a line slightly different from theirs, were two small figures. In the 1850s it was still unusual for two parties to be on the slopes of a big mountain at the same time; it was still more unusual for them not to know of each other's presence. The mystery deepened when Wills and his companions saw that one of the two men carried on his shoulders a young fir tree – root, branches and all.

It was clear that the newcomers were out-flanking the larger party; and since two men move more quickly on a mountain than six it was equally clear who would get first to the top.

Balmat shouted across to them. They shouted back. Wills's fears were soon found to be justified. The two men, Christian Almer, who during the next decades was to become the most famous of all Oberland guides, and his brother-in-law Ulrich Kauffmann, had heard of Wills's departure from Grindelwald and decided that they should be the first to make an ascent of the peak from the village where they lived. No 'flagge' could be found in time, so the fir tree had been brought as a substitute.

Balmat was at first enraged. But in the shouting match across the snows he persuaded Almer and his companion to wait on the edge of the plateau from which the Wetterhörner rise. Here Wills and his guides joined them.

Above, the peak of the Hasle Jungfrau swept up for 800 feet in a snow- and ice-slope of increasing steepness, crowned by a curled-over cornice, from which it was thought that the final peak rose.

At the foot of the slope they held a council of war. It was decided that Lauener should go first, cutting steps in the ice that lay below only an inch or so of snow, and that Simond should follow and enlarge the steps.

The rest of the party waited below as the guides cut up the blindingly white slope, the ice-chips tinkling down in a cascade as the men rose higher and higher.

It was an hour before Lauener called on the rest to follow him. Balmat went first. Behind him there came Wills, followed by Peter Bohren and the two Grindelwald men. All five were roped together. Although the steps had already been cut, they moved slowly, and it was some while before they neared Lauener and Simond who were still hacking their way towards the cornice.

Soon after they started, Wills measured the angle of the slope with the help of his vertical ice-axe. He found it forty-five degrees, an incline which is very much steeper than it sounds; then the slope increased to sixty degrees, and finally to seventy. They seemed to be stepping up an almost vertical ice-wall.

Eventually Lauener neared the cornice, edging up at a point where he could tackle it with his axe; a few blows brought a section crashing down. Then he suddenly shouted: 'I see blue sky.' The cornice was not an advance rampart guarding the way to the actual summit, but the summit itself. A few more blows were necessary. Then Wills stepped through the breach.

The instant before, I had been face to face with a blank wall of ice [he wrote]. One step, and the eye took in a boundless expanse of crag and glacier, peak and precipice, mountain and valley, lake and plain. The whole world seemed to lie at my feet. The next moment, I was almost appalled by the awfulness of our position. The side we had come up was steep; but it was a gentle slope, compared with that which now fell away from where I stood. A few yards of glittering ice at our feet, and then, nothing between us and the green slopes of Grindelwald, nine thousand feet below.

They straddled the narrow ice-ridge and first the iron flagge and then the fir tree were hammered and dug into the snow. Wills dropped a glove which rolled a few yards to the edge of the precipice and was retrieved by Bohren despite orders to stay where he was. Then he waved his hat in the hope of being recognised by his wife and brother-in-law in Grindelwald.

Finally they all started down, finding the descent more difficult than the ascent. Then they remembered they had not drunk the health of the mountain, and halted to take a swig of brandy and snow.

At the foot of the ice-slope they stopped to drink the health of the mountain again – this time in red wine. Then they continued uneventfully down, meeting Mrs Wills and her brother on the lower slopes, and all walking on to Grindelwald itself for the triumphal reception, with cannons firing and the inhabitants confident that the event would be good for trade.

The village landlord had taken the first opportunity to telegraph the news to Berne. Here the largest telescope in the observatory was trained on the summit, and the 'flagge' and the fir tree were quickly identified, a fact which made the exploit famous in the Swiss capital.

However, it was Wills's own account of the climb, given two years later in *Wanderings among the High Alps*, which made famous this particular ascent of the Hasle Jungfrau, or the Wetterhorn as it soon came to be generally known. The peak dominated what had for more than a century been 'the glacier village', visited by scores of travellers who wished to inspect the Upper and Lower ice-falls. Its ascent could be made without any very great difficulty, and the triumph could happily be seen from the village itself.

During the next few decades Christian Almer became not only the greatest of the Oberland guides but also 'the man of the Wetterhorn' in much the same way that Jacques Balmat had been 'the man of Mont Blanc'. He was soon considering it a bad year in which he did not climb the mountain at least once and it became the tradition to take up a fir tree if possible. As new routes were made on the mountain, as iron stanchions were hammered into the exposed places on the Enge to make their passage less dangerous, and as the Gleckstein cave was replaced by the Gleckstein hut, Almer still remained the man who knew more about the Wetterhorn than anyone else.

In 1896, aged seventy, he made his golden-wedding ascent. His wife Margherita, who had never climbed a snow mountain, was one year older. But a golden-wedding ascent without the bride was unthinkable and the party that set out from Grindelwald on 20 June consisted of Almer and his wife; their eldest daughter; two of their sons; a photographer; and the village doctor. They took things easily up to the Gleckstein hut, spent the night and the whole of the following day there, and started out again soon after midnight on the twenty-second. They were on the top in six hours, and although a high wind and great cold quickly forced them down they stayed long enough on the summit to be photographed.

Almer's anniversary ascent was made as Grindelwald was about to add the

Christian Almer and his wife, aged 70 and 71, photographed in Grindelwald before their Golden Wedding ascent of the Wetterhorn.

Right Luc Meynet, Whymper's hunchback tent-bearer.

winter-sports season to its summer round of glacier visiting and mountain climbing, and from the start of the new century the village took its place with Chamonix and Zermatt. Nearness to Interlaken brought the tourists and the opening of the Jungfrau railway with its branchline between the village and the Kleine Scheidegg greatly increased them. Between the wars Grindelwald became a textbook example of tourist exploitation and today, with urban centre, comfy car parks and chalets climbing the slopes like discarded paper bags on the beach, it provides a useful and impressive warning of the problems that face Alpine authorities.

WHYMPER. SC.

CHAPTER EIGHTEEN

The Matterhorn

There is a great similarity between Zermatt, from which Whymper made the first ascent of the Matterhorn in 1865, and the little Pyrenean town of Lourdes, where seven years earlier a vision of the Blessed Virgin is said to have appeared before Bernadette Soubirous. Whymper has for more than a century been the Bernadette of Zermatt. The Matterhorn is the symbol in the sky, and it is significant that the Michelin Guide speaks of the mountain, seen from the village, as being 'the object of almost religious awe'. Just as Lourdes draws more pilgrims than most shrines in the Catholic landscape, so does Zermatt attract more visitors than most other Alpine magnets. And anyone who can stomach what the honest wish to turn an honest penny has done to Lourdes need not fear that he will shrink from the tourist honeypot of Zermatt. For both have qualities that can, and often do, edge out the banal. Even the least devout, even the most sceptical, feel a catch in the throat and metaphorically reach for their rosaries as the Ave Marias rise and fall. In much the same way no man with a knowledge of mountaineering that goes beyond the ascent of Box Hill can see unmoved the awful, ominous, in some ways unbelievable, first silhouette of the Matterhorn from Zermatt.

For centuries, the village was nothing more than a cluster of houses at the upper end of the long valley – Mattertal, Visptal or Nikolaital according to choice – which runs up southwards from Visp towards the Italian frontier twenty miles away. Between the Matterhorn itself and the massif to the east which culminates in Monte Rosa lies the glacier pass of the Théodule, comparatively easy today and even easier in historical times. Across this there came from the Italian valley of Valtournanche smugglers, hardy travellers and, if legend is to be believed, which is not always the case, even Roman soldiers. Few of them gave more than an apprehensive glance at the Matterhorn, and most who did so crossed themselves and looked hurriedly away.

One of the first men to admire rather than blench was the indefatigable de Saussure who came up the Visptal two years after his ascent of Mont Blanc, and whose men built a shelter on the top of the Théodule. He was in no mind to repeat his exploit on Mont Blanc. 'Its precipitous sides', he wrote of the Matterhorn, 'which give no hold to the very snows, are such as to afford no means of access'. Nearly fifty years later Lord Minto, climbing the Breithorn

Smoke-blackened timbers and new concrete cheek-by-jowl in contemporary Zermatt.

which rises to the east of the Théodule, felt much the same thing: 'It is impossible', he wrote, 'for words to convey any idea of the immensity of this pyramid, regular and symmetrical in form, as if it had been designed by an architect, and rising to a prodigious height above the glacier on which it rests.'

Soon after Minto's time Zermatt itself became more popular. Agassiz and his friends, botanists, map-makers, geologists, all came up the valley. But even in the mid-1840s Desor was able to note that the five or six names before his in the visitor's book of Herr Lauber, the village doctor whose home did duty as an inn, 'all belonged to persons known to me, being Swiss botanists and geologists; decidedly this valley is not yet infested by tourists'.

However, things were moving. In 1854 Lauber sold out to Alexander Seiler, an extraordinary man who looked on hotel-keeping as a vocation rather than a profession and who became a key figure in the Golden Age of mountaineering. Seiler took over what Lauber had called the Hôtel du Cervin – after the French name for the Matterhorn – in the season of 1855. Shortly afterwards a strong English party made the first ascent of the highest point of Monte Rosa. Seiler renamed his hotel and thenceforward the Monte Rosa Hotel steadily evolved into the title of Whymper's famous illustration, *The Club-room of Zermatt*.

Seiler epitomised the philosophy of Zermatt's development during the next hundred years. The village has always wished to attract mountaineers; for the last half-century and more it has also wanted to attract winter-sports enthusiasts; and for a rather shorter period it has found it expedient to attract, in their thousands, those who will never set foot on a mountain top without courtesy of funicular, the devout who come to have their look, to visit the accepted Alpine Stations of the Cross, and to complete successfully another pilgrimage. At the same time it has been felt essential to preserve, and not only in a museum sense, the spirit of times past, so that some flavour of Victorian dawn and desperation still lingers even in the more fashionable sections of Zermatt's main street which tend to evoke Bond Street and Fifth Avenue.

This very human desire to have the cake and eat it has resulted in some compromise. The smoke-blackened timbers of the older Zermatt chalets still crouch beside the new blocks that the tower-cranes erect. Horse-drawn carriages and battery-operated luggage carriers instead of hotel buses await arrivals at the station. And only Valais residents can drive up to Zermatt from St Niklaus, leaving the visitors the choice between shanks' pony and the railway that was opened in 1891.

It is some twenty miles from Visp to Zermatt, another eight across the 10,900 feet Théodule to Breuil. Thus, 'starting at a very early hour from Visp', says Murray, 'the traveller might cross the glaciers of the Cervin on the same day, and reach the chalets of Breuil', striking enough testimony to the animal spirits of 'the good old days'. Today the more normal ascent up the valley starts with parking the car near the station at St Niklaus. Thence onwards and upwards both footpath and train pass first through Randa, then Täsch, villages lying in the deep valley trough, cut off from the Saastal on the east by the Mischabel peaks – including the Dom, the highest mountain entirely in

Switzerland – and from the Val d'Hérens on the west by the Weisshorn and the chain of peaks running south-west to the Dent Blanche. Most of these, together with the rest of the high mountains, are effectively concealed from the valley since the slopes above are convex, with summits and most of the snows lying back, revealing themselves only after a stiff pull-up on tracks which zig-zag over the steep lower pastures. There is a distant glimpse of Breithorn, a fleeting sight of the Weisshorn, and just above Täsch the Zinal-Rothhorn can be seen before the train takes to the trees.

But all these are only glimpses of what the conjuror conceals under the black handkerchief. The first view of the Matterhorn is of a different order, a set-piece filling the end of the valley, a confirmation that mountain topo-graphy can really be what the postcard-makers say it is. But how much is conditioned reflex, how much is the view not of the Matterhorn but of the Matterhorn story? It is difficult to say, even when one turns to Whymper. Writing after the conquest of the mountain, he commented that 'ages hence, generations unborn will gaze upon its awful precipices and wonder at its unique form. However exalted may be their ideas, and however exaggerated their expectations, none will come to return disappointed.' But this was for public consumption. Edward Whymper, coming up the Visptal to Zermatt for the first time in 1860, wrote of the Matterhorn in his diary: 'It may be compared to a sugar loaf set upon a table; the sugar loaf should have its head knocked on one side. Grand it is, but beautiful I think it is not.' Even for Whymper the mountain after its conquest was a different piece of sugar loaf from the mountain seen ten years earlier. For most people the Matterhorn is an emotive obelisk. Its spell increases as they find Zermatt churchyard packed with its victims and on the wall of the Monte Rosa Hotel a simple plaque on which a polo-necked middle-aged man glowers out from an en-circling laurel wreath above one word: 'Whymper'.

It is easy to understand the Matterhorn's basically simple geography. The four-faced rock pyramid rises to a height of 14,782 feet on the Italian-Swiss frontier, the four ridges which divide the faces being the Swiss (north-east) and the Furggen (south-east), uniting at the Swiss summit of the mountain; and the Zmutt (north-west) and Italian (south-west) which unite at the Italian summit. The two tops are joined by a hundred-yard rock-and-snow crest.

The Swiss ridge runs down towards Zermatt, falling steeply at first, levelling out at the shoulder, then descending some thousands of feet before rising to the small peak of the Hörnli. On the left is the Furggen, on the right the Zmutt, both shorter than the Swiss ridge and consequently steeper. Out of sight, on the far side of the mountain and descending from the right-hand, or Italian, summit, there stretches the Italian ridge.

Almost all early attempts to climb the mountain were made from the Italian side, many led by Jean-Antoine Carrel, guide of Valtournanche. His aim was to be first on the top, not only as a personal exploit but for the future fame of his valley. Carrel and a party of local men reached about 12,650 feet on the Matterhorn in 1860. The following year Tyndall climbed some three

Plaque on the wall of Zermatt's Monte Rosa Hotel showing Edward Whymper.

Jean-Antoine Carrel, known as the 'Bersagliere'.

245

hundred feet higher, with Carrel's help, and in 1861 Edward Whymper made his first attempt. He failed to get as high as Tyndall. At one point in the contest, in which each party tended to leapfrog the other's earlier efforts, Carrel, going higher than all others, carved his initials on the rocks as a sign of conquest.

Whymper had first come to the Alps in 1860. A businessman-cum-artist aged twenty, he had been commissioned by William Longman to supply drawings for a volume of *Peaks, Passes and Glaciers*, and the work soon roused his passion for mountain scrambling. Like many other climbers of the day, his main interest was in being first, and his obsession with the Matter-horn brought him up hard against Carrel – and, to a lesser extent, against Tyndall, who in 1861 had been first on the Weisshorn, the other great peak that attracted Whymper's special attention.

After the failure of 1861 Whymper returned the following summer to make five attempts on the Matterhorn. On the third he climbed alone, since Carrel and the other guides were occupied in their work-a-day non-guiding duties. This time, climbing in solitary state, he reached 13,400 feet, only some 1,300 feet below the summit, higher than any man had gone before. A few days later Tyndall beat him by five hundred feet.

The following year, 1863, Whymper made another unsuccessful attempt but by the summer of 1865 no one had got higher than Tyndall. In June Whymper tried again and failed again. It was beginning to look as though the Matterhorn might not be for climbing after all.

Then in July chance drew to this one small corner of the Alps four separate parties whose comings and goings have in retrospect an almost contrived air. Few playwrights, assembling characters for a drama, would have dared to create the series of chance encounters which were now to settle the fate of the Matterhorn. Rarely has life aped art so well, providing unity of place, action and time; providing both Whymper and Carrel, locked in rivalry both with themselves and with the mountain. As secondary issues Carrel climbs for the sake of the newly born Italy and the two innkeepers, Seiler at Zermatt and Favre at Breuil await the outcome with commercial interest like stock minor characters to off-set the rising tension. Time after time, moreover, conversa-tion and detailed incident, recorded by those present, have the extraordinary character of dramatic dialogue and fictitious event.

Unknown to Whymper, Carrel had earlier in the summer of 1865 been hired by a group of Italians who wished to make the first ascent of the moun-tain. He had, naturally enough in the circumstances, concealed the fact from Whymper. Thus in the first half of July Whymper was unexpectedly left cooling his heels in Breuil when he had hoped to be out on the Matterhorn with Carrel once more. Far worse, as he realised on the morning of the eleventh, Carrel was working with a strong rival party for whom a supply of rope and provisions had been cached high on the mountain some days previously. 'Bamboozled and humbugged', as he described himself, he was now helpless, with no other guide in the valley willing to jeopardise the success of the Italian party. The weather was set fair; and Whymper's hopes

Edward Whymper (1840–1911) – the youth of twenty-five.

of four years were apparently to be frustrated here as they had been on the Weisshorn.

This would have been enough to deter most men. It might even have deterred Whymper had not a *deus ex machina* arrived over the Théodule from Zermatt in the person of Lord Francis Douglas. A brilliant but relatively inexperienced mountaineer, Douglas was told by Whymper of what had happened. Then Douglas mentioned, almost in passing, that one of the Zermatt guides believed a route might be found up the Swiss ridge of the Matterhorn.

The idea was not really very startling. For the Swiss ridge from Zermatt is seen end-on, and foreshortening thus adds greatly to its appearance of steepness. Whymper had at first been as deceived as most other mountaineers, only after some while had he noticed that snow lay all the year round on parts of the east face which spread out to the left of the ridge. That suggested that the ridge itself was not as steep as it looked, and only the apparent smoothness of the rock – smooth when compared with the broken formation of the Italian ridge – had prevented him from investigating further. But now Old Peter Taugwalder – 'old' to distinguish him from his son, Young Peter – had according to Douglas been some way up the Swiss ridge. And Taugwalder had discovered for himself that the Swiss ridge was not as steep as it looked.

At nine the following morning, 12 July, Whymper and Douglas left the Valtournanche for Zermatt, determined to try the Matterhorn together from the Swiss side. They descended from the Théodule to the Schwarzsee and cached at the little chapel there the supplies of rope and food they would need the following day. Then they continued down to Zermatt, checked in with Seiler, sought out Old Peter, and arranged with him to start for the Matterhorn the following day, Thursday the thirteenth.

And in Zermatt, sitting on the guide's wall before the Monte Rosa, Whymper found Michel Croz, the Chamonix guide who had accompanied him on more than one first ascent during the last few years.

Both Whymper and Croz must have sensed that the other was in Zermatt for only one thing. Croz admitted that he was setting out for the Matterhorn the following morning and shortly afterwards, Whymper saw Croz's new employer come into the long *salle-à-manger*. This was the Rev. Charles Hudson, believed by some to have been the finest mountaineer of the day, a muscular Christian who had been known to walk eighty-six miles in twenty-four hours without undue effort. With Hudson, just twenty-seven, was Douglas Hadow, only nineteen, whom Hudson was introducing to the Alps. Strangely, and with what seems in retrospect to have been some rashness, Hudson was about to introduce him to the Matterhorn.

Now that the Swiss ridge of the Matterhorn has become an Alpine trade route in good conditions – more than a hundred climbers sometimes reach the summit in a single day – the idea that it might be dangerous for two separate parties to be on the ridge at the same time is difficult to understand. Yet a century ago the route was looser than it is today and the hazards were

Above Lord Francis Douglas (1847–1865), one of the three British mountaineers killed in the Matterhorn disaster of 1865; *below* the Rev. Charles Hudson (1828–1865), also a victim of the disaster.

Douglas Hadow (1846–1865), the third victim of the Matterhorn disaster.

virtually unknown. Whymper therefore suggested that Hudson's party and his own should join forces. But he asked what the young Hadow had done in the Alps. Hudson's reply – 'Mr Hadow has done Mont Blanc in less time than most men' – gave a proof of stamina if not of rock-climbing experience. Thus it was settled.

Dawn broke on Thursday, 13 July, with the promise of a diamond-sharp day and soon afterwards the party left the village – Whymper and Lord Francis Douglas, Hudson and Hadow, accompanied by Michel Croz, Old Peter and two of his sons, Joseph and Young Peter, who were expected to go only to the bivouac site.

From the first all went well. They picked up the loads cached at the Schwarzsee the previous afternoon and were soon on the Swiss ridge. Higher up, where they were forced out on to the east face, their beliefs were confirmed. Instead of rising vertically, it sloped back at a considerable angle. As Whymper put it, places which had looked impracticable from below were 'so easy that we could *run about*'.

He appears to have felt only one anxiety and it had nothing to do with the ease or difficulty of the rocks. From time to time he would stop to scan the summit. He did not know what progress the Italians might have made and half-feared the sight of their figures against the sky.

The party camped at about 11,000 feet and with today's experience it seems surprising that they did not press on to the summit that day. But the Matter-horn was still the Matterhorn. Croz and Young Peter, who reconnoitred up above the campsite, reported that the going was still easy; even so they decided to bivouac.

They spent a leisurely twelve hours. Then, soon after 3 am, they set out. Joseph Taugwalder turned back to Zermatt but his brother went on with the rest. The tent was bundled up for Joseph to carry down, but the guides insisted on taking one of the tentpoles. Victory demanded a flag and a flag demanded a flagpole. Whymper protested that this was tempting providence. For once he was disobeyed.

The weather was still perfect, one of those rare days when it is literally possible to light a match on a mountain top and watch the flame burn steady. Quite soon it was clear that most of the upper slopes were little different from the lower – 'a huge natural staircase' as Whymper described them. This was of course a mountaineer's phrase. Even so the rocks were far easier than they had dared hope. Only on the last seven hundred feet or so, where the peak appeared to bend over eastwards like a breaking wave frozen solid, did it seem that difficulties would force them over on to the north face.

It was ten o'clock before they reached the foot of these steepening rocks. At 14,000 feet they were higher – they hoped – than any men had yet been on the Matterhorn. Here they stopped for nearly an hour. Then they roped up – for the first time – and Croz led the way out on to the uppermost seven hundred feet of the mountain's north face.

It was not so much the steepness of the rock as its character which de-manded care. Sheltered from most of the sun, the face held the snow, hard

frozen lumps of it which tended to fill what would otherwise have been hand-
and foot-holds. Below, nothing was to be seen until the eye met the crevasse-
crinkled stretches of the Matterhorn glacier 4,000 feet beneath.

Croz cut steps where necessary. Everyone moved with care, traversing
across the slope for some four hundred feet until the best way upwards was
reached. Then they edged back towards the ridge. It was nearly 1.30 when
they reached it, almost an hour and a half since they had started off across
the face. There was a difficult corner to turn ; then, beyond it, a snow-ridge
sloped gradually upwards towards the sky. There was nothing higher beyond,
and for once all the conventions between guide and master broke down.
Croz, Whymper and Hudson unroped and raced for the top.

'At 1.40 pm the world was at our feet', Whymper wrote, 'and the Matterhorn
was conquered.'

There was no sign of the Italians. But when they walked along the ridge-
pole summit peak to the Italian top they saw them, more than 1,000 feet lower
down – a party so dispirited at the sight of the victors that they decided to retreat.

The English built a cairn. They marvelled at the view, so clear that Monte
Viso, a hundred miles off, could be seen rising clearly above the Italian plain.

The Matterhorn.

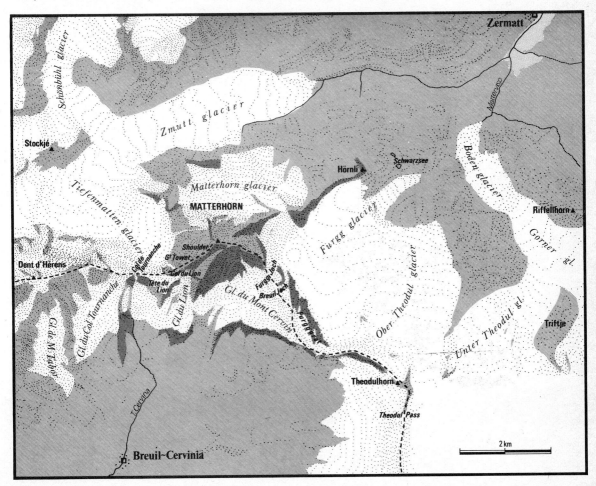

249

Gustav Doré's famous if fanciful engravings showing the final stages in the first ascent of the Matterhorn; and the disastrous mishap on the descent of the mountain.

They planted the tentpole as a flagpost and Croz took off his blue Savoyard smock and hung it in place as a flag. Whymper and his companions spent an hour on the summit. Then they turned to the descent.

There has been a vast amount of learned exegesis on the order in which the members of the party roped up, on the particular ways in which the three different ropes were used, and on the ultimate responsibility for what was about to happen. The most important lesson is that it was a divided party with neither Whymper nor Hudson fully in control.

Croz went first and after him Hadow. Behind Hadow there was Hudson, in the best position to safeguard a novice whose lack of experience was beginning to show. Lord Francis Douglas came fourth with Old Peter Taugwalder at the end of the rope. These five left the summit first. Whymper stayed behind for a moment with Taugwalder's son, to whom he was roped, and then followed the rest of the party, Young Peter bringing up the rear.

The couple reached their companions at the top of the difficult section and tied on to the rest of the party.

Then they all began to move cautiously down, Croz stopping at times and turning round to help place Hadow's feet in their holds. No one spoke, and the silence was broken only by the occasional chink of ice-axe on rock. At the back of the party Whymper and the young Taugwalder could see little of what was happening. All seemed to be secure.

Then, without warning, Hadow and Croz were out of their steps. Their weight dragged down Hudson and the combined weight of the three men

250

pulled down Lord Francis Douglas. The rope between Lord Francis and the elder Taugwalder parted with a snap that Whymper was to remember for the rest of his life.

'For a few seconds we saw our unfortunate companions sliding downwards on their backs, spreading out their hands, endeavouring to save themselves,' he wrote. 'They passed from our sight uninjured, disappeared one by one, and fell from precipice to precipice on to the Matterhorngletscher below, a distance of nearly 4,000 feet in height.'

Whymper and the two Taugwalders, appalled at the accident, moved only slowly down the mountain, reaching the easier slopes so late that they had to bivouac once more. Only on the Saturday morning did they arrive back in Zermatt, Whymper going to his room in the Monte Rosa followed by Seiler who eventually asked: 'What is the matter?'

'The Taugwalders and I have returned,' he replied.

The following day the bodies of Hudson, Hadow and Croz were recovered. That of Lord Francis Douglas was never found. A few days later a Court of Enquiry was held in Zermatt, and here it was disclosed that the cause of the accident appeared to have been a slip by Hadow, whose feet seem to have caught Croz in the small of the back and knocked him from his steps. More important was the revelation that the broken rope, the one which had linked Douglas and Old Peter, was the weakest of three in use on the mountain. Old Peter could easily live down the ridiculous rumour that he had 'cut the rope'; but it was not so simple to rebut the accusation that he had deliberately used a weak rope to link himself with the man next below him on the mountain. Even so evidence and argument lead to an entirely different conclusion: that in the exultation of victory and the confusion of divided command the rope was simply the first that had come to hand.

The death of three Britons and a guide following an already dramatic ascent gave the Matterhorn a notoriety not lessened by the fact that one of the victims was the heir to the Marquess of Queensberry. If it did not, as once claimed, 'set back mountaineering by a whole generation of men', the accident did throw a dark shadow over the sport and bring down the denunciations of the press, popular and otherwise. Thus *The Times* demanded to know what a climber was really seeking. 'What is he doing there, and what right has he to throw away the gift of life and ten thousand golden opportunities in an emulation which he only shares with skylarks, apes, cats and squirrels?' The criticisms continued, although some of them were dissipated five years later when Whymper published his own story in *Scrambles amongst the Alps*, a book which quickly became the best-known mountain epic in the English language.

The Matterhorn disaster gave the Swiss ridge a reputation for difficulty which it did not deserve. Carrel reached the summit by the Italian ridge four days after Whymper. And following a year in which the mountain was left severely alone, three more ascents from Breuil were made in 1867, two by guided English parties and one by Italian guides. But only in 1868 was the second ascent made from Zermatt. Two days later Tyndall climbed the mountain from Breuil and descended by the Swiss ridge.

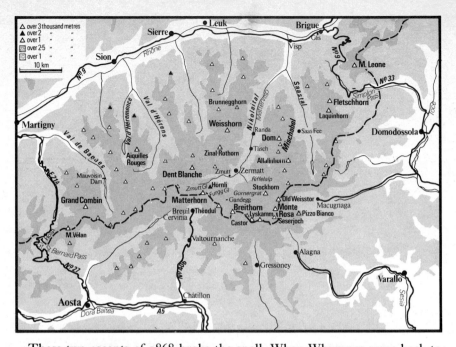

The Central Pennine Alps.

These two ascents of 1868 broke the spell. When Whymper came back to the Matterhorn again in 1874, especially to take photographs, his ascent was the seventy-sixth, and the mountain had already been the target for other firsts. Two years after Lucy Walker's first ascent by a lady in 1871 – and Miss Brevoort's first lady's traverse a few weeks later – Anna and Ellen Pigeon made the first lady's traverse from Breuil to Zermatt, guided by Carrel and Victor Macquignaz; unable to reach the hut by this time built on the Swiss ridge, they spent the night in the open at about 11,000 feet. In 1876 three Englishmen climbed the mountain without guides and six years later Vittorio Sella, in an epic expedition from Breuil, made the first winter ascent. Children climbed the Matterhorn; men climbed it alone; one guide climbed it twice in a single day and another climbed it more than a hundred times. There have also been record-breaking efforts like that of the American who raced up from the hut on the Hörnli in 1930. He took one hour and fifty minutes to reach the top, spent ten minutes on the summit, then returned to the Hörnli in one hour and five minutes, taking three hours five minutes for the journey, hut back to hut. 'The guide was ill for several days after,' noted the *Alpine Journal*, 'and for such crimes the ordinary death penalty is inadequate.'

As early as the 1880s competition between the Swiss and the Italian routes had inspired a table game 'Up, Up the Matterhorn', consisting of a cardboard peak, a dozen tin figures, half guides and half travellers, and a dice.

It was not only the two main routes on the mountain that were soon part of the Matterhorn's history. The north-western or Zmutt ridge with its huge overhanging face, the Nose of Zmutt, was climbed by Mummery in 1879. The Furggen, its counterpart on the left-hand skyline as seen from Zermatt, held out until 1911 although Mummery climbed all but the difficult central section in 1880, and at the turn of the century Guido Rey, whose passion for

The walls of the Pelmo rising above the village of Selva di Cadore.

252

the mountain 'set him aflame', descended the Furggen's difficult pitch on a doubled rope so that his hands were the first to touch the whole ridge. There were also the faces. Simple study of a pyramid shows that a face is, overall, steeper than either of the ridges which contain it; and on a mountain it is apt to be swept by debris coming from both of them. Yet all the four faces of the Matterhorn were scaled in due course; the west or Tiefenmatten face by a lone ascent in 1929, the north and south faces in 1931 and the east face a year later. In 1941, the ultimate came with an ascent *'en spirale'*, involving an ascent to the shoulder on the Swiss ridge, then a traverse round the four faces of the mountain back to the shoulder. In 1959 the north face was climbed solo.

Since Whymper and his ill-fated party stood on the summit many huts have been built on the Matterhorn. The first was the rough refuge at the Cravate on the Italian ridge, built in 1867, followed the next year by a similar shelter on the Swiss ridge. In 1880 there came the Hörnli hut; then a hut on the Italian ridge built at the Great Tower, followed by the Luigi Amadeo hut. During the First World War the Solvay hut, high up on the Swiss ridge, was built as an emergency refuge for those caught by bad weather.

Fixed ropes have been placed in numbers. In good weather the Swiss ridge is a trade route, but year by year the Matterhorn claims a deathroll second only to that of Mont Blanc. A metal cross was carried to the summit in 1902 and in 1965, to celebrate the centenary of the first ascent, a television team reached the top and showed other parties arriving.

On and around the mountain the railways and téléphériques have spread. At the end of the line which takes nearly a million passengers a year to the Gornergrat, that Pennine grandstand with its panorama of Monte Rosa, Breithorn and Matterhorn, enclosed cable-cabins serve a system ending on the Stockhorn. From the southern end of Zermatt a second system runs to the Schwarzsee and a massive self-service restaurant, the concrete block-houses of the cable-way termini and a desolation of construction must all be kept carefully outside photographs of the little chapel where Whymper and Lord Francis cached their supplies. One branch runs to the Trockener Steg, well on the way to the Théodule, and plans are in hand for continuation to the crest of the pass, thus linking it with the Italian cable-way which has served the frontier from Breuil for more than a quarter of a century.

Yet whatever new progress is made in the *vulgarisation des montagnes*, interest obstinately returns to the first ascent of the Matterhorn. Even the least morbid visitor is drawn to the churchyard where the graves of Hadow and Hudson lie; and where by ironic chance there lie the remains of Chamonix-born Michel Croz while Whymper's body rests in Chamonix. One radio play, two films and two novels have been written about the accident as well as several histories. One book of engravings showing nothing but the mountain, one book of photographs, Charles Gos's *Le Cervin*, a breviary of Matterhorn miscellanea, and Guido Rey's magnificent book about the peak return to it again and again as the main theme. The discothèques and the Bar-Dancings exist not only in the shadow of the mountain but because of it. In some ways Zermatt exemplifies the triumph of Matterhorn over matter.

Mont Blanc seen across the Chamonix valley from the summit of the Brévent.

CHAPTER NINETEEN

The Meije and Dauphiné

The approach to the Dauphiné, that island-like knot of peaks which stands apart from the main Alpine chain in the south-west of France, can be the most depressing of any mountain approach in the world. Grenoble is one of the finest cities in Europe, a mountain capital with peak or peaklet at the end of each fine street; but between Grenoble and La Bérarde, the village tucked away between the arms of the main horseshoe of peaks, there lies what Michelin calls *le couloir industriel de la Romanche*, the fifteen-mile stretch of the once glorious river-valley fed by the snows of the Dauphiné.

The Romanche was exploited during the closing years of the last century and the first years of the present when it was most economic to utilise electric power where it was created. This particular area of France could produce vast quantities of 'white oil', the hydro-power that was later to be responsible for damming so many upper valleys. But before the grid, industry came to the power rather than the reverse; and along the Romanche valley, notably between Séchilienne and Rochetaillée, there grew up the complex of electro-chemical and electro-metallurgical works that blacken and brown the air, produce a pollution worthy of Britain's Black Country or Los Angeles, and suggest once again that if the conservationists are to save what is left of the Alps they will have to move fast.

Beyond the industrial corridor is the small provincial town of Bourg d' Oisans, and beyond Bourg lie the mountains. They rise in a huge U-shaped ridge whose ends curl round to give a horseshoe impression on the map. Striking up between the two limbs of the U runs the Vénéon Valley, still granted only the narrowest of lines on the motoring maps, and leading to La Bérarde, in its own quiet way still one of the pleasantest centres in the Alps. Beyond La Bérarde, close under the bottom of the U, rises the beautiful peak of Les Bans. From the northern limb of the U – which gives off a spur to carry the Pelvoux, for long thought to be the highest peak in France – rises the Écrins, highest of all the Dauphiné mountains but difficult to see from the valley-floor; then, after a succession of minor summits, the huge rock wall of the Meije, only slightly lower than the Écrins, a mountain in some ways even more forbidding in appearance than the Matterhorn.

But it is not from Vénéon Valley that the Meije appears at its most im-

Les Ecrins – one of Vittorio Sella's most dramatic photographs.

257

The Meije as drawn by one of its earliest explorers, the Victorian scientist T.G. Bonney (1832–1921)

pressive. The most spectacular view is from the Grenoble-Briançon highway over the Col du Lautaret, one of the few trunk routes from which it is possible to get such an impressive portrait of a great peak. The Lautaret road rises past the Barrage du Chambon, where the snow run-off during one part of the year is held back to work the turbines during winter, and reaches La Grave half-way to the col.

Few mountain walls overshadow the onlooker as the Meije overshadows La Grave. Even from the slopes above the village, where the Chazelet Oratoire stands and from Les Terrasses higher up, the mountain dominates the landscape to the south with its overwhelming personality. To the left is the western peak from which a rocky crest runs to the Pic Central, then on to the eastern and highest summit, also known as the Grand Pic de la Meije, and the Doigt de Dieu. Beyond that the ridge drops steeply towards the Brèche de la Meije, a huge sabre-cut dividing the mountain from the Rateau and reminiscent of the Brèche de Roland in the Pyrenees. From this rocky skyline a frieze of steep slopes drops to snowfields which break into steep glaciers, seamed with crevasses and streaming down towards the valley some thousands of feet below.

The Meije not only looks, but is, formidable, and from the southern side the prospect is little better. This distant face of the mountain can be seen by returning down the Lautaret road, then following up the Vénéon Valley through the village of St Christophe to La Bérarde, whence the Étançons Glen leads up under the southern slopes of the mountain. Here, on the left this time, is the now familiar Brèche de la Meije, first crossed from La Grave to La Bérarde by Whymper, Moore and Walker in 1864. This southern aspect of the Meije presents a face very different but just as vertical, just as repellent or attractive according to taste. The only glacier of note is the tiny hanging Glacier Carré, a pocket-handkerchief of white high up on the face.

While the Valais, the Bernese Oberland and Mont Blanc were all being opened up by mountaineers during the 1850s, this corner of the Alps had only a minor trickle of visitors. Forbes, coming to La Bérarde in 1839, was the first Briton to visit the hamlet. Not many followed in his footsteps. Some valleys remained totally unvisited. When Whymper first arrived in 1861 the only available map was nearly a century old and totally unreliable, while a decade later – when Chamonix, Zermatt and Grindelwald had all become flourishing centres – the few inns in the Dauphiné were 'often filthy beyond description. Rest is seldom obtained in their beds, or decent food found in their kitchens, and guides there are none.'

Whymper's party, having crossed the Brèche de la Meije to La Bérarde, 'a miserable village, without interest, without commerce, and almost without population', went on to make the first ascent of the Écrins. But they left the Meije severely alone. So did everyone else until Coolidge and his aunt arrived in La Grave in 1870.

Coolidge was just twenty, his aunt forty-five. With them as guides they had Christian Almer and Christian's son Ulrich, with a Grindelwald man as porter. They also had Tschingel, who if she was not to reach the top of the Meije was certainly to go higher on it than any dog had ever gone before. There was something slightly outrageous in such a party tackling a peak from which some of the most experienced mountaineers of the day had steered away carefully.

We mounted grass slopes, rocks, moraine, and a little bit of glacier to get to our bivouac which we reached about five. [Coolidge subsequently wrote to his mother]. The afternoon was very hot and we walked very slowly. The men made a flat space for the tent, and turfed it. Then the tent was erected. None of us slept very much, as a wind rose in the night and blew about the canvas of the tent. Yesterday, i.e. Tuesday morning, we left our tent in charge of Tschingel who had accompanied us thus far ... We arrived at the edge of the bergschrund defending the base of the final peak and after some little trouble succeeded in crossing it. Then followed a snow-slope gradually increasing in inclination, ending in a patch of rocks followed by a few steps in bare ice. This Christian considered the most dangerous part of the expedition, especially when we descended it.

We had now arrived at a narrow col between the two teeth of the highest (as we supposed) summit. Turning to the right, we proceeded to wriggle up rocks so steep and smooth that they resembled the rocks of the Matterhorn with the exception that the latter have ropes, the former none. At length to our great joy we gained the summit at 12.10. Imagine our horror at seeing the right-hand peak apparently nearly the same height as ours. Christian decided that it was about twenty feet higher than ours, though I do not agree with him, but think it slightly lower than ours. The French map apparently makes a difference of 250 feet in favour of the right-hand peak, which is manifestly absurd. We built a stone man and left at 12.50.

This was not the first ascent of the Meije. But it was the first ascent of the Pic Central, separated from the highest summit by a ridge which appeared to be extraordinarily difficult. It was a great achievement for Miss Brevoort as well as for her nephew, and from now on her heart was set on the peak. Both returned more than once within the next few years to a La Bérarde that still retained the atmosphere of more primitive days. Once their party had to sleep above the animals in a barn owned by the Rodier who had been one of Forbes's guides more than thirty years earlier – and who still claimed that on a journey to the Midi he himself had seen men with one eye set in the middle of their foreheads.

In the summer of 1876 Coolidge and his aunt were of course in the Alps; but

Miss Brevoort, chaperoning a young niece, was tied to Belalp above the Rhône Valley and her nephew alone arrived beneath the Meije. By this time La Bérarde and La Grave were becoming like Zermatt a decade earlier as attempts on the Matterhorn were nearing their climax. The Pic Central had been reached again more than once. Both British and French parties had tried to discover a way of reaching the Grand Pic which was by now known to be considerably higher. In 1876 the bees were buzzing in numbers round the honeypot.

Coolidge, telling his aunt in a letter that he would let her have news without delay of what happened, received an anguished reply: 'I foresee what your telegram will be,' it went. 'Alas! Alas! and to think of all the others who will be coming and of the *one* who may succeed. Dear Will, give my love to all my dear old friends now in your sight, and especially to that glorious Meije and ask her to keep herself for me.'

That summer everyone again failed to climb the Meije. The following winter Miss Brevoort died, unexpectedly, of rheumatic fever – ironically enough on the day that she received a letter from Henri Duhamel, one of her rivals for the Meije, enclosing a photograph of himself and asking for one of her.

The next summer, in July 1877, Coolidge travelled out to the Dauphiné alone, determined to climb the Grand Pic if not for his own sake then at least in memory of his aunt. The previous month, he learned, the thirteenth and fourteenth attempts had been made by Lord Wentworth. The French were around in force, among them Duhamel and Émmanuel Boileau de Castelnau.

On the twenty-second he left La Bérarde with the two Almers. They reached the Brèche and they tackled the arête as before. Like everyone before them, they got so far and no farther. Coolidge returned: first to La Bérarde and later to London, perhaps not satisfied that the Meije would never be climbed, but confident that it would not be climbed for some time. Only a few weeks later he received news from the Dauphiné: Boileua de Castelnau, with Pierre Gaspard and his son, two local guides from La Bérarde, had got to the top.

This final conquest of the Meije involved some of the most difficult rock-climbing that had so far been carried out in the Alps, in circumstances that pushed the climb well beyond the limits of what was then usually considered justifiable. Early in August de Castelnau and the Gaspards had reached a spot on the mountain higher than anyone before them. Then they had once more been stopped – but not before leaving a strategically placed fixed rope. Later in the month they again reached the same place. Then, above it, they reached the Glacier Carré, the small hanging glacier which is such a prominent feature of the mountain from the Étançons Glen.

Arriving at the farthest edge of the glacier we found ourselves on a little col from which we could see the valley of La Grave, towards which there sloped down a couloir of vertical ice [de Castelnau wrote]. Turning to the right we climbed very rapidly and without difficulty the peak properly called the Meije, keeping all the time on the southern slope of the mountain. Our enemy seemed vanquished until, only a dozen yards from the summit, an unexpected obstacle made us doubt of success. The mountain overhangs on all sides; in other words the line of slabs formed a curve in whose concavity we now found ourselves. To begin with, our efforts were fruitless. Gaspard the elder made the first attempt, and cleared three or four yards. Arrived at that height he found it impossible to advance or retreat; he called on us to give him help and I was able to do so by standing on the shoulders of his son. I arrived just in time, for his strength was running out. Then I tried in my turn but without any more success; then Gaspard the younger succeeded in reaching a point a little higher, but we saw that it would be so difficult to help him to retreat that we signalled him back. He was so exhausted with his efforts that when he got back he was unable to move his limbs and collapsed in tears, so great had been the demands on his nervous energy. Then all three of us, pale and trembling, started to console each other.

The cold was so strong that it drained our energy. The clouds, driven by a wind so violent that it threatened to blow us over, completely enveloped us. We descended a few yards more, ready to give up the struggle after having come to within five or six yards of the summit. Gaspard, furious that his efforts had come to nothing, suggested that we try turning the peak by the north face if that were possible. With great difficulty we did so, clearing a very bad patch in the process. But this time success crowned our perseverance and, at 3.30, we stepped on to the summit having spent two hours in conquering the last few yards.

Gaspard, overjoyed, and with memories of the Oberland and Chamonix men who had been with the English, exclaimed exultantly: 'No foreign guide has got here first.' Then they all set about building a cairn – believing that their success might not be acknowledged if they failed to do so.

Before they could begin the descent, they had to sacrifice a length of rope to negotiate the most difficult pitch. They moved slowly, in what was soon the gathering dusk, feeling their way down rocks that had been difficult enough to ascend in broad daylight.

For a second time they had to leave a fixed rope. Then, unable to see any more, they tied themselves to the rocks, divided out the last of the brandy, and prepared for a night during which the temperature dropped to eleven degrees below zero. About ten o'clock snow began to fall. The heat of their bodies melted it on their clothes; then it froze again, so that soon all three found it difficult to move their limbs within a casing of ice.

First light came at four o'clock and they were soon painfully on the move. For a third time a length of rope had to be sacrificed at a difficult spot. After that they were soon down, first to an *al fresco* breakfast at the head of the Étançons Glen and then on to La Bérarde.

As with other great peaks, one route led to more. The year after Boileau de Castelnau's ascent, the eastern peak was climbed. The Grand Pic was climbed without guides by an English party the following year, and over the decades the peaks, ridges and faces of the Meije became as criss-crossed with routes as others in the Alps. Less than a century ago, when Boileau de Castelnau and the Gaspards at last succeeded, the ways up various parts of the Meije could be counted on the fingers of one hand. Today, the 105 routes up the Groupe de la Meije fill fifty-nine pages of the Groupe de Haute Montagne's guide.

CHAPTER TWENTY

The Pelmo

On the footpath that leads from Cortina, over the Faleria, and down to the Tre Croci Pass, there is a stretch where the view to the south dramatically opens up. Like many around Cortina, it merits most of the travel-merchant adjectives. It is breath-taking, incomparable, magnificent and awe-inspiring; in fact it is rather good, and something more than the almost run-of-the-mill magnificence of the Dolomites. For away slightly west of south there rises something entirely different from the typical mountain spires of the area; something in contrast to Mr Murray's lyrical description of 'sharp peaks or horns, sometimes rising up in pinnacles and obelisks, at others extending in serrated ridges, teethed like the jaw of an alligator; now fencing in the valley with an escarped precipice many thousand feet high, and often cleft with numerous fissures, all running vertically'.

This description is true enough of most Dolomite mountains. The Vajolet Towers in the Rosengarten and the Drei Zinnen above Misurina protrude from the scree as bare rocky teeth which might have been created purely to test the cragsman's ability on vertical rock.

It is certainly true that the Langkofel springs from a foreground of genuinely Alpine meadows. The Brenta Dolomites, among the most westerly, emerge from a rich forested landscape. Yet a majority of the Dolomites do give the impression of gigantic exercise grounds for the rock expert rather than of mountains as the word is understood in other parts of the Alps.

But there are exceptions. One of them can be seen from the Faleria path. Here is what appears to be a broad buttress of a mountain, apparently plateau-topped with a summit shooting up from its western edge; a mass, moreover, which stands apart from its outliers as though keeping them at regal arm's-length. This is the Pelmo, the first of the great Dolomite mountains to be climbed. Closer acquaintance increases rather than diminishes its presence.

A century ago John Ball, who climbed it in 1857, noted in his Guide that it 'shows as a gigantic fortress of the most massive architecture, not fretted into minarets and pinnacles, like most of its rivals, but merely defended by huge bastioned earthworks, whose walls in many places fall in sheer precipices more than 2,000 feet'. This is the impression both from the north-west, where the Val Fiorentina runs up through a string of hamlets from Selva di Cadore,

'…. it was impossible to pass ….' The traverse on the Pelmo.

and from Zoppe to the south. But it is not only impressive form and a land-mark position in the climbing history of the Dolomites that makes the Pelmo of interest, for it stands in an area which has undergone quicker and more violent transformation than any in the Alps. For long it was only these Ampezzo Dolomites, soaring upwards within view of the main road from Venice to Vienna, that were considered worthy of the traveller's comment, and as late as the early years of the present century Coolidge was told that 'there were no Dolomites save in the neighbourhood of Cortina'. Despite this comparative renown, the Pelmo and its surrounding peaks had a hundred years ago the double enchantment of Stephen's Dolomites to the south-west. 'Some strange magic had held the Alpine Club at a distance and, what was more provoking, had cast a profound drowsiness over the dwellers at their feet, and almost prevented them from raising their eyes to these wild summits, or bestowing names on them.' All this when Zermatt, Grindelwald and Chamonix were rustling alive to the name of Mr Cook.

But just as the Dolomites were roused late from their happy lack of history, so was the thoroughness of their transformation very quick when it did start. After the end of the First World War, when the frontier was thrust north to make Cortina and Bolzano Italian, great efforts were made to capitalise the area's possibilities. The advent of Mussolini, and the modernising of the Dolomite road as a major attraction, carried the process a step further and such efforts were doubled and redoubled after 1945. Thus the Dolomites are today perhaps more tourist-conscious, more apt to present their peaks on a visual platter, than any other mountains between the Maritimes and the Julians. Despite this, the charm hangs on in many places, and nowhere more tenaciously than round the Pelmo.

The mountain can be viewed to advantage from Selva di Cadore, virtually on the road which runs from Caprile up over the Giau Pass *en route* to Cortina, or from Borca di Cadore on the eastern side of the peak, where John Ball prepared for his climb in September 1857. From both places the horizontal terraces which break up the face are very prominent; many are wide enough to give easy passage to experienced mountaineers and long before 1857 the local chamois-hunters had become familiar with many routes along and across them.

One such hunter accompanied Ball as he left Borca in the early hours of 19 September. With the assiduous observation of most Victorians, Ball noted that 'Venus rose behind a rock so bright as to throw a decided shadow. Jupiter overhead.' Then, as the dawn came up, they reached a shepherd's hut which Ball claimed was housing five hundred sheep, many goats, some pigs, four men and two boys. One knows how he felt.

Here he carried out the equivalent of changing into his climbing gear. What he did, in his own words, was to screw in points to his boots, a job which took him half an hour and is a good indication of contemporary equipment.

From here the outlook was distinctly unpromising. Above them, the south face rose in long battlemented cascades for some 5,000 feet. Up these, passing from ledge to ledge, many laden with the debris of earlier rock falls, the two men slowly made their way for an hour and a half.

'You soon come to a place', Ball noted, 'which my guide expected was to turn me back. The ledge gives way, and there are a few broken pieces below by which you pass and regain it.' Here he unslung his botanical box, unwound his plaid, and the guide stowed them in a cranny in the rocks.

The ledge now took them round three deep bays – 'tolerable footing except here and there', as Ball describes it. In the third, he goes on, 'is the *pons asinorum*. The rock projects, leaving the shelf but $1\frac{1}{2}$ feet high. The guide, leaving traps, went forward to see how the land lay. After a few minutes he returned, saying that it was impossible to pass, that the "croda" had given way on the other side, which before had offered assistance.'

It is possible that this was so. But it seems more likely that the local hunter-cum-guide had made extravagant claims in the hope that his client would call a halt once he saw the difficulties. He had reckoned without John Ball.

We examined the face of the bay below us to see if it were possible to reach another more practicable ledge, but no go [Ball went on]. Before giving it up I said I would look, and I found that I could pass, which I did, leaving one leg outside to catch the edges. The guide passed the traps in succession on to me, and followed, absolutely crawling on his face; it is too low for hands and knees, which serve in another place.

The guide told me [he says], that that was as far as we could go, and on my pointing to a ridge terminating in a rock eighty or a hundred feet higher, he said there was no use in going there, as the view was interrupted by a higher and inaccessible point. I said, 'Let us go there at all events.' The rock and another immediately behind were very shattered. I began to examine them to see if I could not manage to ascend. The guide implored me to desist, saying it was *croda morta*, not *viva*, very unsafe, etc. I assured him I would run no risk, and began to remove all moveable pieces of rock, and then found the thing quite manageable, and proceeded, in spite of renewed entreaties from the guide. This was the very top ridge. With a little caution in passing from one jagged and rotten tooth to another I gained the ridge – easy and safe, about two hundred yards long.

The character of the ascent now changed, the route going up over scree, easier ridges and patches of snow. Above this, steeper snow led up on to a small platform from which Ball could look towards the Antelao and, in the other direction, down and across the Valle di Zoldo.

Ball surveyed the view, noted that he had seen pine needles about a thousand feet below leaves of larch and even of beech, and recorded the presence of many ptarmigan. By early afternoon they were down without difficulty.

Today both the Val Fiorentina on the north-west and the Valle di Zoldo on the south are picture-book valleys replete with picture-book hamlets. They are on a road; they are listed in *Alpine Resorts in Italy* and no doubt elsewhere. Yet for some reason this stretch of country has retained – or had done so until 1970 – an extraordinary measure of likable innocence. Perhaps Cortina and the Dolomite road to the north tend to siphon off the worst of the crowds. Perhaps the Marmolada cable-way, not so very far to the west, deals with many of the rest. Whatever the reason John Ball, and possibly even Leslie Stephen, would today find it difficult to raise more than a sniff of disapproval.

CHAPTER TWENTY-ONE

The Top of Europe

The car-ferry terminus is down the valley at Le Fayet. The casino stands on the south side of the town square in which Jacques Balmat, arm outstretched, dramatically shows an equally statuesque de Saussure where the rounded white summit of Mont Blanc rises above the knick-knack shops. In Michelin the columns for *sports et distractions* are full beside Chamonix–Mont Blanc: swimming, golf, skating, ski-school, mountaineering of course, and no less than thirty-six *remontées mécaniques* by which visitors are hauled uphill for the downhill run. All this, and much more besides, because Mont Blanc pushes its brow nearly six hundred feet higher than Monte Rosa, its nearest rival in Europe.

At least, partly because of this. Mont Blanc, and the long trough of the Chamonix Valley through which the River Arve runs to the north of it, has certainly had the drawing-power of all record-breaking natural features for more than two hundred years. It has also had a good deal more, as though an omnipotent travel agent, handing out the gifts when geological history was being made, had set aside the best features for Mont Blanc. The glaciers, if not the longest in the Alps, have characteristics which make them unique. The peaks surrounding Mont Blanc itself, Mont Blanc du Tacul, the Aiguille Verte, the Grandes Jorasses, are superb mountains in their own right, and the rock-peaks of the Dru and the Géant are impressive – quite apart from the famous line of Aiguilles, whose spikey bits are as spikey as the most enthusiastic would wish. The granite of Mont Blanc's architecture is as fine to climb as to look at, while the forests setting off the glaciers grow in the right artistic places, as though they had been planted on the best principles by John Ruskin himself. As if this were not enough, the Aiguilles Rouges to the north rise as grandstand *fauteuils*. Paths, tracks and near-tracks lead even the least adventurous to new viewpoints, and to the 'Tour of Mont Blanc', from which the walker can survey the mountain from each point of the compass.

It is enough to turn a mountain's head. Yet Mont Blanc gives the impression of being totally unimplicated – in the helicopters buzzing through the air with supplies to its huts, in the queues waiting for cable-way cars, or the convoys clipping miles off a journey by disappearing into the tunnel which debouches beside the Glacier des Bossons. Mont Blanc can afford to be un-

The south face of Mont Blanc seen from the forests above Pré St Didier, photographed by Vittorio Sella at the end of the 19th century.

Above Jacques Balmat (1762–1834) the Chamonix crystal-hunter who with Dr Michel Gabriel Paccard, *below*, made the first ascent of Mont Blanc on 8 August 1786.

implicated. In the bad weather that can descend any day of the year all the combined technology of the 1970s can fail to extricate a man from his difficulties, and the mountain continues to claim as many victims as any in the Alps.

The classic view of Mont Blanc is obtained from the Brévent, reached from Chamonix in forty-five minutes by téléphérique or some five hours on foot. Looking across the valley, the most intriguing single feature is not the Mont Blanc but the long white tongue of the Glacier des Bossons, thrusting down between the forested ridge of the Montagne de la Côte and the Aiguille du Midi. To the west of the Montagne de la Côte is the Glacier de Taconnaz and above its junction with the Bossons the narrowish rock-rib of the Grands Mulets, which has seen a succession of rough shelter, small hut, large hut and hotel. Higher still the snows merge into the huge reservoir of the Grand Plateau from which rise the summit slopes. To the west, the skyline descends over the Dôme and the Aiguille du Goûter, the line of the St Gervais route. To the east the Mer de Glace peeps from behind the Aiguilles and beyond that again, rise the Dru and the Verte.

This scene was the stage for the early attempts to climb the mountain. In 1775 a party of guides reached the Montagne de la Côte and appear to have gone as far as the Grand Plateau. Nine years later another party of Chamonix men descended the valley to St Gervais, then followed the western spur, up over the Aiguille de Goûter to the Dôme, but failed to push on to the top. More topographical knowledge of the mountain, experience, hardiness – and the will to win – was still needed.

The combination was provided by the two men who set out from Chamonix on an August evening in 1786. They were an ill-assorted pair. One was Dr Michel Paccard, twenty-nine-year-old son of a Chamonix lawyer, who had long been intrigued by de Saussure's belief that valuable observations could be made from the summit. His companion was Jacques Balmat, five years younger, a crystal-hunter who knew the lower slopes of the mountain well. Two months earlier Balmat had spent a night out on the snow and his face had been badly snow-burnt. He had gone to Paccard for advice and soon afterwards the two men agreed to join forces. But their aims were very different. Paccard was moved almost exclusively by scientific inquiry, Balmat by the hope of reward; this alone would have provided fuel for the Paccard-Balmat controversy, one of the bitter arguments which rumble through Alpine history at regular intervals.

On 7 August they decided that the time for the great attempt had come, and at five that evening they kissed their wives goodbye and left the village – taking routes on different sides of the river so that no one might suspect their intentions. Downstream, at the hamlet of La Côte, they joined forces and took the rough track which zig-zags up the crest of the Montagne de la Côte. Near the top they found a shelter among the rocks, and settled down for the night.

'At two the white line of the dawn appeared', Balmat wrote 'and soon the sun rose without a cloud, brilliant and beautiful, a promise of a glorious day!

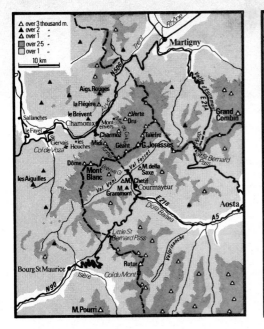
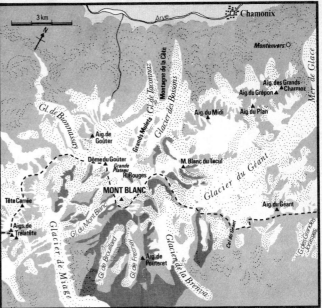

I awoke the doctor and we began our day's march.'

They were quickly on the glacier and made across it towards the Grands Mulets. Here Jacques Balmat carved his initials on a rock – a mark of ownership like the initials Jean-Antoine Carrel later cut on the Matterhorn. Years afterwards the rock was discovered and taken down to the Chamonix museum. The two men then moved on and up, buffetted by a rising wind and going more slowly. Eventually they reached the Grand Plateau. Before them there soared the final snowy dome of Mont Blanc, with broken slopes ahead and to the west, and on the east two parallel lines of rock running up towards the left-hand skyline. These are the Rochers Rouges, and above them lie the steep snow and ice of the *ancien passage*. This was the route picked by Balmat; direct, but dangerously exposed to avalanches and now rarely taken.

Here Balmat – according to his account later given to Alexandre Dumas – realised that he might be seen from the valley and remembered, in particular, a shop-keeper from whom he had bought supplies. 'Taking out my glass, there, twelve thousand feet below, was our gossiping friend and fifty others snatching a glass from hand to hand to look at us,' he claimed.

Balmat waved back. Then Paccard and he moved on again. They had no special equipment, they were dressed as though for a rough country stroll; they had no ice-axes, and they were utterly alone on the mountain, a situation whose danger it is difficult to appreciate fully today. It was already afternoon when they came to the end of the *ancien passage* and turned right up the final slopes towards the Calotte, the huge dome of snow forming the summit.

Many of Balmat's details are suspect. Paccard is more often on his knees than his feet; all would have been lost but for the heroic unaided efforts of Balmat. Nevertheless some echo of genuine feeling comes through in Balmat's description of the last few plodding feet. Every ten steps he had to stop for breath. But he went on, head down, walking upward, watching only the snow at his feet.

Then he realised that they were on the top of Mont Blanc. 'I looked round, trembling for fear that there might be some further new unattainable *aiguille*. But no! no! I had no longer any strength to go higher; the muscles of my legs seemed only held together by my trousers. But behold I was at the end of my journey; I was on a spot where no living being had ever been before, no eagle nor even a chamois! I was the monarch of Mont Blanc! I was the statue on this unique pedestal!'

He turned towards Chamonix and waved his hat on the end of his long alpenstock. 'My subjects in the valley perceived,' he said. 'The whole village was gathered together in the market-place.',

It was now nearly 5.30 and the two men knew it would be dark in three hours. But the sun still shone and all the Alps seemed to be stretched out around them, 'its four hundred glaciers shining in the sunlight', as Balmat recalled.

At seven they left the summit, following down the ridge the little round holes that their alpenstocks had left in the snow. As they descended, the shadows came up to meet them; by the time they reached the far edge of the Grand Plateau they were almost in the dark. The light sky still helped, but for the last hour of their journey down the glacier all was black – and a nightmare journey it must have been.

At eleven they reached the top of the Montagne de la Côte, found that one of Balmat's hands and both of Paccard's were frost-bitten, and wrapped themselves in their rug. It was six in the morning when Balmat was woken by Paccard and found himself suffering so badly from the previous day's snow-glare that he could hardly see.

The two men made their way back into Chamonix with difficulty. They had worn no dark glasses, nor the dark veils used in the days before glacier creams. 'I was quite unrecognisable,' said Balmat. 'My eyes were red, my face black and my lips blue. Every time I laughed or yawned the blood spouted out from my lips and cheeks, and in addition I was half blind.'

Even today, when every inch of Mont Blanc has been mapped, and every particular danger assessed, few men would care to follow in Paccard's and Balmat's footsteps with only their primitive equipment. The mountaineering achievement had been unique, and the misrepresentations that followed were almost as singular.

Today there is no doubt that the ascent was a co-operative effort in which the experience of the 'professional' Balmat complemented the planning abilities of the 'amateur' Paccard. But the difference in status between the competent guide and the village doctor was not as great as the words may suggest; both contributed in equal measure to success, much as guides and amateurs of later decades contributed to the conquests of the Golden Age.

But this was not how the first ascent of Mont Blanc was presented to the world. More than a century was to pass before the truth was unravelled and

Above Grindelwald,
Bernese Oberland; a new
house rises next to the old,
built more amply but still
in the traditional style with
traditional materials.

even today Chamonix sometimes gives pride of place to only two names – Balmat and de Saussure. The first misrepresentation came a few weeks after the ascent when a Genevese artist, Marc Théodore Bourrit, wrote a long version of the climb as told him by Balmat. Bourrit was a mountain wanderer in his own right, a man who had made a number of unsuccessful expeditions on Mont Blanc and was soon to publish a three-volume description of the Alps. To Bourrit it was bearable that a local guide could succeed, but insupportable that Paccard, a professional man like himself, could have played a significant part in the expedition. Thus in Bourrit's story it was Balmat who discovered the route, Balmat who led the way and reached the top first, Balmat who went back to help the incapable Paccard on to the summit.

Dr Paccard is believed to have written his own version in reply. But this, the famous Paccard manuscript, was never published and has never been found. Balmat was thus left in command of the literary field. His position was further buttressed almost half a century later when in 1832 – five years after Paccard's death – he was interviewed in Chamonix by Alexandre Dumas. Balmat was then seventy. He was suitably primed by Dumas who wanted a good story. The result, published in *Impressions de voyage* the following year, fixed for the rest of the century the picture of a heroic Balmat leading an almost helpless Paccard.

Only in the early 1900s, with the researches of the American H. F. Montagnier, the Swiss Dr Dübi and a number of Englishmen including Douglas Freshfield, did a totally different picture emerge. Paccard's diary was discovered. Quite as important, Dr Dübi found the diary of a Baron von Gersdorf, who had watched the ascent through a telescope from Chamonix. What the baron had seen was Paccard and Balmat taking the lead turn and turn about – and Paccard taking thermometer and barometer readings on the summit for half an hour. Later material added detail, and the whole story of the first ascent of Europe's highest summit was finally and definitively described 170 years after it was made in a book that is both a work of scholarship and an Alpine detective tale – *The First Ascent of Mont Blanc* by Graham Brown and Sir Gavin de Beer.

Just how lucky Paccard and Balmat had been in their adventure was demonstrated less than a fortnight later when de Saussure, who had been sent news of the climb, arrived in Chamonix, anxious to repeat it as soon as possible. De Saussure set out at once but got no further than the Montagne de la Côte: the weather broke, and snow and rain continuously obscured the upper slopes. Paccard and Balmat could hardly have survived had this happened beyond their point of no return.

De Saussure came back the following year, arriving in Chamonix early in July. Balmat had been to the summit for a second time a few days earlier but, as in 1786, de Saussure brought bad weather with him and was able to set out only on 1 August.

The party which made this third ascent was impressively, if not dangerously, large. With de Saussure went his valet; Balmat; and seventeen other guides who carried provisions, a tent, a mattress for de Saussure, a large

Early morning light on the Dôme du Goûter, Mont Blanc.

273

John Auldjo's ascent of
Mont Blanc.

barometer and numerous other instruments with which observations were to
be made on the summit.

Like Balmat and Paccard the previous year, de Saussure slept at the top of
the Montagne de la Côte. Everyone took it easy the following day and bivouacked on the Petit Plateau, a smaller snow-basin lying near the upper end of
the Grands Mulets. The following morning, the third out from Chamonix,
they left late; but, following the same route as Balmat, they were on the top
by eleven. Here de Saussure spent four and a half hours with his instruments,
after which the whole party made a leisurely descent to the Rochers Rouges
where the third night was spent. By 9.30 the following morning they were all
back safe and sound on the rocks at the top of the Montagne de la Côte.

The expedition had passed off almost without incident, in the finest of
weather. One of the guides had a lucky escape from disaster when he fell into a
crevasse through a broken snow-bridge. The barometer fell into another
crevasse, but was retrieved. On the descent they were shocked by the collapse
of a great group of séracs on the upper reaches of the Bionnasey Glacier. But
the unwieldly party returned safely, a tribute to Balmat's organising ability
and to the good luck that smiled on many of the early men of Mont Blanc.

De Saussure's ascent of the highest mountain in Europe showed what
could be done. Less than a week later he was followed by Colonel Mark
Beaufoy, a Coldstreamer who climbed despite the warnings of the guides.
The following year the fifth ascent was made by another Englishman, a Mr

274

Woodley. Then the Napoleonic Wars tended to eclipse interest in Mont Blanc – although in 1809 the local girl, Maria Paradis, became the first woman to reach the summit. Only after 1815 did the ascent become an almost fashionable if still hazardous exploit, often made on the grand tour.

Captain Undrell, Royal Navy, borrowed scientific apparatus from Dr Paccard and took it to the top. Frederick Clissold climbed Mont Blanc, 'having frequently ascended Snowdon without guides', and feeling 'in some measure prepared for the critical circumstances attending mountain excursions'. Dr Edmund Clark buried near the summit rocks a glass tube containing an olive branch and a paper carrying the signature of George IV. Henriette d'Angeville, the lady, followed in the steps of Maria Paradis, the peasant woman.

Climbing Mont Blanc was still an exploit, almost a stunt, and was still usually undertaken by men who rarely went up another mountain. Yet two ascents, made in 1820 and 1827, were of special importance for the future. In 1820 a Russian, Dr Hamel, and two Oxford students were ascending the *ancien passage* with eight guides when without warning an avalanche swept the whole party down the slope, killing three of the local men. Then in 1827 a route was discovered which was comparatively free of avalanche danger and left the Grand Plateau below the Rochers Rouges along slopes christened the Corridor.

Thus there were now two routes up the mountain. Until mid-century few serious attempts were made to add to them, and those who ascended Mont Blanc did so much as they would carry out any other sightseeing exploit, an attitude which changed from the 1850s onwards as sporting mountaineering came into its own. A dividing line between the two epochs, each with its own outlook, was drawn by the extraordinary ascent of Albert Smith, which influenced the history of the mountain – and its popularity with the general public – more than any other event since Paccard and Balmat's climb.

Albert Smith was obsessed from youth with a passion for Mont Blanc – set alight when he read *The Peasants of Chamouni*, which described the accident to the Hamel party. He was also journalist and editor, a traveller and deviser of public entertainments who retained all his life a genuine mountain enthusiasm. In 1851 Smith travelled to Chamonix. Here he met three other young Englishmen and with them set out early in August for the top of Mont Blanc.

Smith's party was the largest, as well as the most publicised, which ever set foot on the mountain. In addition to him and his three companions, there were sixteen guides and about a score of porters and other volunteers who accompanied them for varying distances. The commissariat included sixty bottles of *vin ordinaire*, six bottles of Bordeaux, ten bottles of St George, fifteen bottles of St Jean, two bottles of Champagne and three bottles of Cognac. Food included thirty-five small and eleven large fowls, four legs and four shoulders of mutton, as well as veal and beef, ten cheeses and twenty loaves.

This exploit was not only the centre-piece of Smith's *The Story of Mont Blanc*, which he quickly wrote on return to England. There was also *The*

Title page from *Ten Scenes in the last ascent of Mont Blanc....*
Dedicated to the Nine Guides of Chamonix.

Albert Smith, who ascended Mont Blanc in 1851.

The hut on the Grands
Mulets.

'Provisions for the Ascent
of Mont Blanc'

PROVISIONS FOR THE ASCENT OF MONT BLANC.

Hôtel de Londres, Chamouni,
August 12, 1851.

			Francs.
60 bottles of Vin Ordinaire	... ...	...	60
6 do. Bordeaux	... ...	...	36
10 bottles of St. George	... ...	...	30
15 do. St. Jean ...	... ...	...	30
3 do. Cognac ...	... ...	...	15
1 do. syrup of raspberries	... ...	...	3
6 do. lemonade	... ...	...	6
2 do. champagne	... ...	...	14
20 loaves	... ...	...	30
10 small cheeses ...	... ...	...	8
6 packets of chocolate	... ...	...	9
6 do. sugar	... ...	...	6
4 do. prunes ...	... ...	...	6
4 do. raisins ...	... ...	...	6
2 do. salt	... ...	...	1
4 wax candles	... ...	...	4
6 lemons	... ...	...	1
4 legs of mutton	... ...	...	24
4 shoulders, do.	... ...	...	12
6 pieces of veal ...	... ...	...	30
1 piece of beef ...	... ...	...	5
11 large fowls	... ...	...	30
35 small do.	... ...	...	87
	Total		456

Ascent of Mont Blanc, an entertainment produced in the Egyptian Hall, Piccadilly, which ran without break for six years. Three royal-command performances were given – to the Prince of Wales in London and to Queen Victoria at Osborne and Windsor. The entertainment, in which Smith described the climb with the help of dioramic views and a supporting cast that included St Bernard dogs and girls in local costume, was not all. *The Game of Mont Blanc*, something like an Alpine snakes-and-ladders, sold by the thousand. The 'Mont Blanc Quadrille' and the 'Chamonix Polka' were among the fashionable tunes of the day. Simultaneously, there was an increase in the panoramas, dioramas and cosmoramas which even before Albert Smith had given ordinary people a fairground impression of the Alps. In London the lure of the Alps was even utilised at the Baker Street Glaciarum where, all the year round, skaters could perform on 3,000 square feet 'amidst Alpine scenery, covered with snow and hoar frost'.

All this upsurge of interest in the Alps of which *The Ascent of Mont Blanc* was partly the symptom, partly the cause, was distressing to what was hardening into an Alpine Establishment. It was claimed that Albert Smith's initials represented merely two thirds of the truth. Dickens resigned from the Garrick Club when he was elected. Nevertheless Smith gave many thousands of people an awareness of the Alps in general, and of Mont Blanc in particular, which they would otherwise have lacked. Thus he helped to draw to Mont Blanc hundreds of travellers, a few of whom did more than look at the mountain, more than climb it in the usual way, and who during the next decades began to lace the massif with new routes.

In 1855, while Smith was drawing crowds to the Egyptian Hall, Sir James Ramsay made a brave attempt to force a completely new way up the mountain, crossing the Col de Géant from Courmayeur, bivouacking out at the foot of the Aiguille du Midi and then joining the usual route at the Mur de la Côte. Only the threat of being benighted forced the party back an hour from the summit. Shortly afterwards E. S. Kennedy and a strong party tackled the mountain from St Gervais without guides, ascending over the Aiguille and Dôme du Goûter. Here, however, they considered the snowy dome of the Bosses as being impracticable, descended to the Grand Plateau and finished the ascent by the usual route of the corridor and the Mur de la Côte. While they had thus made the first guideless ascent of the mountain they had not made the 'purist's' route from St Gervais – 'over the skyline' all the way. This was left to Leslie Stephen in 1861. Two years later the eastern route, so nearly completed by Ramsay, was followed to the summit, while another two years on, Moore and his companions climbed the mountain by the Brenva, the first of three separate routes from the south made within the next few years.

In January 1876 the first winter ascent of the mountain was made by Miss Straton, the rich young Englishwoman who married one of her guides and lived happily every after.

On arriving at the Rochers Foudroyés we met the north wind; it blew very hard and increased much on the first Bosse [she wrote]. When we got on the top of it two of my fingers were frost-bitten, and they had to be rubbed with snow and brandy for three quarters of an hour before it was thought prudent to continue the ascent. When we turned to resume our upward course, the wind seemed to mock our efforts; it sent the snow curling in clouds along the arête. By dint of very great perseverance we attained the summit of Mont Blanc at 3.00 pm. The thermometer showed 10 degrees below zero. The view was magnificent beyond all anticipation.

By this time the hut-building which has now produced a multitude of shelters, was already under way. De Saussure's rough construction on the

'.... Her ....'

Grands Mulets had been replaced in 1853 by a proper building whose official opening was attended by Albert Smith. Three years later a hut was erected on the Aiguille du Goûter – at 13,000 feet compared with the 10,000 feet of the Grands Mulets – and first one and then a second hut were built on the Italian side. In 1866 the Grands Mulets hut was drastically enlarged to contain a dining-room, a kitchen and two bedrooms; soon there was a second hut, then a resident housekeeper. Today the Grands Mulets is, in a mountaineering sense, as good a place as the Café de la Paix or Piccadilly to see everyone in the world in due time.

Although Mont Blanc will always retain a special savour that does not rest entirely on its position at the top of the altitude league, its story, and that of its supporting summits, has accurately reflected the developments that can be traced out elsewhere. Perhaps the problems have been usually that bit more extreme than those faced in other places; perhaps the solutions often had a touch of excess, as when in 1878 Lord Wentworth tried to climb the Dent du Géant, the huge tooth overlooking the Col, with the help of a cannon that was to have sent a rocket and rope across the summit in the manner of a lifeboat rescue line. His failure left the way open for the Italian Sella family four years later. The Sellas' guides drilled holes in the rock, hammered in wooden pegs, tied on some 500 feet of fixed rope, and in the shape of what was contemptuously called 'Sella's staircase' created an artificial route that would raise eyebrows even in our own more sophisticated days.

The blind who have climbed in the area run from Sir Francis Campbell who climbed the Matterhorn, the Eiger and the Jungfrau as well as Mont Blanc, to Mlle Colette Richard, who a decade ago climbed Mont Tondu and Mont Blanc du Tacul.

There are also the youngest and the oldest. Elsewhere in the Alps Gerald Noelting, in 1934 at the age of thirteen, climbed the Aiguille du Tour, Mont Blanc de Seilon and the Aiguille de la Tsa. At the upper limit there was Benjamin Fosson, the guide who climbed Castor in 1947 at the age of ninety and General Sir Aylmer Haldane who before the last war climbed the Piz Languard from Pontresina at the age of seventy-six. As companion, he had the eighty-one-year-old Edgar Foa. But while such achievements have come elsewhere almost as a casual by-product from the enthusiasms of youth or old age, Mont Blanc has been a natural magnet for the instinctive record-breaker. Myles Mathews reached the top at the age of thirteen, while Durier's history records climbs by a descendant of de Saussure at the age of fourteen, by Charles Rand, an American aged fifteen, and by Aline Loppé, who went up at the age of sixteen and made a second ascent two years later. By this time Lucabella Hare had at the age of fifteen reached the top of the Aiguille du Goûter with her brother Theodore. This was in 1856 and it is clear that both would have gone on had they not promised their mother to stop short of the top. And five years later Captain Paget took his wife and children – Claude aged nine and Hardol aged eleven – as far as the Grands Mulets.

As to elderly climbers, there have been many since the Marquis de Turenne's ascent in 1875 at the age of seventy-two. Few if any have equalled the record of Monsieur H. Brulle, a Foreign Member of the Alpine Club. In 1932 he made his third ascent of the mountain at the age of seventy-nine; the following year he made his fourth ascent; and he was prevented only by bad weather from completing his fifth ascent at the age of eighty-three, shortly before his death.

In other ways Mont Blanc and Chamonix have continued to mirror, usually in extreme forms, the developments which have transformed the rest of the Alps. When, after the First World War, a new generation of guideless climbers set out – Pierre Dalloz's adventurers to whom climbing came as a revelation – the members of the French Groupe de Haute Montagne showed in the Mont Blanc range just how far such dedication could be taken. Contrariwise, as a new sort of guide began to emerge, it was among the Chamonix men that the epitome of the type could be seen.

As huts throughout the Alps tended to get bigger and more elaborate, that at the Couvercle above the Mer de Glace was expanded, after the Second World War, to accommodate no less than 150. In the age of the téléphérique, Chamonix could boast not only the highest in Europe, taking visitors to the summit of the Aiguille du Midi – raising in an acute form Bourdillon's question: 'Are the snow-peak and the glacier the place for the masses of mankind?' – but a bus service of a cable-way providing a four-hour package journey to Italy and back. Its road tunnel, opened in 1965 bringing Courmayeur within twenty kilometres of Chamonix, was almost inevitably the longest of its kind in the world.

All this, and the development of Chamonix itself into a winter-sports centre of almost Butlin-like proportions; all this, and yet much of the magic remains. It is difficult to explain except for the presence of some continuing spirit which has moved the men of Mont Blanc; Paccard and Balmat with a determination that survived their differences; Albert Smith, of such sublime enthusiasm that not even the Alpine Establishment could really call him vulgar; Dent, making a steely-eyed twelfth attempt on the Dru, and the young French parachutist who landed plump on the summit in 1961 as two companions landed nearby. All these have succumbed to the magic of this particular mountain, have heard the same voices as Henriette d'Angeville, exultantly lifted on to her guides' shoulders so that she was even higher than Mont Blanc. Here, by the mountain, all appear of the same company; here all ghosts are brothers. One can hear them uniting to ask, on the top of some existential summit, what is to happen to the Alps, all confident that an answer to the challenge will be found.

Last Words: A Final Fling

There is still a place not so far from the triangle of trade routes formed by the Grimsel, the Furka and the Susten Passes where it is possible to see nothing but mountains. Below the Viso it can seem as desolate as the remoter Scottish glens, and in some of the lesser by-ways of the Graians you can still hear talk of peaks and pastures much as in Whymper's day. At times, in certain areas, and with luck, the Alps continue to do the trick. Like the inhabitant of a city before the final stages of a siege, the traveller can still walk without seeing a sign of the besiegers.

How long this will go on depends partly on the outcome of minor battles now being fought by local inhabitants. In the Alps, more than in most areas, today's environmental climate is fashioned by the immediate past; the victories or defeats of one generation determine whether the next will see a mountain skyline or a grid of cables aping the electricity industry at its worst.

There are signs that at the last minute of the last hour the balance is beginning to change, and not only in Switzerland, where the Swiss Alpine Club, the Ligue Suisse pour la Protection de la Nature and a host of smaller bodies are making themselves felt more strongly. Local opinion, supported by the Club Alpin Français and other organisations, has eventualy blocked a scheme which would have created 35,000 new tourist beds in the area of the Vanoise National Park. A plan by Paris financiers to build a téléphérique from Les Houches in the Chamonix Valley to the summit of the Aiguille du Goûter, whence guides were to take travellers to the top of Mont Blanc, has also been abandoned; though here the chance of a tourist disaster may have come into the equation.

The citizens of Bagnes, meeting in the Swiss way that enables them to decide their own fate, decided by 310 votes to 64 that the commune should sign an agreement under which sites in 155 square kilometres should be given special protection. The citizens of Ayer, controlling key areas in the Val d'Anniviers, decisively voted down an army request for facilities in the valley – after listening to a spirited debate between an army spokesman and their own representative. The little commune of Vouvry decided off its own bat to sign an agreement with three conservation societies to protect the Lac de Tanay and its surrounding summits, endangered as they had become by 'the establishment of téléphériques, a tourist route and haphazard camping sites'. These are pointers to the way the wind is blowing but they would not be significant were not their numbers, as shown by the notes in *Les Alpes*, both considerable and growing.

As far as the tourist is concerned, this is not an either/or problem. The Swiss have lived to a considerable extent on their visitors for more than a century and other countries whose territory includes part of the Alps have taken their share of the pickings. Thus no one concerned with servicing the millions who come here every year has any interest in putting the Alps behind bars or in driving Alpine addicts further afield, and despite the occasional hint to the contrary, very few genuine mountaineers wish to deny the mass of mankind the joys of the Alps. Thus the apparent conflict of interest between those who think that they alone should be allowed to destroy the silence and those for whom more is better in tourism as in education is not as deep as it sometimes appears.

There is much common ground, including acceptance of the fact that un-controlled exploitation will be increasingly self-destructive. For here, before long, man will be so isolated from his environment that he is no longer able fully to appreciate the dangers and the joys of the world in which he lives. The mountaineers will go first – and are indeed already moving off as the more distant ranges of the world become more accessible. The walkers will leave for fresh pastures and eventually those who come to admire merely from coach or téléphérique will feel that one viewpoint is much like another and turn to different titillations. It will not, of course, be quite as quick as that. But the process is inevitable unless the countries concerned first formulate, then implement, some scheme to limit the continuing scenic destruction.

Piecemeal attempts have been made to carry out some suggestions. The most hopeful extend some form of zoning. This can, for instance, allow virtually unrestricted tourist development in specific places; restrict it else-where; designate certain areas where both tourist and industrial building is severely limited; and extend the areas of national parks in which all develop-ment is forbidden.

Any such plans are likely to be met with vigorous opposition, not only from the financial interests involved but also from the shorter-sighted of the national tourist industries. Yet those constantly at grips with the problem, watching the transformation that the latest travel techniques make inevitable, see some resemblance between visitors with mountain interests, participant or spectator, and the hunters who over the last few decades have been seeking out the last of the big game.

Unless the camera finally replaces the rifle as a weapon, this century will probably see the end of the 'great cats'; in all, nearly a thousand species of animals and birds are threatened, and throughout the world roughly 20,000 species of plants, one in ten of those known, are in danger from the human predator.

So, less dramatically but just as certainly, are the Alps.

Bibliography

Alpine bibliographies can run not only to pages but to volumes. The reader's problem is that of selection rather than discovery, and since each reader wants to make his own choice any list presented here must be in the nature of a bran-tub into which the interested plunge an arm for the lucky dip.

But whether on foot or on wheels, some detailed knowledge of the roads and places will be required, and Michelin's paperbacked green guides *Switzerland, Alpes* (the French Alps, and only published in French), *Austria*, and *Italy* are all useful. So is Baedeker, and if editions long out-of-date have an antique air and are useless for finding accommodation they have a wealth of background information that can add enjoyment to the view. Even the téléphériques have not moved the mountains and the long pull-out panoramas, a feature of early Baedekers (not to be consulted in a high wind) can still settle arguments.

Most climbers will know where to look for what they want in detailed guides to special areas, but not all may yet be aware that West Col Productions (of 1 Meadow Close, Goring, Berks.) cover so many groups with titles ranging from *Maritime Alps* at one end of the range to *Karwendel* at the other. The Zermatt and Chamonix district guides published by Constable are of use to the non-mountaineer.

As a mine of information on all things Alpine, Coolidge's *The Alps in Nature and History* has an all-embracing pedantry which is more than counter-balanced by its information on all that happened up to the start of the present century. Claire Eliane-Engel's *A History of Mountaineering in the Alps* is the best all-over one-volume survey in English, and Sir Gavin de Beer's *Travellers in Switzerland* an astonishingly readable display of erudition whose bibliography could keep an enthusiast deep in his armchair for much of his life. His *Early Travellers in the Alps*, together with Francis Gribble's *The Early Mountaineers*, are the best accounts of what happened before the nineteenth century for those unwilling to grapple with Coolidge's *Josias Simler et les origines de l'alpinisme jusqu'en 1600*. De Beer's *Escape to Switzerland* and his story of *Hannibal* are good value by any reader's standards.

Of the individual stories of the pioneers, Edward Whymper's *Scrambles amongst the Alps*, Alfred Wills's *Wanderings among the High Alps*, A. W.

Moore's *The Alps in 1864*, Leslie Stephen's *The Playground of Europe*, and A. F. Mummery's *My Climbs in the Alps and Caucasus* are the accepted classics. Guido Rey's *The Matterhorn* tells the story of one man's involvement with one mountain; *The First Ascent of Mont Blanc* by de Beer and the late Graham Brown is the last word on that famous climb; Heinrich Harrer's *The White Spider* tells the story of the Eigerwand; and my *The Day the Rope Broke* is a detailed account of events before, during and after the Matterhorn disaster. None of Geoffrey Winthrop Young's books dealing with the Alps can be read without learning a great deal that is worth while, and the same is true of more than a century's issues of the *Alpine Journal*. All of Martin Conway is rewarding; so is all of Arnold Lunn, especially on the history of skiing.

Until recent years few guides wrote their stories, but two worthwhile exceptions are Christian Klucker's *Adventures of an Alpine Guide* and Mattias Zurbriggen's *From the Alps to the Andes*. Their modern counterparts include Armand Charlet's *Vocation Alpine* and more than one book by Gaston Rebuffat.

For the specialist, Anthony Huxley's *Mountain Flowers* and Douglas Milner's *Mountain Photography* are unrivalled; so, for the motorist, is Hugh Merrick's *The Passes of the Alps*, and those who can lay their hands on out-of-print books can compare it with Freeston's *The High-Roads of the Alps*, published in 1910. *A Woman's Reach* by Nea Morin gives an admirable account of near-contemporary mountaineering by women, *The Book of European Skiing* edited by Malcolm Milne and Mark Hellen packs an extremely diverse amount of information between two covers, while *Geiger and the Alps* is an engaging account of great work that almost disarms criticism of aircraft in the mountains. Of anthologies, Lunn's *The Englishman in the Alps* (hard to obtain) and R. L. G. Irving's *The Mountain Way* (which deals mainly, although not exclusively, with the Alps) are among the best.

As with other subjects, really desirable books on the Alps have a habit of being out of print or otherwise unobtainable, a problem hardly helped by the fact that in the whole of Britain there are only a few specialist Alpine booksellers, notably Mr Louis Baume of Gaston's Alpine Books, 134 Kenton Road, Harrow, Middlesex.

Index

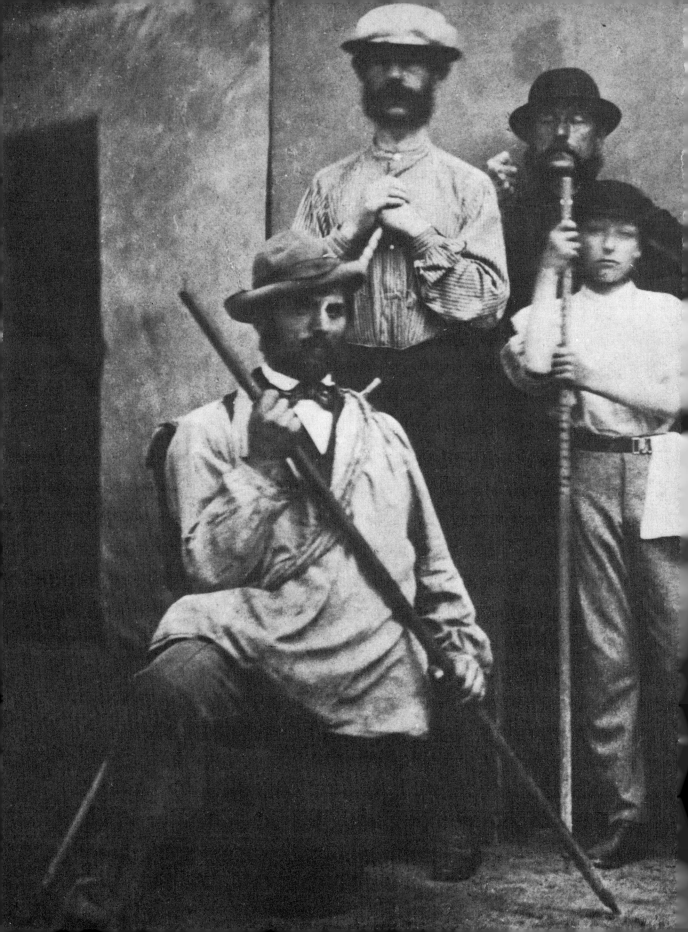